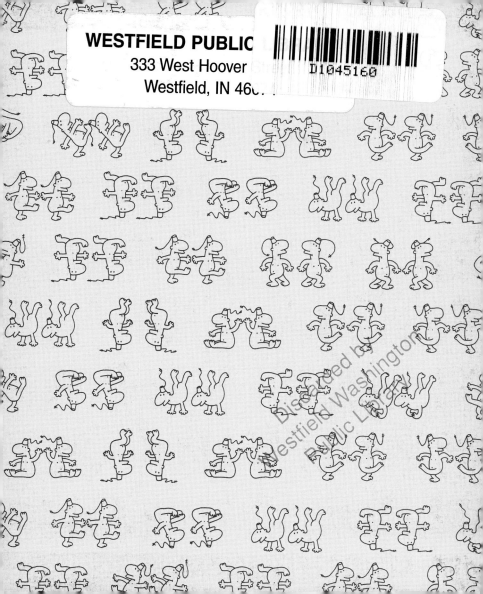

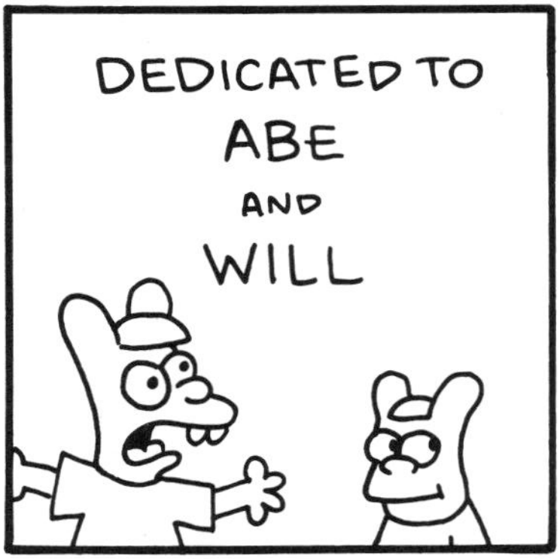
DEDICATED TO
ABE
AND
WILL

BINKY'S GUIDE TO

Love™

A CARTOON BOOK BY MATT GROENING

Harper

An Imprint of HarperCollinsPublishers

ORIGINALLY PUBLISHED IN 1994 BY HARPERCOLLINS PUBLISHERS.

BINKY'S GUIDE TO LOVE. COPYRIGHT © 1994, 2006 BY MATT GROENING. ALL RIGHTS
RESERVED. PRINTED IN THE UNITED STATES OF AMERICA. NO PART OF THIS BOOK MAY
BE USED OR REPRODUCED IN ANY MANNER WHATSOEVER WITHOUT WRITTEN PERMISSION
EXCEPT IN THE CASE OF BRIEF QUOTATIONS EMBODIED IN CRITICAL ARTICLES AND
REVIEWS. FOR INFORMATION ADDRESS HARPERCOLLINS PUBLISHERS,
10 EAST 53RD STREET, NEW YORK, NY 10022.

HARPERCOLLINS BOOKS MAY BE PURCHASED FOR EDUCATIONAL, BUSINESS, OR SALES
PROMOTIONAL USE. FOR INFORMATION PLEASE WRITE: SPECIAL MARKETS DEPARTMENT,
HARPERCOLLINS PUBLISHERS, 10 EAST 53RD STREET, NEW YORK, NY 10022.

FIRST HARPER PAPERBACK PUBLISHED 2006.

LIBRARY OF CONGRESS CATALOGING-IN-PUBLICATION DATA IS AVAILABLE UPON REQUEST.

ISBN-10: 0-06-112493-1
ISBN-13: 978-0-06-112493-8

06 07 08 09 10 ❖/RRD 10 9 8 7 6 5 4 3 2 1

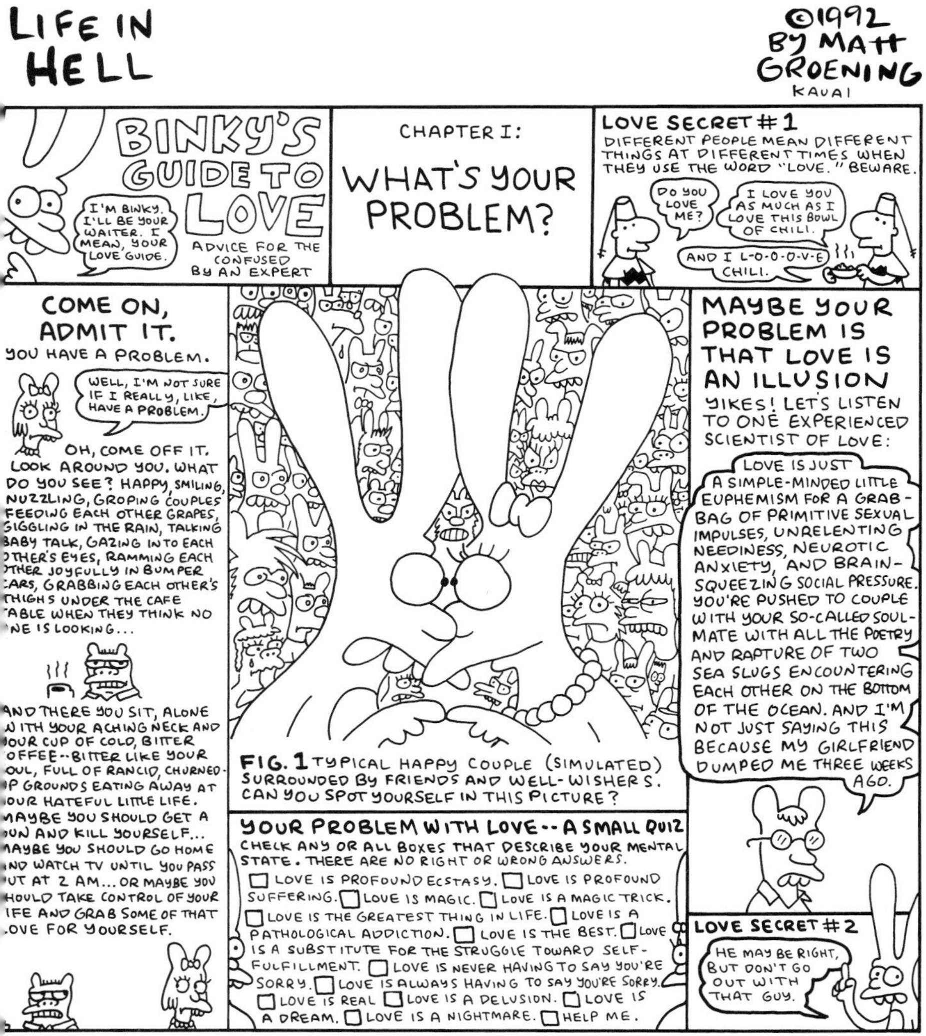

LIFE IN HELL
©1992 BY MATT GROENING
KAUAI
BINKY'S GUIDE TO LOVE
I'M BINKY. I'LL BE YOUR WAITER. I MEAN, YOUR LOVE GUIDE.
ADVICE FOR THE CONFUSED BY AN EXPERT
CHAPTER I:
WHAT'S YOUR PROBLEM?
LOVE SECRET #1
DIFFERENT PEOPLE MEAN DIFFERENT THINGS AT DIFFERENT TIMES WHEN THEY USE THE WORD "LOVE." BEWARE.
DO YOU LOVE ME?
I LOVE YOU AS MUCH AS I LOVE THIS BOWL OF CHILI.
AND I L-O-O-O-V-E CHILI.
COME ON, ADMIT IT.
YOU HAVE A PROBLEM.
WELL, I'M NOT SURE IF I REALLY, LIKE, HAVE A PROBLEM.
OH, COME OFF IT. LOOK AROUND YOU. WHAT DO YOU SEE? HAPPY, SMILING, NUZZLING, GROPING COUPLES FEEDING EACH OTHER GRAPES, GIGGLING IN THE RAIN, TALKING BABY TALK, GAZING INTO EACH OTHER'S EYES, RAMMING EACH OTHER JOYFULLY IN BUMPER CARS, GRABBING EACH OTHER'S THIGHS UNDER THE CAFE TABLE WHEN THEY THINK NO ONE IS LOOKING...
AND THERE YOU SIT, ALONE WITH YOUR ACHING NECK AND YOUR CUP OF COLD, BITTER COFFEE--BITTER LIKE YOUR SOUL, FULL OF RANCID, CHURNED-UP GROUNDS EATING AWAY AT YOUR HATEFUL LITTLE LIFE. MAYBE YOU SHOULD GET A GUN AND KILL YOURSELF... MAYBE YOU SHOULD GO HOME AND WATCH TV UNTIL YOU PASS OUT AT 2 AM... OR MAYBE YOU SHOULD TAKE CONTROL OF YOUR LIFE AND GRAB SOME OF THAT LOVE FOR YOURSELF.
FIG. 1 TYPICAL HAPPY COUPLE (SIMULATED) SURROUNDED BY FRIENDS AND WELL-WISHERS. CAN YOU SPOT YOURSELF IN THIS PICTURE?
MAYBE YOUR PROBLEM IS THAT LOVE IS AN ILLUSION
YIKES! LET'S LISTEN TO ONE EXPERIENCED SCIENTIST OF LOVE:
LOVE IS JUST A SIMPLE-MINDED LITTLE EUPHEMISM FOR A GRAB-BAG OF PRIMITIVE SEXUAL IMPULSES, UNRELENTING NEEDINESS, NEUROTIC ANXIETY, AND BRAIN-SQUEEZING SOCIAL PRESSURE. YOU'RE PUSHED TO COUPLE WITH YOUR SO-CALLED SOUL-MATE WITH ALL THE POETRY AND RAPTURE OF TWO SEA SLUGS ENCOUNTERING EACH OTHER ON THE BOTTOM OF THE OCEAN. AND I'M NOT JUST SAYING THIS BECAUSE MY GIRLFRIEND DUMPED ME THREE WEEKS AGO.
YOUR PROBLEM WITH LOVE--A SMALL QUIZ
CHECK ANY OR ALL BOXES THAT DESCRIBE YOUR MENTAL STATE. THERE ARE NO RIGHT OR WRONG ANSWERS.
☐ LOVE IS PROFOUND ECSTASY. ☐ LOVE IS PROFOUND SUFFERING. ☐ LOVE IS MAGIC. ☐ LOVE IS A MAGIC TRICK. ☐ LOVE IS THE GREATEST THING IN LIFE. ☐ LOVE IS A PATHOLOGICAL ADDICTION. ☐ LOVE IS THE BEST. ☐ LOVE IS A SUBSTITUTE FOR THE STRUGGLE TOWARD SELF-FULFILLMENT. ☐ LOVE IS NEVER HAVING TO SAY YOU'RE SORRY. ☐ LOVE IS ALWAYS HAVING TO SAY YOU'RE SORRY. ☐ LOVE IS REAL ☐ LOVE IS A DELUSION. ☐ LOVE IS A DREAM. ☐ LOVE IS A NIGHTMARE. ☐ HELP ME.
LOVE SECRET #2
HE MAY BE RIGHT, BUT DON'T GO OUT WITH THAT GUY.

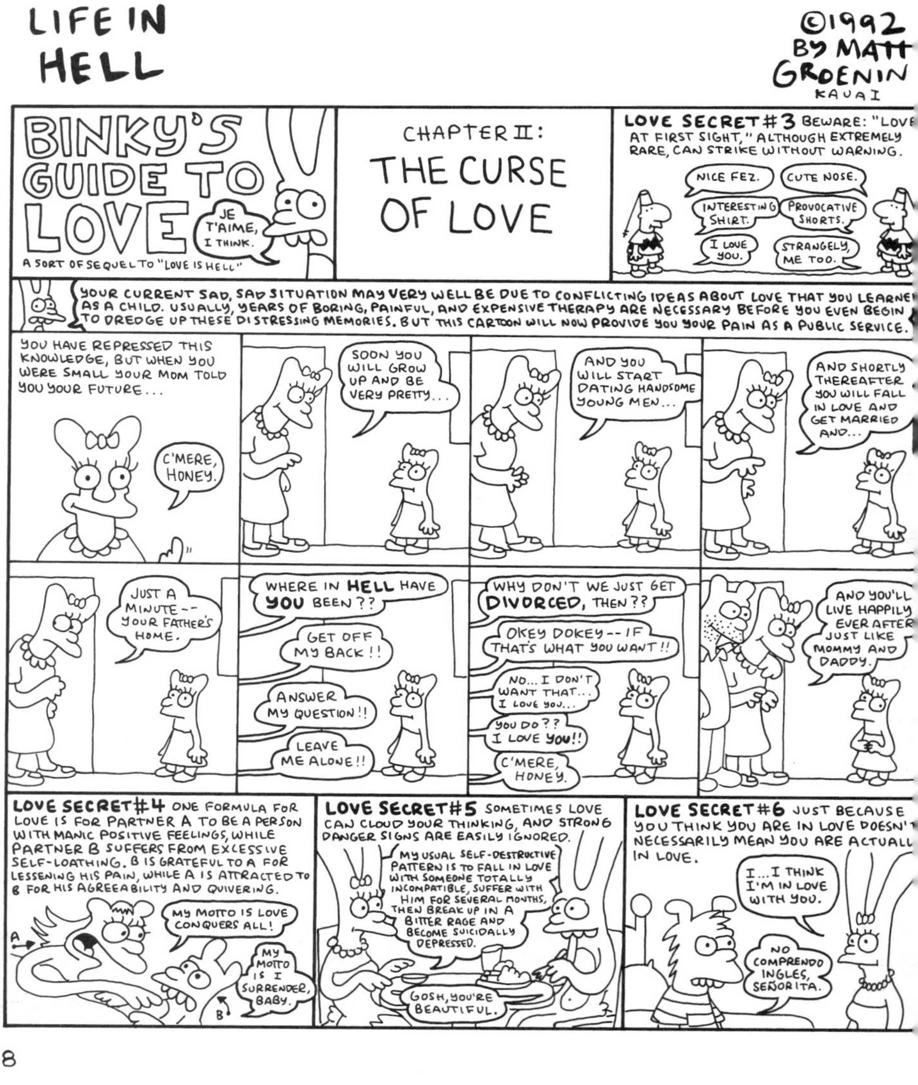
LIFE IN HELL
©1992 BY MATT GROENING KAUAI
BINKY'S GUIDE TO LOVE
JE T'AIME, I THINK.
A SORT OF SEQUEL TO "LOVE IS HELL"
CHAPTER II: THE CURSE OF LOVE
LOVE SECRET #3 BEWARE: "LOVE AT FIRST SIGHT," ALTHOUGH EXTREMELY RARE, CAN STRIKE WITHOUT WARNING.
NICE FEZ.
CUTE NOSE.
INTERESTING SHIRT.
PROVOCATIVE SHORTS.
I LOVE YOU.
STRANGELY, ME TOO.
YOUR CURRENT SAD, SAD SITUATION MAY VERY WELL BE DUE TO CONFLICTING IDEAS ABOUT LOVE THAT YOU LEARNED AS A CHILD. USUALLY, YEARS OF BORING, PAINFUL, AND EXPENSIVE THERAPY ARE NECESSARY BEFORE YOU EVEN BEGIN TO DREDGE UP THESE DISTRESSING MEMORIES. BUT THIS CARTOON WILL NOW PROVIDE YOU YOUR PAIN AS A PUBLIC SERVICE.
YOU HAVE REPRESSED THIS KNOWLEDGE, BUT WHEN YOU WERE SMALL YOUR MOM TOLD YOU YOUR FUTURE...
C'MERE, HONEY.
SOON YOU WILL GROW UP AND BE VERY PRETTY...
AND YOU WILL START DATING HANDSOME YOUNG MEN...
AND SHORTLY THEREAFTER YOU WILL FALL IN LOVE AND GET MARRIED AND...
JUST A MINUTE -- YOUR FATHER'S HOME.
WHERE IN HELL HAVE YOU BEEN??
GET OFF MY BACK!!
ANSWER MY QUESTION!!
LEAVE ME ALONE!!
WHY DON'T WE JUST GET DIVORCED, THEN??
OKEY DOKEY -- IF THAT'S WHAT YOU WANT!!
NO... I DON'T WANT THAT... I LOVE YOU...
YOU DO?? I LOVE YOU!!
C'MERE, HONEY.
AND YOU'LL LIVE HAPPILY EVER AFTER JUST LIKE MOMMY AND DADDY.
LOVE SECRET #4 ONE FORMULA FOR LOVE IS FOR PARTNER A TO BE A PERSON WITH MANIC POSITIVE FEELINGS, WHILE PARTNER B SUFFERS FROM EXCESSIVE SELF-LOATHING. B IS GRATEFUL TO A FOR LESSENING HIS PAIN, WHILE A IS ATTRACTED TO B FOR HIS AGREEABILITY AND QUIVERING.
A
MY MOTTO IS LOVE CONQUERS ALL!
MY MOTTO IS I SURRENDER, BABY.
B
LOVE SECRET #5 SOMETIMES LOVE CAN CLOUD YOUR THINKING, AND STRONG DANGER SIGNS ARE EASILY IGNORED.
MY USUAL SELF-DESTRUCTIVE PATTERN IS TO FALL IN LOVE WITH SOMEONE TOTALLY INCOMPATIBLE, SUFFER WITH HIM FOR SEVERAL MONTHS, THEN BREAK UP IN A BITTER RAGE AND BECOME SUICIDALLY DEPRESSED.
GOSH, YOU'RE BEAUTIFUL.
LOVE SECRET #6 JUST BECAUSE YOU THINK YOU ARE IN LOVE DOESN'T NECESSARILY MEAN YOU ARE ACTUALLY IN LOVE.
I... I THINK I'M IN LOVE WITH YOU.
NO COMPRENDO INGLES, SEÑORITA.

LIFE IN HELL

©1992 BY MATT GROENING

BYE BYE KAUAI

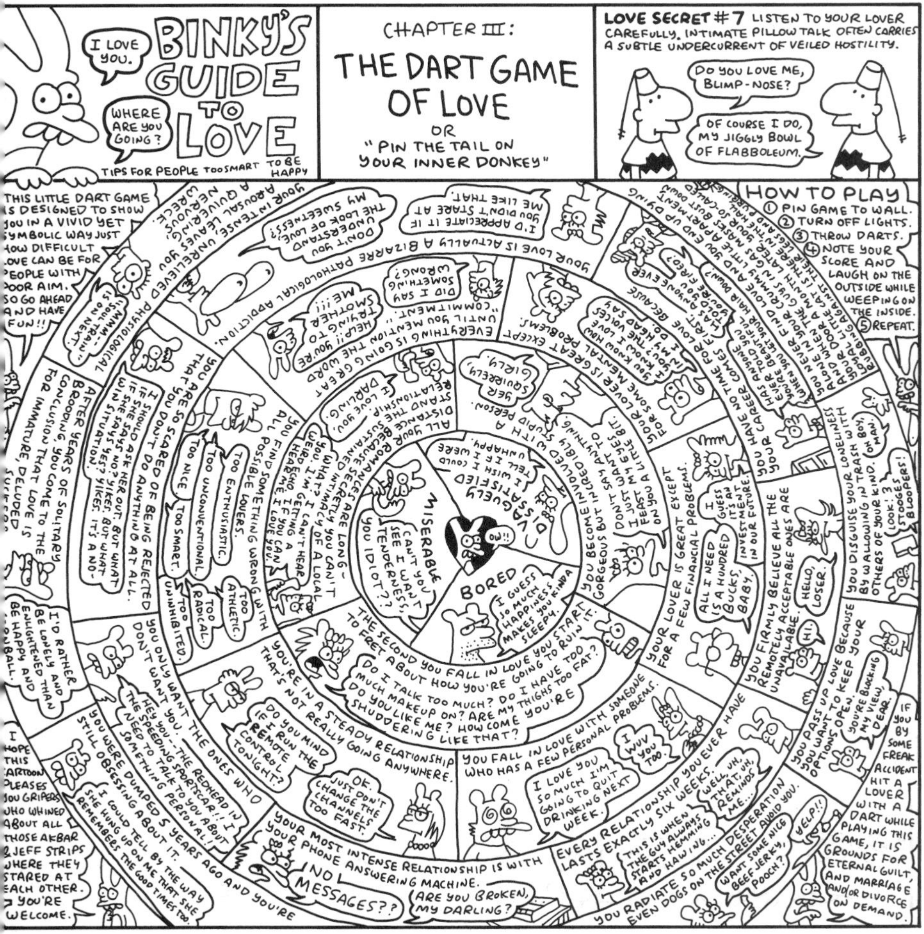
I LOVE YOU.
WHERE ARE YOU GOING?
BINKY'S GUIDE TO LOVE
TIPS FOR PEOPLE TOO SMART TO BE HAPPY
CHAPTER III:
THE DART GAME OF LOVE
OR
"PIN THE TAIL ON YOUR INNER DONKEY"
LOVE SECRET #7 LISTEN TO YOUR LOVER CAREFULLY. INTIMATE PILLOW TALK OFTEN CARRIES A SUBTLE UNDERCURRENT OF VEILED HOSTILITY.
DO YOU LOVE ME, BLIMP-NOSE?
OF COURSE I DO, MY JIGGLY BOWL OF FLABBOLEUM.
THIS LITTLE DART GAME IS DESIGNED TO SHOW YOU IN A VIVID YET SYMBOLIC WAY JUST HOW DIFFICULT LOVE CAN BE FOR PEOPLE WITH POOR AIM. SO GO AHEAD AND HAVE FUN!!
HOW TO PLAY
① PIN GAME TO WALL.
② TURN OFF LIGHTS.
③ THROW DARTS.
④ NOTE YOUR SCORE AND LAUGH ON THE OUTSIDE WHILE WEEPING ON THE INSIDE.
⑤ REPEAT.
MISERABLE
CAN'T YOU SEE I WANT TENDERNESS, YOU IDIOT??
DISSATISFIED VAGUELY
I WISH I COULD TELL IF I WERE UNHAPPY.
OW!!
BORED
I GUESS SO MUCH HAPPINESS MAKES YOU KINDA SLEEPY.
YOUR LOVE IS ACTUALLY A BIZARRE PATHOLOGICAL ADDICTION.
DON'T YOU UNDERSTAND THE LOOK OF LOVE, MY SWEETNESS?
I'D APPRECIATE IT IF YOU DIDN'T STARE AT ME LIKE THAT.
YOUR INTENSE, UNRELIEVED PHYSIOLOGICAL AROUSAL LEAVES YOU A QUIVERING, NERVOUS WRECK.
MMM...SOUL TRAIN IS ON NEXT.
YOU LOVE AND END UP DYING ALONE IN A LITTLE APARTMENT WITH YOUR CAT, WHICH EATS YOUR FACE.
YOU HAVE NO TIME FOR LOVE BECAUSE YOUR CAREER COMES FIRST.
YOU WILL NEVER FIND LOVE BECAUSE YOU'RE TOO PICKY.
EVERYTHING IS GOING GREAT UNTIL YOU MENTION THE WORD "COMMITMENT."
HELP!! YOU'RE TRYING TO SMOTHER ME!!!
DID I SAY SOMETHING WRONG?
YOUR LOVER IS GREAT EXCEPT FOR SOME MENTAL PROBLEMS.
YER SQUIRRELY, GIRLY.
YOU KNOW HOW I LOVE YOU? THE VOICES IN MY HEAD SAY I DO.
YOU BECOME INVOLVED WITH A STUPID PERSON.
DON'T SAY ANYTHING. I JUST WANT TO FEAST MY EYES ON YOU A LITTLE BIT.
YOU BECOME INCREDIBLY GORGEOUS BUT STUPID.
ALL YOUR ROMANCES ARE LONG-DISTANCE AND THE RELATIONSHIP IS SUSTAINED BY...
I LOVE YOU, DARLING.
YOU FIND SOMETHING WRONG WITH ALL POSSIBLE LOVERS.
TOO ENTHUSIASTIC.
TOO UNCONVENTIONAL.
TOO NICE.
TOO SMART.
TOO ATHLETIC.
TOO RADICAL.
TOO UNINHIBITED.
YOU ARE SO SCARED OF BEING REJECTED THAT YOU DON'T DO ANYTHING AT ALL.
I SHOULD ASK HER OUT. BUT WHAT IF SHE SAYS NO? YIKES. BUT WHAT IF SHE SAYS YES? YIKES. IT'S A NO-WIN SITUATION.
AFTER YEARS OF SOLITARY BROODING, YOU COME TO THE CONCLUSION THAT LOVE IS FOR IMMATURE, DELUDED SUCKERS.
I'D RATHER BE LONELY AND ENLIGHTENED THAN BE HAPPY AND A SCREWBALL.
YOU ONLY WANT THE ONES WHO DON'T WANT YOU.
HEY YOU--THE REDHEAD IN THE SPEEDING SPORTSCAR!! I NEED TO TALK TO YOU ABOUT SOMETHING PERSONAL!
THE SECOND YOU FALL IN LOVE YOU START TO FRET ABOUT HOW YOU'RE GOING TO RUIN IT.
DO I TALK TOO MUCH? DO I HAVE TOO MUCH MAKEUP ON? ARE MY THIGHS TOO FAT? DO YOU LIKE ME? HOW COME YOU'RE SHUDDERING LIKE THAT?
YOU'RE IN A STEADY RELATIONSHIP THAT'S NOT REALLY GOING ANYWHERE.
DO YOU MIND IF I RUN THE REMOTE CONTROL TONIGHT?
OK. JUST DON'T CHANGE THE CHANNELS TOO FAST.
YOUR LOVER IS GREAT EXCEPT FOR A FEW FINANCIAL PROBLEMS.
ALL I NEED IS A HUNDRED BUCKS, BABY.
I GUESS IT'S AN INVESTMENT IN OUR FUTURE.
YOU FIRMLY BELIEVE ALL THE REMOTELY ACCEPTABLE ONES ARE UNAVAILABLE.
HELLO, LOSER.
HI.
YOU DISGUISE YOUR LONELINESS BY WALLOWING IN TRASH WITH OTHERS OF YOUR KIND.
OH BOY, MAN.
LOOK: 3 STOOGES BLOOPERS!
YOU PASS UP LOVE BECAUSE YOU WANT TO KEEP YOUR OPTIONS OPEN.
YOU'RE BLOCKING MY VIEW, DEAR.
YOU FALL IN LOVE WITH SOMEONE WHO HAS A FEW PERSONAL PROBLEMS.
I WUV YOU TOO.
I LOVE YOU SO MUCH I'M GOING TO QUIT DRINKING NEXT WEEK.
EVERY RELATIONSHIP YOU EVER HAVE LASTS EXACTLY SIX WEEKS.
THIS IS WHEN THE GUY ALWAYS STARTS HEMMING AND HAWING...
WELL, UH, THAT, UH, REMINDS ME...
YOU RADIATE SO MUCH DESPERATION EVEN DOGS ON THE STREET AVOID YOU.
WANT SOME NICE BEEF JERKY, POOCH?
YELP!!
YOUR MOST INTENSE RELATIONSHIP IS WITH YOUR PHONE ANSWERING MACHINE.
NO MESSAGES??
ARE YOU BROKEN, MY DARLING?
YOU WERE DUMPED 5 YEARS AGO AND YOU'RE STILL OBSESSING ABOUT IT.
I COULD TELL BY THE WAY SHE HUNG UP ON ME THAT SHE REMEMBERS THE GOOD TIMES TOO.
I HOPE THIS CARTOON PLEASES YOU GRIPERS WHO WHINED ABOUT ALL THOSE AKBAR & JEFF STRIPS WHERE THEY STARED AT EACH OTHER. YOU'RE WELCOME.
IF YOU BY SOME FREAK ACCIDENT HIT A LOVER WITH A DART WHILE PLAYING THIS GAME, IT IS GROUNDS FOR ETERNAL GUILT, AND MARRIAGE AND/OR DIVORCE ON DEMAND.

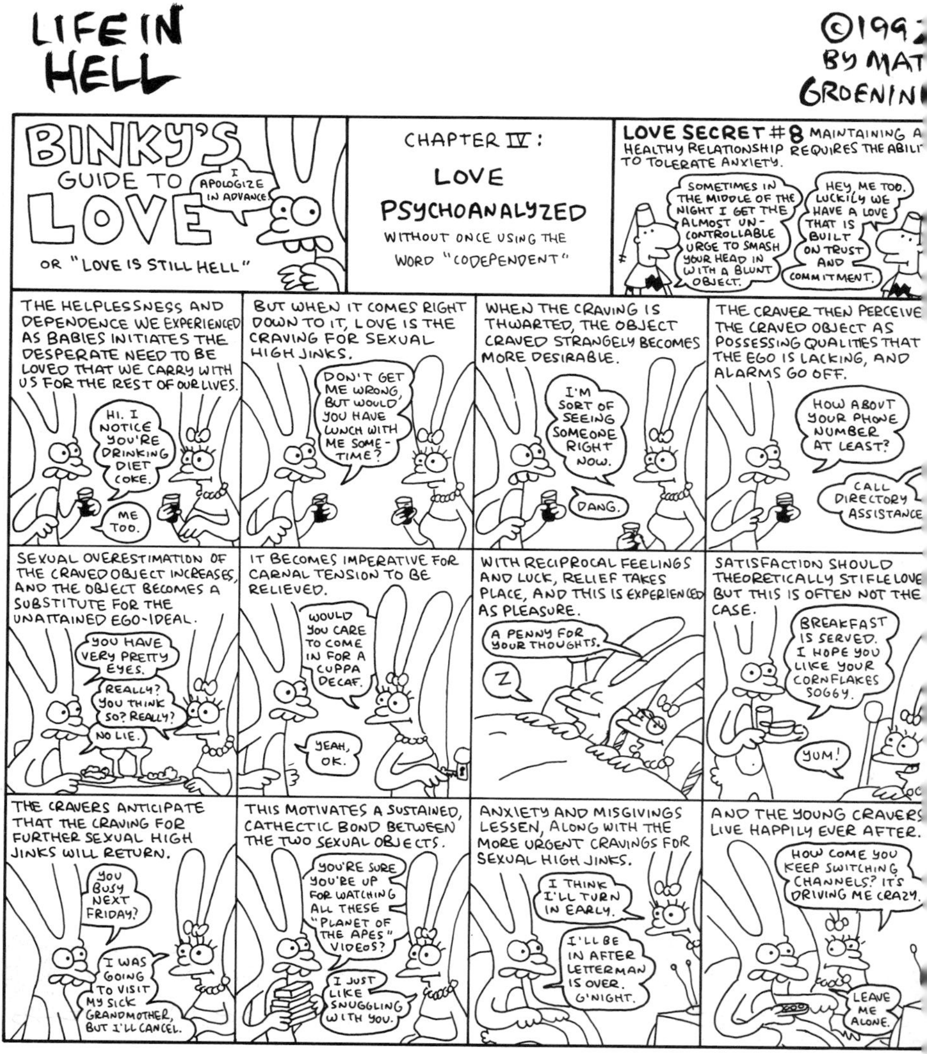
LIFE IN HELL
©199
BY MAT
GROENIN
BINKY'S GUIDE TO LOVE
I APOLOGIZE IN ADVANCE.
OR "LOVE IS STILL HELL"
CHAPTER IV:
LOVE PSYCHOANALYZED
WITHOUT ONCE USING THE WORD "CODEPENDENT"
LOVE SECRET #8 MAINTAINING A HEALTHY RELATIONSHIP REQUIRES THE ABILI TO TOLERATE ANXIETY.
SOMETIMES IN THE MIDDLE OF THE NIGHT I GET THE ALMOST UN-CONTROLLABLE URGE TO SMASH YOUR HEAD IN WITH A BLUNT OBJECT.
HEY, ME TOO. LUCKILY WE HAVE A LOVE THAT IS BUILT ON TRUST AND COMMITMENT.
THE HELPLESSNESS AND DEPENDENCE WE EXPERIENCED AS BABIES INITIATES THE DESPERATE NEED TO BE LOVED THAT WE CARRY WITH US FOR THE REST OF OUR LIVES.
HI. I NOTICE YOU'RE DRINKING DIET COKE.
ME TOO.
BUT WHEN IT COMES RIGHT DOWN TO IT, LOVE IS THE CRAVING FOR SEXUAL HIGH JINKS.
DON'T GET ME WRONG, BUT WOULD YOU HAVE LUNCH WITH ME SOME-TIME?
WHEN THE CRAVING IS THWARTED, THE OBJECT CRAVED STRANGELY BECOMES MORE DESIRABLE.
I'M SORT OF SEEING SOMEONE RIGHT NOW.
DANG.
THE CRAVER THEN PERCEIVE THE CRAVED OBJECT AS POSSESSING QUALITIES THAT THE EGO IS LACKING, AND ALARMS GO OFF.
HOW ABOUT YOUR PHONE NUMBER AT LEAST?
CALL DIRECTORY ASSISTANCE
SEXUAL OVERESTIMATION OF THE CRAVED OBJECT INCREASES, AND THE OBJECT BECOMES A SUBSTITUTE FOR THE UNATTAINED EGO-IDEAL.
YOU HAVE VERY PRETTY EYES.
REALLY? YOU THINK SO? REALLY?
NO LIE.
IT BECOMES IMPERATIVE FOR CARNAL TENSION TO BE RELIEVED.
WOULD YOU CARE TO COME IN FOR A CUPPA DECAF.
YEAH, OK.
WITH RECIPROCAL FEELINGS AND LUCK, RELIEF TAKES PLACE, AND THIS IS EXPERIENCED AS PLEASURE.
A PENNY FOR YOUR THOUGHTS.
Z
SATISFACTION SHOULD THEORETICALLY STIFLE LOVE BUT THIS IS OFTEN NOT THE CASE.
BREAKFAST IS SERVED. I HOPE YOU LIKE YOUR CORNFLAKES SOGGY.
YUM!
THE CRAVERS ANTICIPATE THAT THE CRAVING FOR FURTHER SEXUAL HIGH JINKS WILL RETURN.
YOU BUSY NEXT FRIDAY?
I WAS GOING TO VISIT MY SICK GRANDMOTHER, BUT I'LL CANCEL.
THIS MOTIVATES A SUSTAINED, CATHECTIC BOND BETWEEN THE TWO SEXUAL OBJECTS.
YOU'RE SURE YOU'RE UP FOR WATCHING ALL THESE "PLANET OF THE APES" VIDEOS?
I JUST LIKE SNUGGLING WITH YOU.
ANXIETY AND MISGIVINGS LESSEN, ALONG WITH THE MORE URGENT CRAVINGS FOR SEXUAL HIGH JINKS.
I THINK I'LL TURN IN EARLY.
I'LL BE IN AFTER LETTERMAN IS OVER. G'NIGHT.
AND THE YOUNG CRAVERS LIVE HAPPILY EVER AFTER.
HOW COME YOU KEEP SWITCHING CHANNELS? IT'S DRIVING ME CRAZY.
LEAVE ME ALONE.

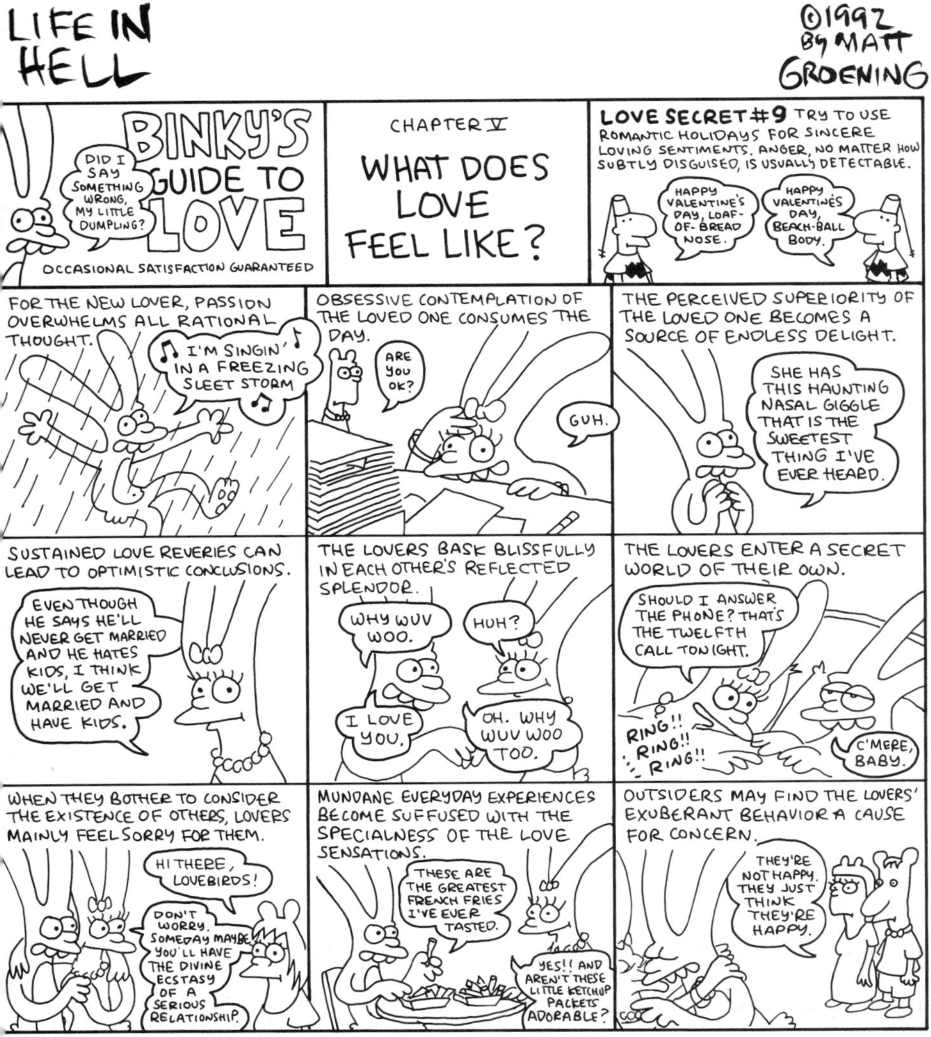
LIFE IN HELL
©1992 BY MATT GROENING
BINKY'S GUIDE TO LOVE
DID I SAY SOMETHING WRONG, MY LITTLE DUMPLING?
OCCASIONAL SATISFACTION GUARANTEED
CHAPTER V
WHAT DOES LOVE FEEL LIKE?
LOVE SECRET #9 TRY TO USE ROMANTIC HOLIDAYS FOR SINCERE LOVING SENTIMENTS. ANGER, NO MATTER HOW SUBTLY DISGUISED, IS USUALLY DETECTABLE.
HAPPY VALENTINE'S DAY, LOAF-OF-BREAD NOSE.
HAPPY VALENTINE'S DAY, BEACH-BALL BODY.
FOR THE NEW LOVER, PASSION OVERWHELMS ALL RATIONAL THOUGHT.
I'M SINGIN' IN A FREEZING SLEET STORM
OBSESSIVE CONTEMPLATION OF THE LOVED ONE CONSUMES THE DAY.
ARE YOU OK?
GUH.
THE PERCEIVED SUPERIORITY OF THE LOVED ONE BECOMES A SOURCE OF ENDLESS DELIGHT.
SHE HAS THIS HAUNTING NASAL GIGGLE THAT IS THE SWEETEST THING I'VE EVER HEARD.
SUSTAINED LOVE REVERIES CAN LEAD TO OPTIMISTIC CONCLUSIONS.
EVEN THOUGH HE SAYS HE'LL NEVER GET MARRIED AND HE HATES KIDS, I THINK WE'LL GET MARRIED AND HAVE KIDS.
THE LOVERS BASK BLISSFULLY IN EACH OTHER'S REFLECTED SPLENDOR.
WHY WUV WOO.
HUH?
I LOVE YOU.
OH. WHY WUV WOO TOO.
THE LOVERS ENTER A SECRET WORLD OF THEIR OWN.
SHOULD I ANSWER THE PHONE? THAT'S THE TWELFTH CALL TONIGHT.
RING!! RING!! RING!!
C'MERE, BABY.
WHEN THEY BOTHER TO CONSIDER THE EXISTENCE OF OTHERS, LOVERS MAINLY FEEL SORRY FOR THEM.
HI THERE, LOVEBIRDS!
DON'T WORRY. SOMEDAY MAYBE YOU'LL HAVE THE DIVINE ECSTASY OF A SERIOUS RELATIONSHIP.
MUNDANE EVERYDAY EXPERIENCES BECOME SUFFUSED WITH THE SPECIALNESS OF THE LOVE SENSATIONS.
THESE ARE THE GREATEST FRENCH FRIES I'VE EVER TASTED.
YES!! AND AREN'T THESE LITTLE KETCHUP PACKETS ADORABLE?
OUTSIDERS MAY FIND THE LOVERS' EXUBERANT BEHAVIOR A CAUSE FOR CONCERN.
THEY'RE NOT HAPPY. THEY JUST THINK THEY'RE HAPPY.

LIFE IN HELL

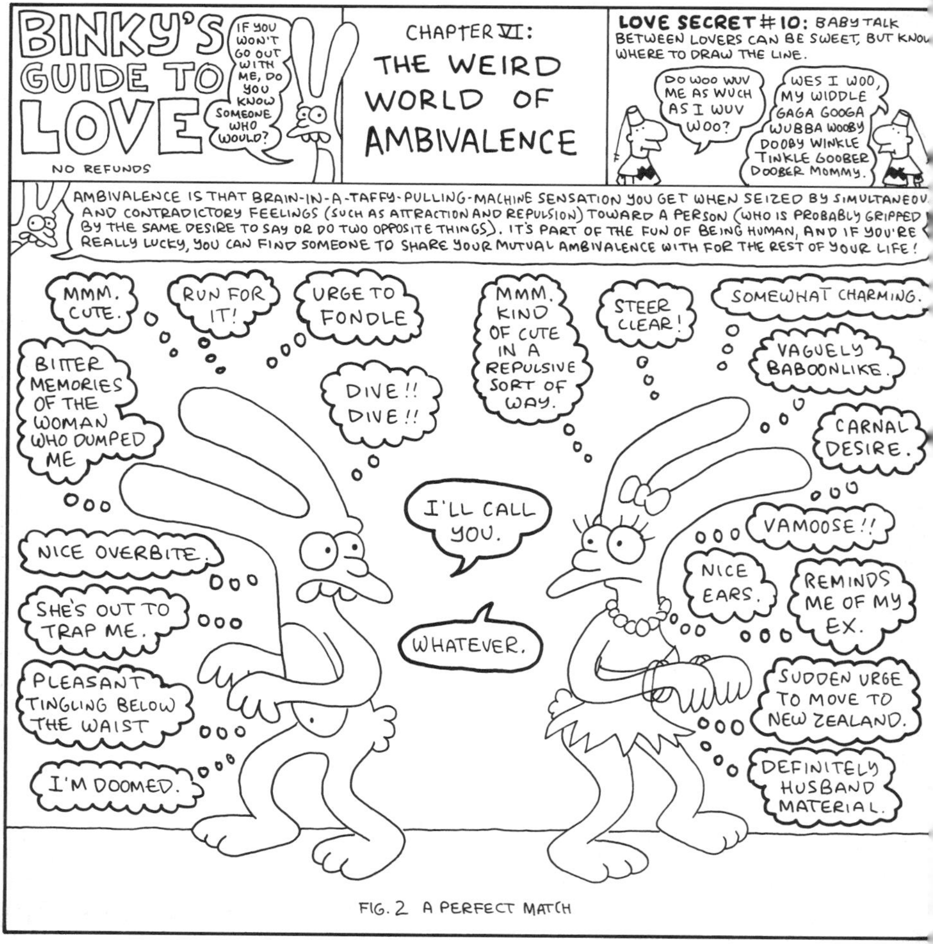
BINKY'S GUIDE TO LOVE
IF YOU WON'T GO OUT WITH ME, DO YOU KNOW SOMEONE WHO WOULD?
NO REFUNDS
CHAPTER VI: THE WEIRD WORLD OF AMBIVALENCE
LOVE SECRET #10: BABY TALK BETWEEN LOVERS CAN BE SWEET, BUT KNO
WHERE TO DRAW THE LINE.
DO WOO WUV ME AS WUCH AS I WUV WOO?
WES I WOO, MY WIDDLE GAGA GOOGA WUBBA WOOBY DOOBY WINKLE TINKLE GOOBER DOOBER MOMMY.
AMBIVALENCE IS THAT BRAIN-IN-A-TAFFY-PULLING-MACHINE SENSATION YOU GET WHEN SEIZED BY SIMULTANEOU
AND CONTRADICTORY FEELINGS (SUCH AS ATTRACTION AND REPULSION) TOWARD A PERSON (WHO IS PROBABLY GRIPPED
BY THE SAME DESIRE TO SAY OR DO TWO OPPOSITE THINGS). IT'S PART OF THE FUN OF BEING HUMAN, AND IF YOU'RE
REALLY LUCKY, YOU CAN FIND SOMEONE TO SHARE YOUR MUTUAL AMBIVALENCE WITH FOR THE REST OF YOUR LIFE!
MMM. CUTE.
RUN FOR IT!
URGE TO FONDLE
BITTER MEMORIES OF THE WOMAN WHO DUMPED ME
DIVE!! DIVE!!
NICE OVERBITE.
SHE'S OUT TO TRAP ME.
PLEASANT TINGLING BELOW THE WAIST
I'M DOOMED.
I'LL CALL YOU.
WHATEVER.
MMM. KIND OF CUTE IN A REPULSIVE SORT OF WAY.
STEER CLEAR!
SOMEWHAT CHARMING.
VAGUELY BABOONLIKE.
CARNAL DESIRE.
VAMOOSE!!
NICE EARS.
REMINDS ME OF MY EX.
SUDDEN URGE TO MOVE TO NEW ZEALAND.
DEFINITELY HUSBAND MATERIAL.

FIG. 2 A PERFECT MATCH

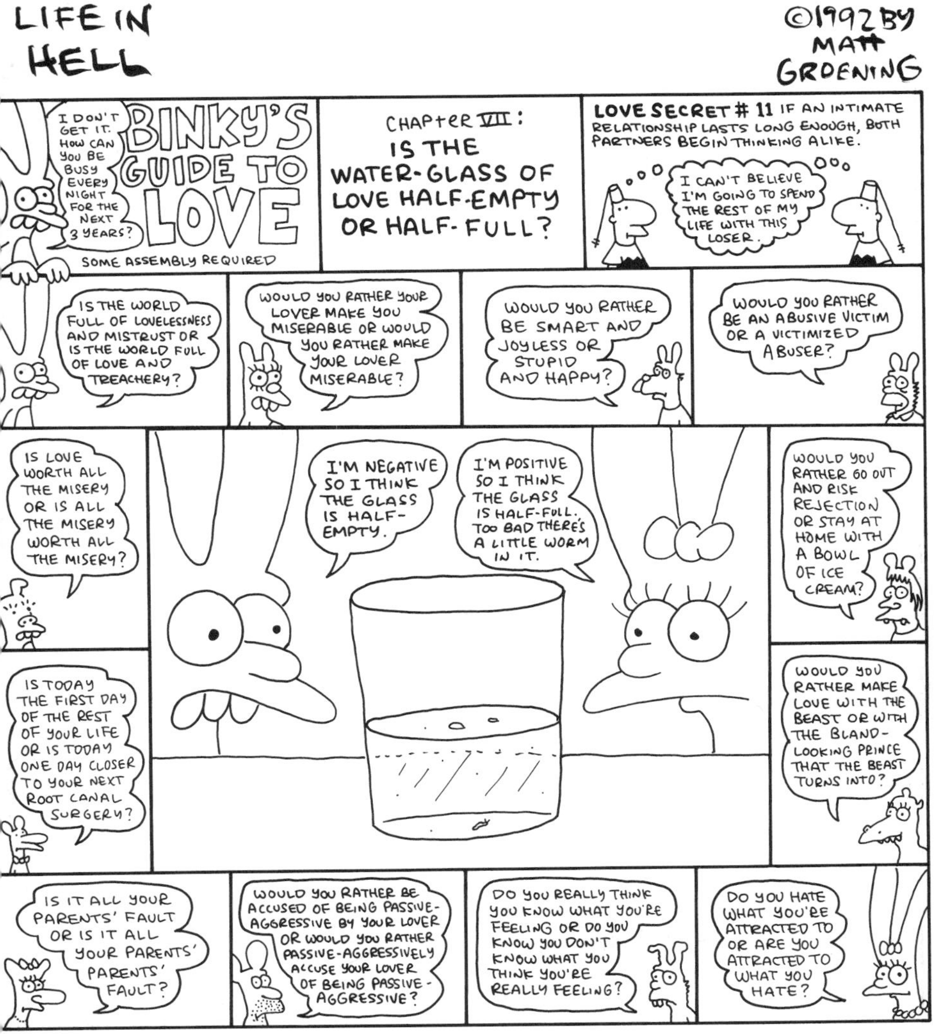

LIFE IN HELL
©1992 BY MATT GROENING
I DON'T GET IT. HOW CAN YOU BE BUSY EVERY NIGHT FOR THE NEXT 3 YEARS?
BINKY'S GUIDE TO LOVE
SOME ASSEMBLY REQUIRED
CHAPTER VII: IS THE WATER-GLASS OF LOVE HALF-EMPTY OR HALF-FULL?
LOVE SECRET # 11 IF AN INTIMATE RELATIONSHIP LASTS LONG ENOUGH, BOTH PARTNERS BEGIN THINKING ALIKE.
I CAN'T BELIEVE I'M GOING TO SPEND THE REST OF MY LIFE WITH THIS LOSER.
IS THE WORLD FULL OF LOVELESSNESS AND MISTRUST OR IS THE WORLD FULL OF LOVE AND TREACHERY?
WOULD YOU RATHER YOUR LOVER MAKE YOU MISERABLE OR WOULD YOU RATHER MAKE YOUR LOVER MISERABLE?
WOULD YOU RATHER BE SMART AND JOYLESS OR STUPID AND HAPPY?
WOULD YOU RATHER BE AN ABUSIVE VICTIM OR A VICTIMIZED ABUSER?
IS LOVE WORTH ALL THE MISERY OR IS ALL THE MISERY WORTH ALL THE MISERY?
I'M NEGATIVE SO I THINK THE GLASS IS HALF-EMPTY.
I'M POSITIVE SO I THINK THE GLASS IS HALF-FULL. TOO BAD THERE'S A LITTLE WORM IN IT.
WOULD YOU RATHER GO OUT AND RISK REJECTION OR STAY AT HOME WITH A BOWL OF ICE CREAM?
IS TODAY THE FIRST DAY OF THE REST OF YOUR LIFE OR IS TODAY ONE DAY CLOSER TO YOUR NEXT ROOT CANAL SURGERY?
WOULD YOU RATHER MAKE LOVE WITH THE BEAST OR WITH THE BLAND-LOOKING PRINCE THAT THE BEAST TURNS INTO?
IS IT ALL YOUR PARENTS' FAULT OR IS IT ALL YOUR PARENTS' PARENTS' FAULT?
WOULD YOU RATHER BE ACCUSED OF BEING PASSIVE-AGGRESSIVE BY YOUR LOVER OR WOULD YOU RATHER PASSIVE-AGGRESSIVELY ACCUSE YOUR LOVER OF BEING PASSIVE-AGGRESSIVE?
DO YOU REALLY THINK YOU KNOW WHAT YOU'RE FEELING OR DO YOU KNOW YOU DON'T KNOW WHAT YOU THINK YOU'RE REALLY FEELING?
DO YOU HATE WHAT YOU'RE ATTRACTED TO OR ARE YOU ATTRACTED TO WHAT YOU HATE?

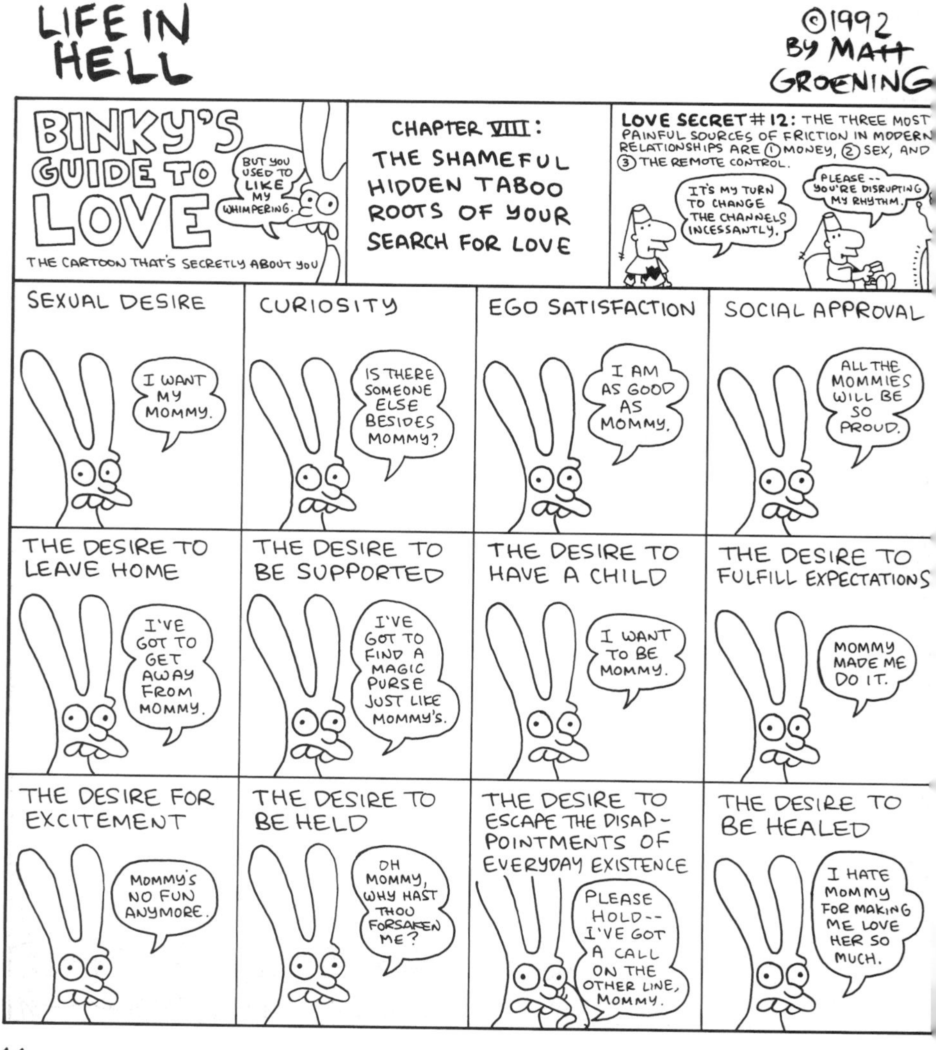
LIFE IN HELL
©1992 BY MATT GROENING
BINKY'S GUIDE TO LOVE
THE CARTOON THAT'S SECRETLY ABOUT YOU
BUT YOU USED TO LIKE MY WHIMPERING.
CHAPTER VIII: THE SHAMEFUL HIDDEN TABOO ROOTS OF YOUR SEARCH FOR LOVE
LOVE SECRET #12: THE THREE MOST PAINFUL SOURCES OF FRICTION IN MODERN RELATIONSHIPS ARE ① MONEY, ② SEX, AND ③ THE REMOTE CONTROL.
IT'S MY TURN TO CHANGE THE CHANNELS INCESSANTLY.
PLEASE -- YOU'RE DISRUPTING MY RHYTHM.
SEXUAL DESIRE
I WANT MY MOMMY.
CURIOSITY
IS THERE SOMEONE ELSE BESIDES MOMMY?
EGO SATISFACTION
I AM AS GOOD AS MOMMY.
SOCIAL APPROVAL
ALL THE MOMMIES WILL BE SO PROUD.
THE DESIRE TO LEAVE HOME
I'VE GOT TO GET AWAY FROM MOMMY.
THE DESIRE TO BE SUPPORTED
I'VE GOT TO FIND A MAGIC PURSE JUST LIKE MOMMY'S.
THE DESIRE TO HAVE A CHILD
I WANT TO BE MOMMY.
THE DESIRE TO FULFILL EXPECTATIONS
MOMMY MADE ME DO IT.
THE DESIRE FOR EXCITEMENT
MOMMY'S NO FUN ANYMORE.
THE DESIRE TO BE HELD
OH MOMMY, WHY HAST THOU FORSAKEN ME?
THE DESIRE TO ESCAPE THE DISAPPOINTMENTS OF EVERYDAY EXISTENCE
PLEASE HOLD -- I'VE GOT A CALL ON THE OTHER LINE, MOMMY.
THE DESIRE TO BE HEALED
I HATE MOMMY FOR MAKING ME LOVE HER SO MUCH.

LIFE IN HELL

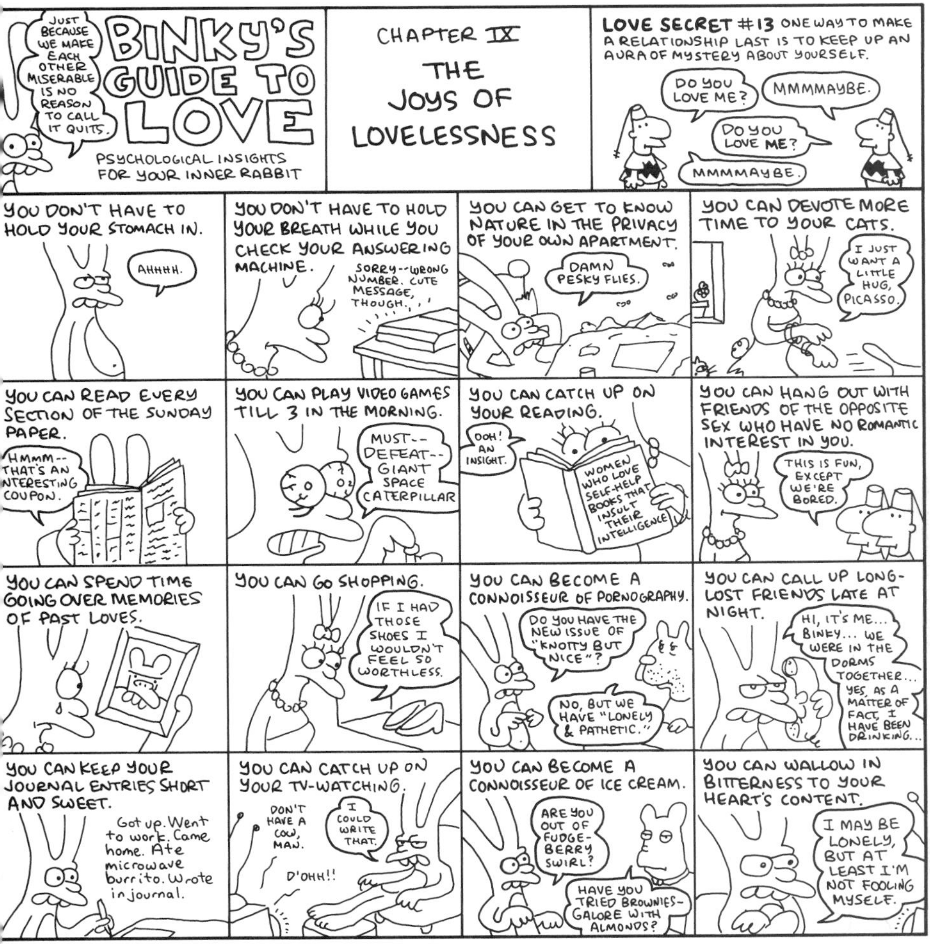
JUST BECAUSE WE MAKE EACH OTHER MISERABLE IS NO REASON TO CALL IT QUITS.
BINKY'S GUIDE TO LOVE
PSYCHOLOGICAL INSIGHTS FOR YOUR INNER RABBIT
CHAPTER IX
THE JOYS OF LOVELESSNESS
LOVE SECRET #13 ONE WAY TO MAKE A RELATIONSHIP LAST IS TO KEEP UP AN AURA OF MYSTERY ABOUT YOURSELF.
DO YOU LOVE ME?
MMMMAYBE.
DO YOU LOVE ME?
MMMMAYBE.
YOU DON'T HAVE TO HOLD YOUR STOMACH IN.
AHHHH.
YOU DON'T HAVE TO HOLD YOUR BREATH WHILE YOU CHECK YOUR ANSWERING MACHINE.
SORRY--WRONG NUMBER. CUTE MESSAGE, THOUGH.
YOU CAN GET TO KNOW NATURE IN THE PRIVACY OF YOUR OWN APARTMENT.
DAMN PESKY FLIES.
YOU CAN DEVOTE MORE TIME TO YOUR CATS.
I JUST WANT A LITTLE HUG, PICASSO.
YOU CAN READ EVERY SECTION OF THE SUNDAY PAPER.
HMMM-- THAT'S AN INTERESTING COUPON.
YOU CAN PLAY VIDEO GAMES TILL 3 IN THE MORNING.
MUST-- DEFEAT-- GIANT SPACE CATERPILLAR
YOU CAN CATCH UP ON YOUR READING.
OOH! AN INSIGHT.
WOMEN WHO LOVE SELF-HELP BOOKS THAT INSULT THEIR INTELLIGENCE
YOU CAN HANG OUT WITH FRIENDS OF THE OPPOSITE SEX WHO HAVE NO ROMANTIC INTEREST IN YOU.
THIS IS FUN, EXCEPT WE'RE BORED.
YOU CAN SPEND TIME GOING OVER MEMORIES OF PAST LOVES.
YOU CAN GO SHOPPING.
IF I HAD THOSE SHOES I WOULDN'T FEEL SO WORTHLESS.
YOU CAN BECOME A CONNOISSEUR OF PORNOGRAPHY.
DO YOU HAVE THE NEW ISSUE OF "KNOTTY BUT NICE"?
NO, BUT WE HAVE "LONELY & PATHETIC."
YOU CAN CALL UP LONG-LOST FRIENDS LATE AT NIGHT.
HI, IT'S ME... BINKY... WE WERE IN THE DORMS TOGETHER... YES, AS A MATTER OF FACT, I HAVE BEEN DRINKING...
YOU CAN KEEP YOUR JOURNAL ENTRIES SHORT AND SWEET.
Got up. Went to work. Came home. Ate microwave burrito. Wrote in journal.
YOU CAN CATCH UP ON YOUR TV-WATCHING.
DON'T HAVE A COW, MAN.
D'OHH!!
I COULD WRITE THAT.
YOU CAN BECOME A CONNOISSEUR OF ICE CREAM.
ARE YOU OUT OF FUDGE-BERRY SWIRL?
HAVE YOU TRIED BROWNIES-GALORE WITH ALMONDS?
YOU CAN WALLOW IN BITTERNESS TO YOUR HEART'S CONTENT.
I MAY BE LONELY, BUT AT LEAST I'M NOT FOOLING MYSELF.

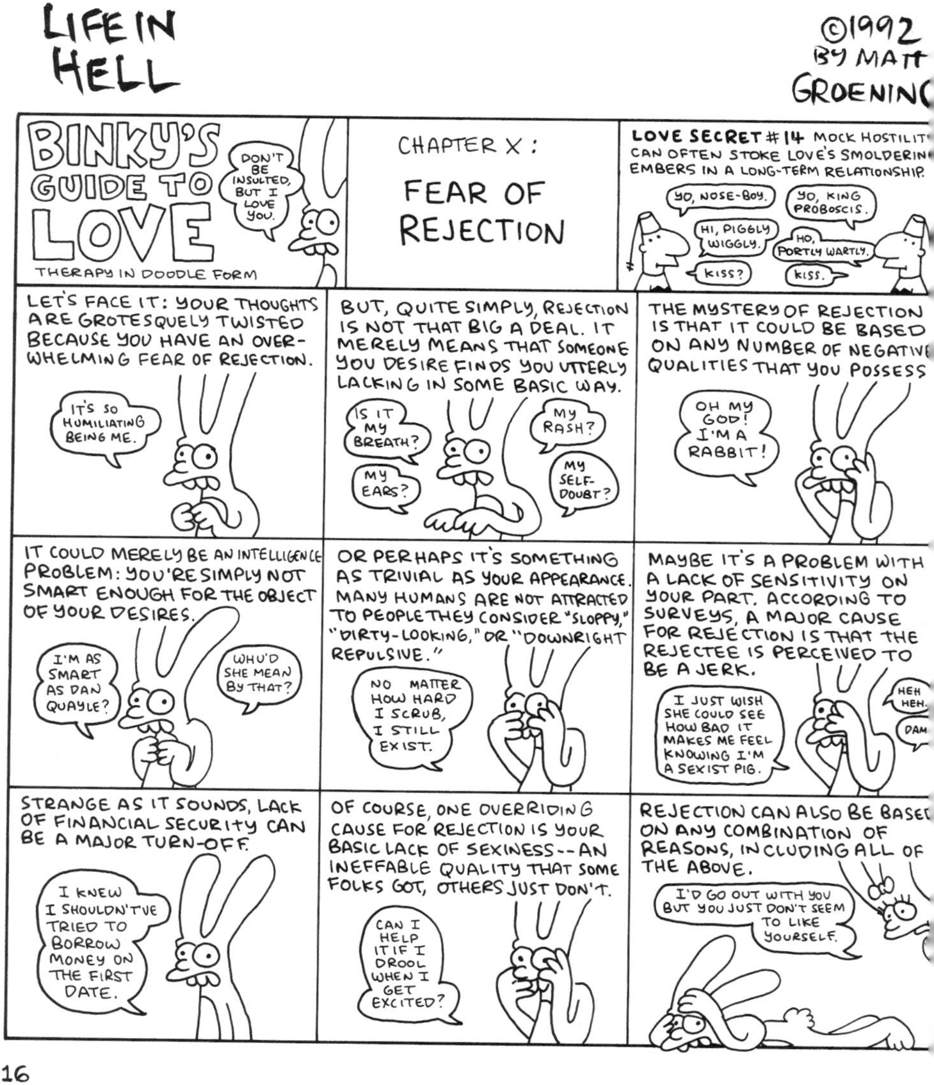
LIFE IN HELL
©1992 BY MATT GROENING
BINKY'S GUIDE TO LOVE
THERAPY IN DOODLE FORM
DON'T BE INSULTED, BUT I LOVE YOU.
CHAPTER X:
FEAR OF REJECTION
LOVE SECRET #14 MOCK HOSTILITY CAN OFTEN STOKE LOVE'S SMOLDERING EMBERS IN A LONG-TERM RELATIONSHIP.
YO, NOSE-BOY.
YO, KING PROBOSCIS.
HI, PIGGLY WIGGLY.
HO, PORTLY WARTLY.
KISS?
KISS.
LET'S FACE IT: YOUR THOUGHTS ARE GROTESQUELY TWISTED BECAUSE YOU HAVE AN OVERWHELMING FEAR OF REJECTION.
IT'S SO HUMILIATING BEING ME.
BUT, QUITE SIMPLY, REJECTION IS NOT THAT BIG A DEAL. IT MERELY MEANS THAT SOMEONE YOU DESIRE FINDS YOU UTTERLY LACKING IN SOME BASIC WAY.
IS IT MY BREATH?
MY RASH?
MY EARS?
MY SELF-DOUBT?
THE MYSTERY OF REJECTION IS THAT IT COULD BE BASED ON ANY NUMBER OF NEGATIVE QUALITIES THAT YOU POSSESS.
OH MY GOD! I'M A RABBIT!
IT COULD MERELY BE AN INTELLIGENCE PROBLEM: YOU'RE SIMPLY NOT SMART ENOUGH FOR THE OBJECT OF YOUR DESIRES.
I'M AS SMART AS DAN QUAYLE?
WHU'D SHE MEAN BY THAT?
OR PERHAPS IT'S SOMETHING AS TRIVIAL AS YOUR APPEARANCE. MANY HUMANS ARE NOT ATTRACTED TO PEOPLE THEY CONSIDER "SLOPPY," "DIRTY-LOOKING," OR "DOWNRIGHT REPULSIVE."
NO MATTER HOW HARD I SCRUB, I STILL EXIST.
MAYBE IT'S A PROBLEM WITH A LACK OF SENSITIVITY ON YOUR PART. ACCORDING TO SURVEYS, A MAJOR CAUSE FOR REJECTION IS THAT THE REJECTEE IS PERCEIVED TO BE A JERK.
I JUST WISH SHE COULD SEE HOW BAD IT MAKES ME FEEL KNOWING I'M A SEXIST PIG.
HEH HEH.
STRANGE AS IT SOUNDS, LACK OF FINANCIAL SECURITY CAN BE A MAJOR TURN-OFF.
I KNEW I SHOULDN'T'VE TRIED TO BORROW MONEY ON THE FIRST DATE.
OF COURSE, ONE OVERRIDING CAUSE FOR REJECTION IS YOUR BASIC LACK OF SEXINESS--AN INEFFABLE QUALITY THAT SOME FOLKS GOT, OTHERS JUST DON'T.
CAN I HELP IT IF I DROOL WHEN I GET EXCITED?
REJECTION CAN ALSO BE BASED ON ANY COMBINATION OF REASONS, INCLUDING ALL OF THE ABOVE.
I'D GO OUT WITH YOU BUT YOU JUST DON'T SEEM TO LIKE YOURSELF.

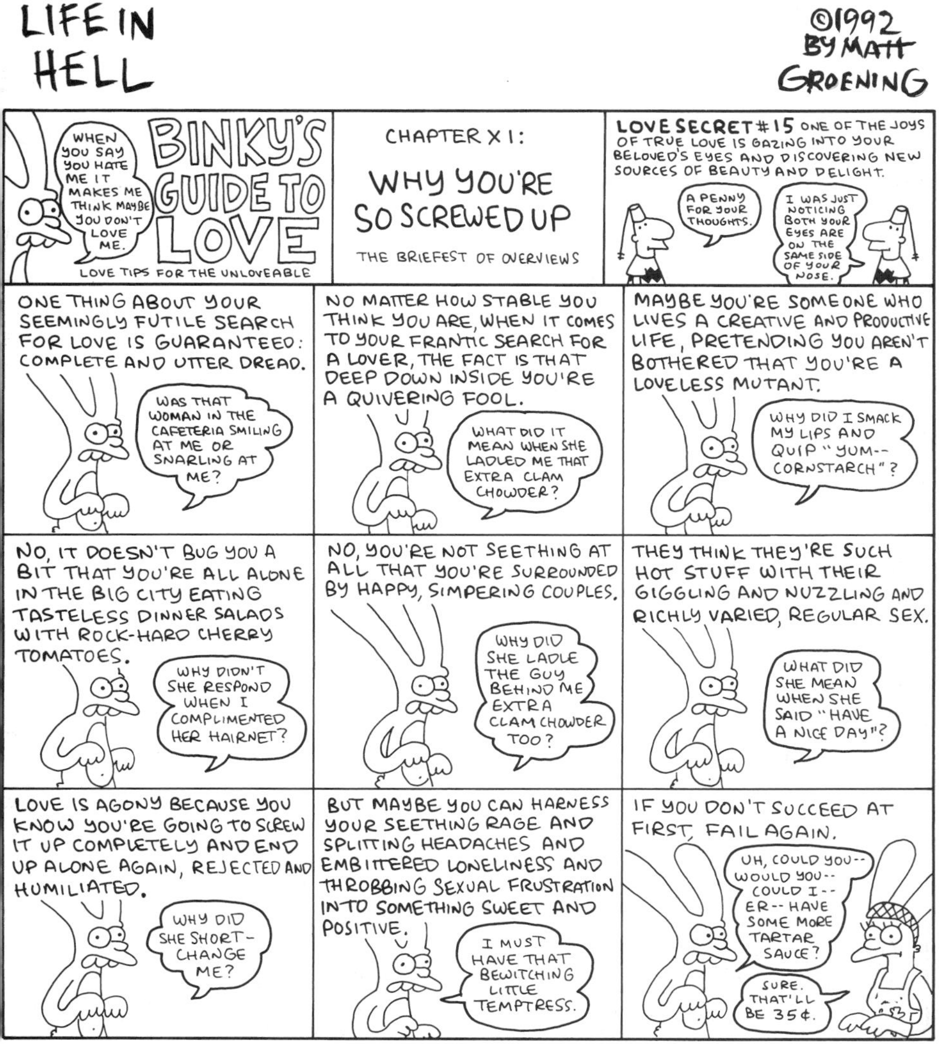
LIFE IN HELL
©1992 BY MATT GROENING
WHEN YOU SAY YOU HATE ME IT MAKES ME THINK MAYBE YOU DON'T LOVE ME.
BINKY'S GUIDE TO LOVE
LOVE TIPS FOR THE UNLOVEABLE
CHAPTER XI:
WHY YOU'RE SO SCREWED UP
THE BRIEFEST OF OVERVIEWS
LOVE SECRET #15 ONE OF THE JOYS OF TRUE LOVE IS GAZING INTO YOUR BELOVED'S EYES AND DISCOVERING NEW SOURCES OF BEAUTY AND DELIGHT.
A PENNY FOR YOUR THOUGHTS.
I WAS JUST NOTICING BOTH YOUR EYES ARE ON THE SAME SIDE OF YOUR NOSE.
ONE THING ABOUT YOUR SEEMINGLY FUTILE SEARCH FOR LOVE IS GUARANTEED: COMPLETE AND UTTER DREAD.
WAS THAT WOMAN IN THE CAFETERIA SMILING AT ME OR SNARLING AT ME?
NO MATTER HOW STABLE YOU THINK YOU ARE, WHEN IT COMES TO YOUR FRANTIC SEARCH FOR A LOVER, THE FACT IS THAT DEEP DOWN INSIDE YOU'RE A QUIVERING FOOL.
WHAT DID IT MEAN WHEN SHE LADLED ME THAT EXTRA CLAM CHOWDER?
MAYBE YOU'RE SOMEONE WHO LIVES A CREATIVE AND PRODUCTIVE LIFE, PRETENDING YOU AREN'T BOTHERED THAT YOU'RE A LOVELESS MUTANT.
WHY DID I SMACK MY LIPS AND QUIP "YUM--CORNSTARCH"?
NO, IT DOESN'T BUG YOU A BIT THAT YOU'RE ALL ALONE IN THE BIG CITY EATING TASTELESS DINNER SALADS WITH ROCK-HARD CHERRY TOMATOES.
WHY DIDN'T SHE RESPOND WHEN I COMPLIMENTED HER HAIRNET?
NO, YOU'RE NOT SEETHING AT ALL THAT YOU'RE SURROUNDED BY HAPPY, SIMPERING COUPLES.
WHY DID SHE LADLE THE GUY BEHIND ME EXTRA CLAM CHOWDER TOO?
THEY THINK THEY'RE SUCH HOT STUFF WITH THEIR GIGGLING AND NUZZLING AND RICHLY VARIED, REGULAR SEX.
WHAT DID SHE MEAN WHEN SHE SAID "HAVE A NICE DAY"?
LOVE IS AGONY BECAUSE YOU KNOW YOU'RE GOING TO SCREW IT UP COMPLETELY AND END UP ALONE AGAIN, REJECTED AND HUMILIATED.
WHY DID SHE SHORT-CHANGE ME?
BUT MAYBE YOU CAN HARNESS YOUR SEETHING RAGE AND SPLITTING HEADACHES AND EMBITTERED LONELINESS AND THROBBING SEXUAL FRUSTRATION INTO SOMETHING SWEET AND POSITIVE.
I MUST HAVE THAT BEWITCHING LITTLE TEMPTRESS.
IF YOU DON'T SUCCEED AT FIRST, FAIL AGAIN.
UH, COULD YOU-- WOULD YOU-- COULD I-- ER-- HAVE SOME MORE TARTAR SAUCE?
SURE. THAT'LL BE 35¢.

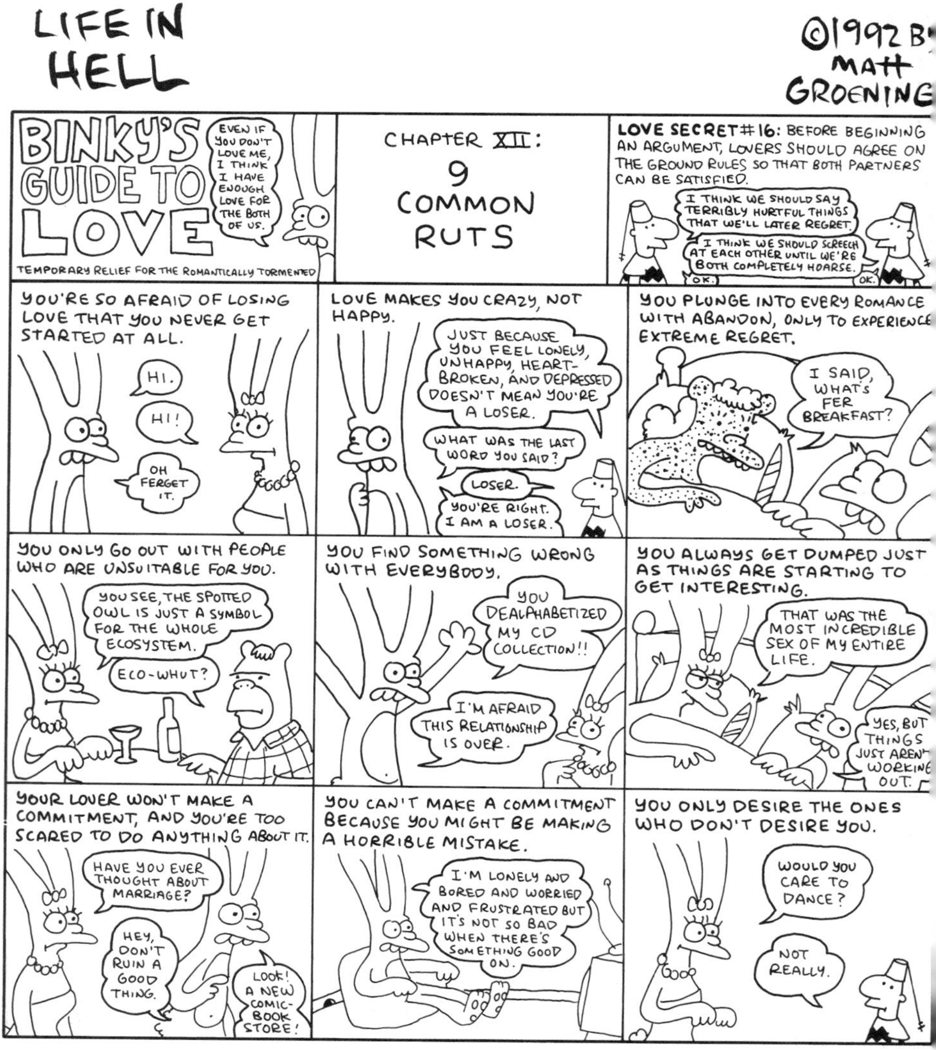
LIFE IN HELL
©1992 BY MATT GROENING
BINKY'S GUIDE TO LOVE
EVEN IF YOU DON'T LOVE ME, I THINK I HAVE ENOUGH LOVE FOR THE BOTH OF US.
TEMPORARY RELIEF FOR THE ROMANTICALLY TORMENTED
CHAPTER XII: 9 COMMON RUTS
LOVE SECRET #16: BEFORE BEGINNING AN ARGUMENT, LOVERS SHOULD AGREE ON THE GROUND RULES SO THAT BOTH PARTNERS CAN BE SATISFIED.
I THINK WE SHOULD SAY TERRIBLY HURTFUL THINGS THAT WE'LL LATER REGRET.
I THINK WE SHOULD SCREECH AT EACH OTHER UNTIL WE'RE BOTH COMPLETELY HOARSE.
OK.
OK.
YOU'RE SO AFRAID OF LOSING LOVE THAT YOU NEVER GET STARTED AT ALL.
HI.
HI!
OH FERGET IT.
LOVE MAKES YOU CRAZY, NOT HAPPY.
JUST BECAUSE YOU FEEL LONELY, UNHAPPY, HEART-BROKEN, AND DEPRESSED DOESN'T MEAN YOU'RE A LOSER.
WHAT WAS THE LAST WORD YOU SAID?
LOSER.
YOU'RE RIGHT. I AM A LOSER.
YOU PLUNGE INTO EVERY ROMANCE WITH ABANDON, ONLY TO EXPERIENCE EXTREME REGRET.
I SAID, WHAT'S FER BREAKFAST?
YOU ONLY GO OUT WITH PEOPLE WHO ARE UNSUITABLE FOR YOU.
YOU SEE, THE SPOTTED OWL IS JUST A SYMBOL FOR THE WHOLE ECOSYSTEM.
ECO-WHUT?
YOU FIND SOMETHING WRONG WITH EVERYBODY.
YOU DEALPHABETIZED MY CD COLLECTION!!
I'M AFRAID THIS RELATIONSHIP IS OVER.
YOU ALWAYS GET DUMPED JUST AS THINGS ARE STARTING TO GET INTERESTING.
THAT WAS THE MOST INCREDIBLE SEX OF MY ENTIRE LIFE.
YES, BUT THINGS JUST AREN'T WORKING OUT.
YOUR LOVER WON'T MAKE A COMMITMENT, AND YOU'RE TOO SCARED TO DO ANYTHING ABOUT IT.
HAVE YOU EVER THOUGHT ABOUT MARRIAGE?
HEY, DON'T RUIN A GOOD THING.
LOOK! A NEW COMIC-BOOK STORE!
YOU CAN'T MAKE A COMMITMENT BECAUSE YOU MIGHT BE MAKING A HORRIBLE MISTAKE.
I'M LONELY AND BORED AND WORRIED AND FRUSTRATED BUT IT'S NOT SO BAD WHEN THERE'S SOMETHING GOOD ON.
YOU ONLY DESIRE THE ONES WHO DON'T DESIRE YOU.
WOULD YOU CARE TO DANCE?
NOT REALLY.

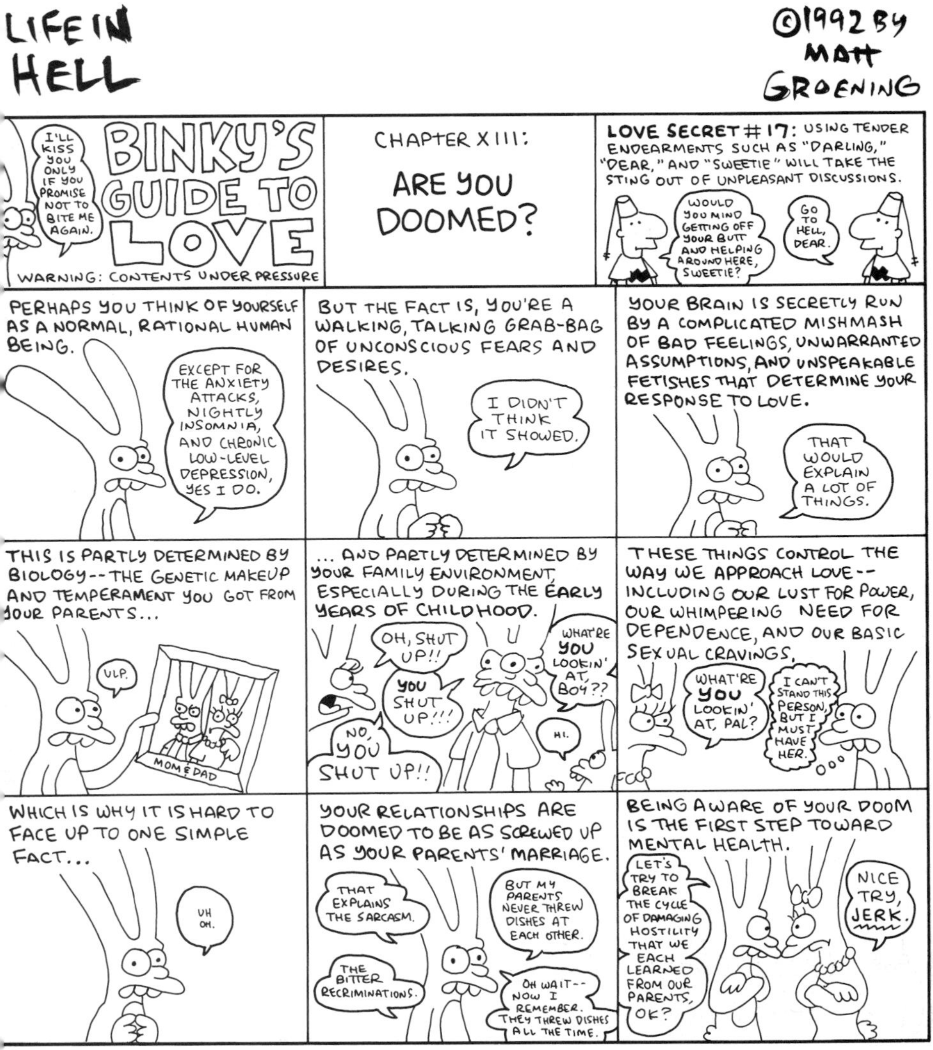
LIFE IN HELL
©1992 BY MATT GROENING
I'LL KISS YOU ONLY IF YOU PROMISE NOT TO BITE ME AGAIN.
BINKY'S GUIDE TO LOVE
WARNING: CONTENTS UNDER PRESSURE
CHAPTER XIII:
ARE YOU DOOMED?
LOVE SECRET #17: USING TENDER ENDEARMENTS SUCH AS "DARLING," "DEAR," AND "SWEETIE" WILL TAKE THE STING OUT OF UNPLEASANT DISCUSSIONS.
WOULD YOU MIND GETTING OFF YOUR BUTT AND HELPING AROUND HERE, SWEETIE?
GO TO HELL, DEAR.
PERHAPS YOU THINK OF YOURSELF AS A NORMAL, RATIONAL HUMAN BEING.
EXCEPT FOR THE ANXIETY ATTACKS, NIGHTLY INSOMNIA, AND CHRONIC LOW-LEVEL DEPRESSION, YES I DO.
BUT THE FACT IS, YOU'RE A WALKING, TALKING GRAB-BAG OF UNCONSCIOUS FEARS AND DESIRES.
I DIDN'T THINK IT SHOWED.
YOUR BRAIN IS SECRETLY RUN BY A COMPLICATED MISHMASH OF BAD FEELINGS, UNWARRANTED ASSUMPTIONS, AND UNSPEAKABLE FETISHES THAT DETERMINE YOUR RESPONSE TO LOVE.
THAT WOULD EXPLAIN A LOT OF THINGS.
THIS IS PARTLY DETERMINED BY BIOLOGY--THE GENETIC MAKEUP AND TEMPERAMENT YOU GOT FROM YOUR PARENTS...
ULP.
MOM & DAD
... AND PARTLY DETERMINED BY YOUR FAMILY ENVIRONMENT, ESPECIALLY DURING THE EARLY YEARS OF CHILDHOOD.
OH, SHUT UP!!
YOU SHUT UP!!!
NO, YOU SHUT UP!!
WHAT'RE YOU LOOKIN' AT, BOY??
HI.
THESE THINGS CONTROL THE WAY WE APPROACH LOVE-- INCLUDING OUR LUST FOR POWER, OUR WHIMPERING NEED FOR DEPENDENCE, AND OUR BASIC SEXUAL CRAVINGS,
WHAT'RE YOU LOOKIN' AT, PAL?
I CAN'T STAND THIS PERSON, BUT I MUST HAVE HER.
WHICH IS WHY IT IS HARD TO FACE UP TO ONE SIMPLE FACT...
UH OH.
YOUR RELATIONSHIPS ARE DOOMED TO BE AS SCREWED UP AS YOUR PARENTS' MARRIAGE.
THAT EXPLAINS THE SARCASM.
THE BITTER RECRIMINATIONS.
BUT MY PARENTS NEVER THREW DISHES AT EACH OTHER.
OH WAIT-- NOW I REMEMBER. THEY THREW DISHES ALL THE TIME.
BEING AWARE OF YOUR DOOM IS THE FIRST STEP TOWARD MENTAL HEALTH.
LET'S TRY TO BREAK THE CYCLE OF DAMAGING HOSTILITY THAT WE EACH LEARNED FROM OUR PARENTS, OK?
NICE TRY, JERK.

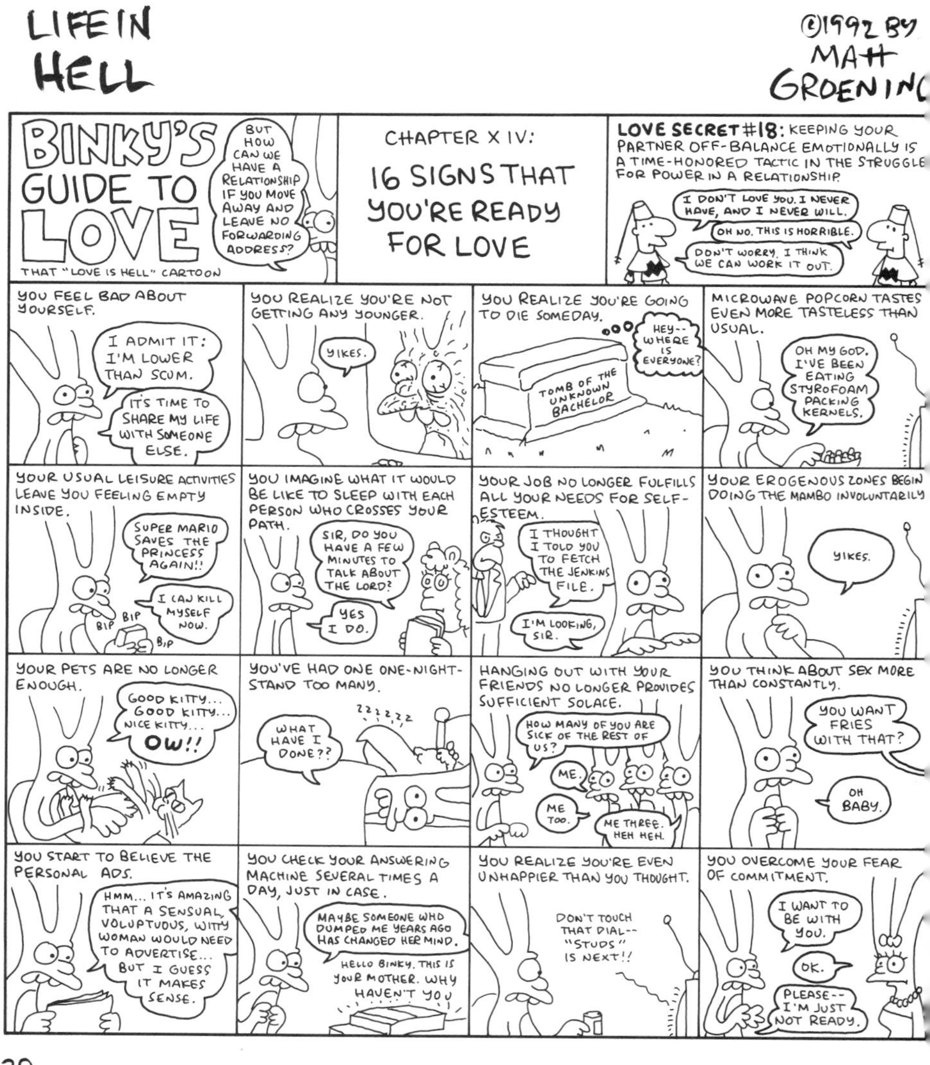
LIFE IN HELL
©1992 BY MATT GROENING
BINKY'S GUIDE TO LOVE
THAT "LOVE IS HELL" CARTOON
BUT HOW CAN WE HAVE A RELATIONSHIP IF YOU MOVE AWAY AND LEAVE NO FORWARDING ADDRESS?
CHAPTER XIV:
16 SIGNS THAT YOU'RE READY FOR LOVE
LOVE SECRET #18: KEEPING YOUR PARTNER OFF-BALANCE EMOTIONALLY IS A TIME-HONORED TACTIC IN THE STRUGGLE FOR POWER IN A RELATIONSHIP.
I DON'T LOVE YOU. I NEVER HAVE, AND I NEVER WILL.
OH NO. THIS IS HORRIBLE.
DON'T WORRY. I THINK WE CAN WORK IT OUT.
YOU FEEL BAD ABOUT YOURSELF.
I ADMIT IT: I'M LOWER THAN SCUM.
IT'S TIME TO SHARE MY LIFE WITH SOMEONE ELSE.
YOU REALIZE YOU'RE NOT GETTING ANY YOUNGER.
YIKES.
YOU REALIZE YOU'RE GOING TO DIE SOMEDAY.
HEY-- WHERE IS EVERYONE?
TOMB OF THE UNKNOWN BACHELOR
MICROWAVE POPCORN TASTES EVEN MORE TASTELESS THAN USUAL.
OH MY GOD. I'VE BEEN EATING STYROFOAM PACKING KERNELS.
YOUR USUAL LEISURE ACTIVITIES LEAVE YOU FEELING EMPTY INSIDE.
SUPER MARIO SAVES THE PRINCESS AGAIN!!
I CAN KILL MYSELF NOW.
BIP BIP BIP
YOU IMAGINE WHAT IT WOULD BE LIKE TO SLEEP WITH EACH PERSON WHO CROSSES YOUR PATH.
SIR, DO YOU HAVE A FEW MINUTES TO TALK ABOUT THE LORD?
YES I DO.
YOUR JOB NO LONGER FULFILLS ALL YOUR NEEDS FOR SELF-ESTEEM.
I THOUGHT I TOLD YOU TO FETCH THE JENKINS FILE.
I'M LOOKING, SIR.
YOUR EROGENOUS ZONES BEGIN DOING THE MAMBO INVOLUNTARILY.
YIKES.
YOUR PETS ARE NO LONGER ENOUGH.
GOOD KITTY... GOOD KITTY... NICE KITTY... OW!!
YOU'VE HAD ONE ONE-NIGHT-STAND TOO MANY.
WHAT HAVE I DONE??
ZZZZZZZ
HANGING OUT WITH YOUR FRIENDS NO LONGER PROVIDES SUFFICIENT SOLACE.
HOW MANY OF YOU ARE SICK OF THE REST OF US?
ME.
ME TOO.
ME THREE. HEH HEH.
YOU THINK ABOUT SEX MORE THAN CONSTANTLY.
YOU WANT FRIES WITH THAT?
OH BABY.
YOU START TO BELIEVE THE PERSONAL ADS.
HMM... IT'S AMAZING THAT A SENSUAL, VOLUPTUOUS, WITTY WOMAN WOULD NEED TO ADVERTISE... BUT I GUESS IT MAKES SENSE.
YOU CHECK YOUR ANSWERING MACHINE SEVERAL TIMES A DAY, JUST IN CASE.
MAYBE SOMEONE WHO DUMPED ME YEARS AGO HAS CHANGED HER MIND.
HELLO BINKY. THIS IS YOUR MOTHER. WHY HAVEN'T YOU
YOU REALIZE YOU'RE EVEN UNHAPPIER THAN YOU THOUGHT.
DON'T TOUCH THAT DIAL-- "STUDS" IS NEXT!!
YOU OVERCOME YOUR FEAR OF COMMITMENT.
I WANT TO BE WITH YOU.
OK.
PLEASE-- I'M JUST NOT READY.

LIFE IN HELL

©1992 BY MATT GROENING

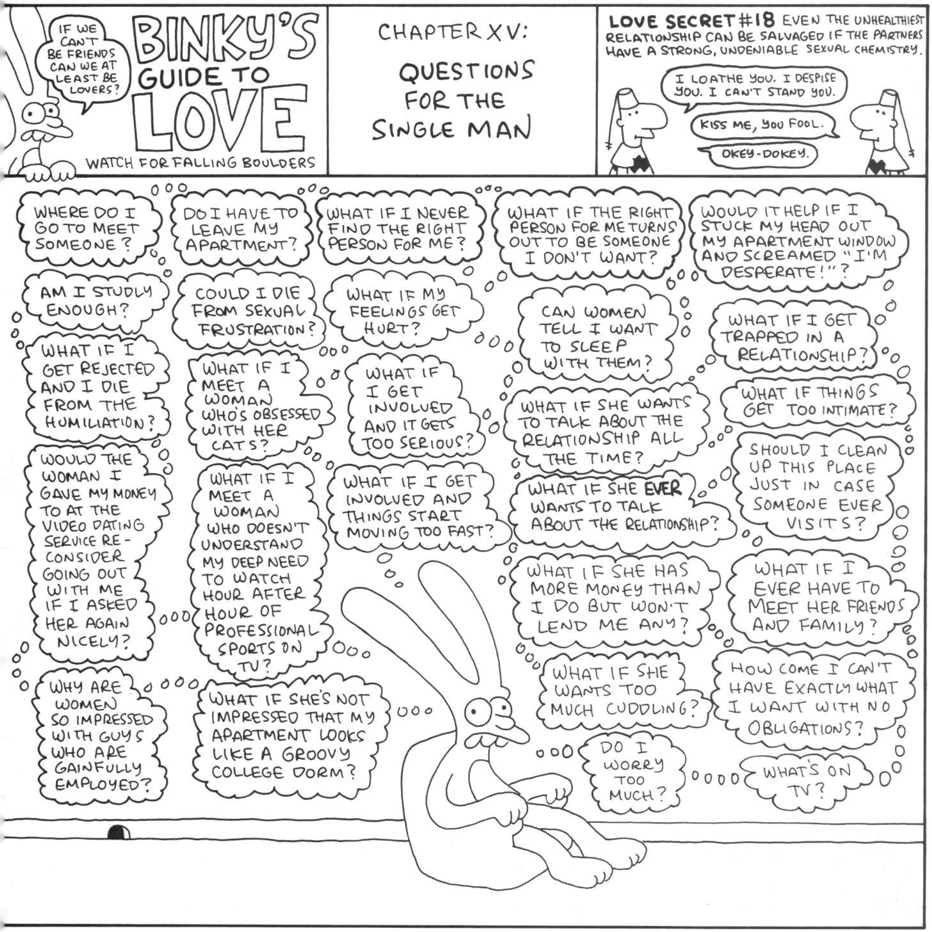

IF WE CAN'T BE FRIENDS CAN WE AT LEAST BE LOVERS?
BINKY'S GUIDE TO LOVE
WATCH FOR FALLING BOULDERS
CHAPTER XV:
QUESTIONS FOR THE SINGLE MAN
LOVE SECRET #18 EVEN THE UNHEALTHIEST RELATIONSHIP CAN BE SALVAGED IF THE PARTNERS HAVE A STRONG, UNDENIABLE SEXUAL CHEMISTRY.
I LOATHE YOU. I DESPISE YOU. I CAN'T STAND YOU.
KISS ME, YOU FOOL.
OKEY-DOKEY.
WHERE DO I GO TO MEET SOMEONE?
AM I STUDLY ENOUGH?
WHAT IF I GET REJECTED AND I DIE FROM THE HUMILIATION?
WOULD THE WOMAN I GAVE MY MONEY TO AT THE VIDEO DATING SERVICE RECONSIDER GOING OUT WITH ME IF I ASKED HER AGAIN NICELY?
WHY ARE WOMEN SO IMPRESSED WITH GUYS WHO ARE GAINFULLY EMPLOYED?
DO I HAVE TO LEAVE MY APARTMENT?
COULD I DIE FROM SEXUAL FRUSTRATION?
WHAT IF I MEET A WOMAN WHO'S OBSESSED WITH HER CATS?
WHAT IF I MEET A WOMAN WHO DOESN'T UNDERSTAND MY DEEP NEED TO WATCH HOUR AFTER HOUR OF PROFESSIONAL SPORTS ON TV?
WHAT IF SHE'S NOT IMPRESSED THAT MY APARTMENT LOOKS LIKE A GROOVY COLLEGE DORM?
WHAT IF I NEVER FIND THE RIGHT PERSON FOR ME?
WHAT IF MY FEELINGS GET HURT?
WHAT IF I GET INVOLVED AND IT GETS TOO SERIOUS?
WHAT IF I GET INVOLVED AND THINGS START MOVING TOO FAST?
WHAT IF THE RIGHT PERSON FOR ME TURNS OUT TO BE SOMEONE I DON'T WANT?
CAN WOMEN TELL I WANT TO SLEEP WITH THEM?
WHAT IF SHE WANTS TO TALK ABOUT THE RELATIONSHIP ALL THE TIME?
WHAT IF SHE EVER WANTS TO TALK ABOUT THE RELATIONSHIP?
WHAT IF SHE HAS MORE MONEY THAN I DO BUT WON'T LEND ME ANY?
WHAT IF SHE WANTS TOO MUCH CUDDLING?
DO I WORRY TOO MUCH?
WOULD IT HELP IF I STUCK MY HEAD OUT MY APARTMENT WINDOW AND SCREAMED "I'M DESPERATE!"?
WHAT IF I GET TRAPPED IN A RELATIONSHIP?
WHAT IF THINGS GET TOO INTIMATE?
SHOULD I CLEAN UP THIS PLACE JUST IN CASE SOMEONE EVER VISITS?
WHAT IF I EVER HAVE TO MEET HER FRIENDS AND FAMILY?
HOW COME I CAN'T HAVE EXACTLY WHAT I WANT WITH NO OBLIGATIONS?
WHAT'S ON TV?

LIFE IN HELL

©1992 BY MATT GROENING

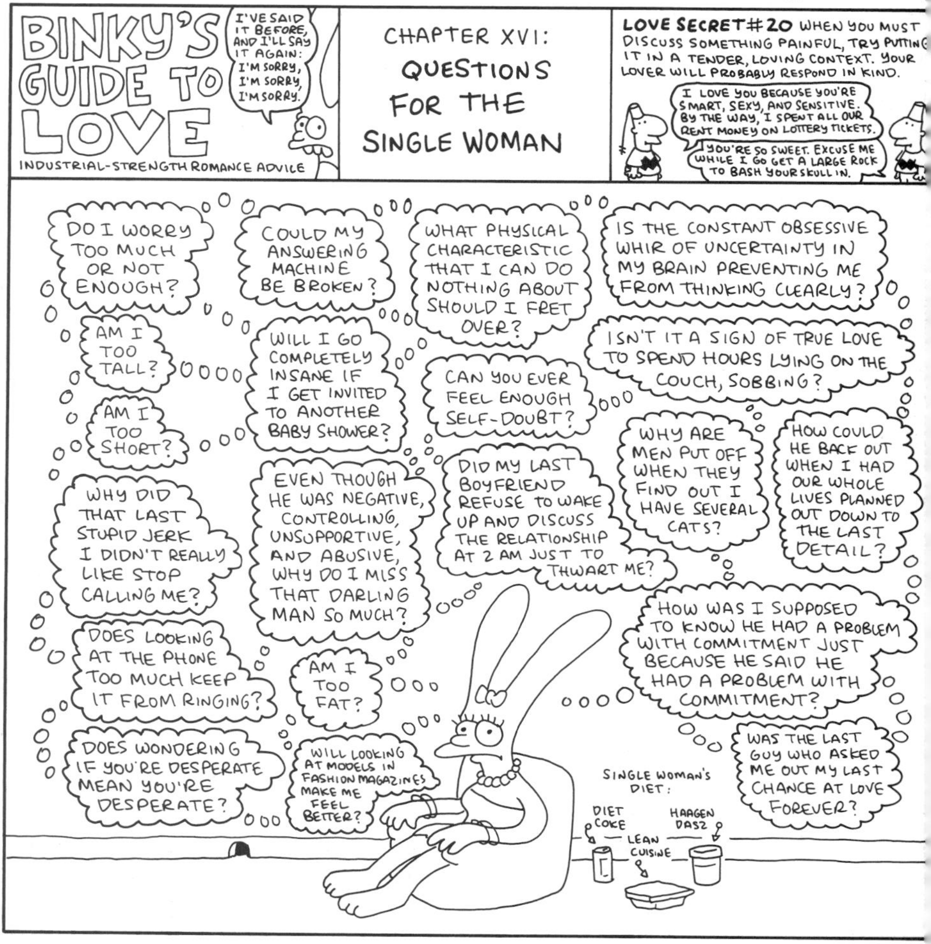

BINKY'S GUIDE TO LOVE
INDUSTRIAL-STRENGTH ROMANCE ADVICE
I'VE SAID IT BEFORE, AND I'LL SAY IT AGAIN: I'M SORRY, I'M SORRY, I'M SORRY.
CHAPTER XVI: QUESTIONS FOR THE SINGLE WOMAN
LOVE SECRET #20 WHEN YOU MUST DISCUSS SOMETHING PAINFUL, TRY PUTTING IT IN A TENDER, LOVING CONTEXT. YOUR LOVER WILL PROBABLY RESPOND IN KIND.
I LOVE YOU BECAUSE YOU'RE SMART, SEXY, AND SENSITIVE. BY THE WAY, I SPENT ALL OUR RENT MONEY ON LOTTERY TICKETS.
YOU'RE SO SWEET. EXCUSE ME WHILE I GO GET A LARGE ROCK TO BASH YOUR SKULL IN.
DO I WORRY TOO MUCH OR NOT ENOUGH?
COULD MY ANSWERING MACHINE BE BROKEN?
WHAT PHYSICAL CHARACTERISTIC THAT I CAN DO NOTHING ABOUT SHOULD I FRET OVER?
IS THE CONSTANT OBSESSIVE WHIR OF UNCERTAINTY IN MY BRAIN PREVENTING ME FROM THINKING CLEARLY?
AM I TOO TALL?
WILL I GO COMPLETELY INSANE IF I GET INVITED TO ANOTHER BABY SHOWER?
ISN'T IT A SIGN OF TRUE LOVE TO SPEND HOURS LYING ON THE COUCH, SOBBING?
CAN YOU EVER FEEL ENOUGH SELF-DOUBT?
AM I TOO SHORT?
WHY ARE MEN PUT OFF WHEN THEY FIND OUT I HAVE SEVERAL CATS?
HOW COULD HE BACK OUT WHEN I HAD OUR WHOLE LIVES PLANNED OUT DOWN TO THE LAST DETAIL?
WHY DID THAT LAST STUPID JERK I DIDN'T REALLY LIKE STOP CALLING ME?
EVEN THOUGH HE WAS NEGATIVE, CONTROLLING, UNSUPPORTIVE, AND ABUSIVE, WHY DO I MISS THAT DARLING MAN SO MUCH?
DID MY LAST BOYFRIEND REFUSE TO WAKE UP AND DISCUSS THE RELATIONSHIP AT 2 AM JUST TO THWART ME?
HOW WAS I SUPPOSED TO KNOW HE HAD A PROBLEM WITH COMMITMENT JUST BECAUSE HE SAID HE HAD A PROBLEM WITH COMMITMENT?
DOES LOOKING AT THE PHONE TOO MUCH KEEP IT FROM RINGING?
AM I TOO FAT?
DOES WONDERING IF YOU'RE DESPERATE MEAN YOU'RE DESPERATE?
WILL LOOKING AT MODELS IN FASHION MAGAZINES MAKE ME FEEL BETTER?
WAS THE LAST GUY WHO ASKED ME OUT MY LAST CHANCE AT LOVE FOREVER?
SINGLE WOMAN'S DIET:
DIET COKE
LEAN CUISINE
HAAGEN DASZ

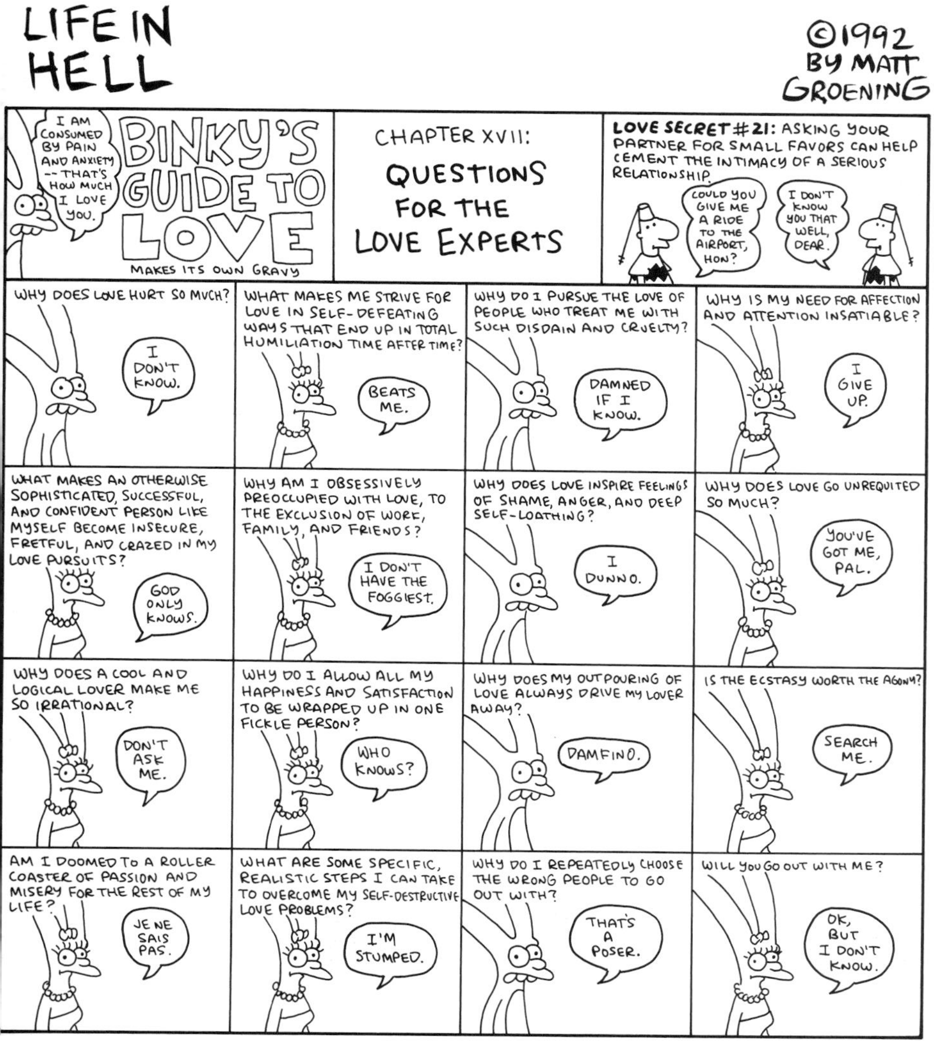
LIFE IN HELL
©1992 BY MATT GROENING
I AM CONSUMED BY PAIN AND ANXIETY -- THAT'S HOW MUCH I LOVE YOU.
BINKY'S GUIDE TO LOVE
MAKES ITS OWN GRAVY
CHAPTER XVII:
QUESTIONS FOR THE LOVE EXPERTS
LOVE SECRET #21: ASKING YOUR PARTNER FOR SMALL FAVORS CAN HELP CEMENT THE INTIMACY OF A SERIOUS RELATIONSHIP.
COULD YOU GIVE ME A RIDE TO THE AIRPORT, HON?
I DON'T KNOW YOU THAT WELL, DEAR.
WHY DOES LOVE HURT SO MUCH?
I DON'T KNOW.
WHAT MAKES ME STRIVE FOR LOVE IN SELF-DEFEATING WAYS THAT END UP IN TOTAL HUMILIATION TIME AFTER TIME?
BEATS ME.
WHY DO I PURSUE THE LOVE OF PEOPLE WHO TREAT ME WITH SUCH DISDAIN AND CRUELTY?
DAMNED IF I KNOW.
WHY IS MY NEED FOR AFFECTION AND ATTENTION INSATIABLE?
I GIVE UP.
WHAT MAKES AN OTHERWISE SOPHISTICATED, SUCCESSFUL, AND CONFIDENT PERSON LIKE MYSELF BECOME INSECURE, FRETFUL, AND CRAZED IN MY LOVE PURSUITS?
GOD ONLY KNOWS.
WHY AM I OBSESSIVELY PREOCCUPIED WITH LOVE, TO THE EXCLUSION OF WORK, FAMILY, AND FRIENDS?
I DON'T HAVE THE FOGGIEST.
WHY DOES LOVE INSPIRE FEELINGS OF SHAME, ANGER, AND DEEP SELF-LOATHING?
I DUNNO.
WHY DOES LOVE GO UNREQUITED SO MUCH?
YOU'VE GOT ME, PAL.
WHY DOES A COOL AND LOGICAL LOVER MAKE ME SO IRRATIONAL?
DON'T ASK ME.
WHY DO I ALLOW ALL MY HAPPINESS AND SATISFACTION TO BE WRAPPED UP IN ONE FICKLE PERSON?
WHO KNOWS?
WHY DOES MY OUTPOURING OF LOVE ALWAYS DRIVE MY LOVER AWAY?
DAMFINO.
IS THE ECSTASY WORTH THE AGONY?
SEARCH ME.
AM I DOOMED TO A ROLLER COASTER OF PASSION AND MISERY FOR THE REST OF MY LIFE?
JE NE SAIS PAS.
WHAT ARE SOME SPECIFIC, REALISTIC STEPS I CAN TAKE TO OVERCOME MY SELF-DESTRUCTIVE LOVE PROBLEMS?
I'M STUMPED.
WHY DO I REPEATEDLY CHOOSE THE WRONG PEOPLE TO GO OUT WITH?
THAT'S A POSER.
WILL YOU GO OUT WITH ME?
OK, BUT I DON'T KNOW.

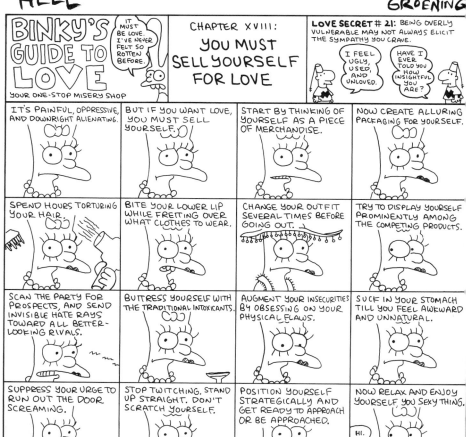

LIFE IN HELL

© 1992 BY MATT GROENING

BINKY'S GUIDE TO LOVE
YOUR ONE-STOP MISERY SHOP

IT MUST BE LOVE. I'VE NEVER FELT SO ROTTEN BEFORE.

CHAPTER XVIII:
YOU MUST SELL YOURSELF FOR LOVE

LOVE SECRET #21: BEING OVERLY VULNERABLE MAY NOT ALWAYS ELICIT THE SYMPATHY YOU CRAVE.

I FEEL UGLY, USED, AND UNLOVED.

HAVE I EVER TOLD YOU HOW INSIGHTFUL YOU ARE?

IT'S PAINFUL, OPPRESSIVE, AND DOWNRIGHT ALIENATING.

BUT IF YOU WANT LOVE, YOU MUST SELL YOURSELF.

START BY THINKING OF YOURSELF AS A PIECE OF MERCHANDISE.

NOW CREATE ALLURING PACKAGING FOR YOURSELF.

SPEND HOURS TORTURING YOUR HAIR.

BITE YOUR LOWER LIP WHILE FRETTING OVER WHAT CLOTHES TO WEAR.

CHANGE YOUR OUTFIT SEVERAL TIMES BEFORE GOING OUT.

TRY TO DISPLAY YOURSELF PROMINENTLY AMONG THE COMPETING PRODUCTS.

SCAN THE PARTY FOR PROSPECTS, AND SEND INVISIBLE HATE RAYS TOWARD ALL BETTER-LOOKING RIVALS.

BUTTRESS YOURSELF WITH THE TRADITIONAL INTOXICANTS.

AUGMENT YOUR INSECURITIES BY OBSESSING ON YOUR PHYSICAL FLAWS.

SUCK IN YOUR STOMACH TILL YOU FEEL AWKWARD AND UNNATURAL.

SUPPRESS YOUR URGE TO RUN OUT THE DOOR SCREAMING.

STOP TWITCHING. STAND UP STRAIGHT. DON'T SCRATCH YOURSELF.

POSITION YOURSELF STRATEGICALLY AND GET READY TO APPROACH OR BE APPROACHED.

NOW RELAX AND ENJOY YOURSELF YOU SEXY THING.

HI.

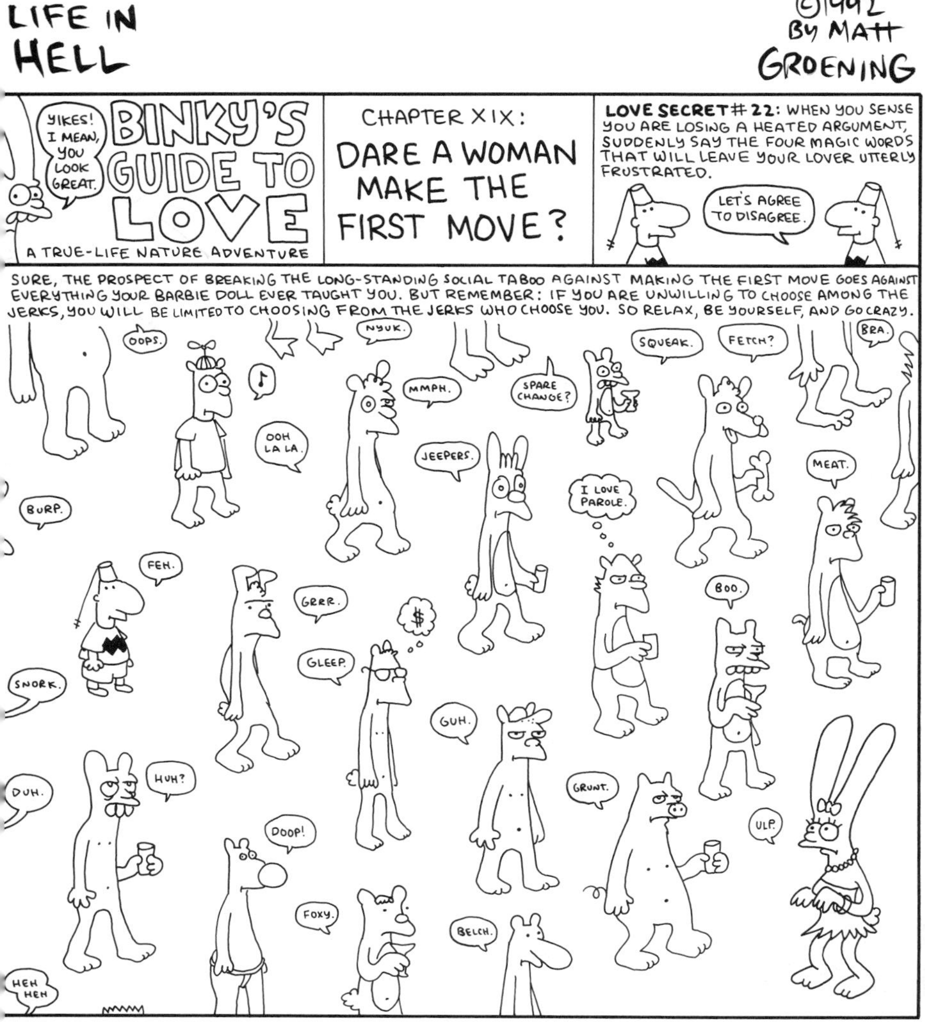
LIFE IN HELL
©1992 BY MATT GROENING
YIKES! I MEAN, YOU LOOK GREAT.
BINKY'S GUIDE TO LOVE
A TRUE-LIFE NATURE ADVENTURE
CHAPTER XIX:
DARE A WOMAN MAKE THE FIRST MOVE?
LOVE SECRET #22: WHEN YOU SENSE YOU ARE LOSING A HEATED ARGUMENT, SUDDENLY SAY THE FOUR MAGIC WORDS THAT WILL LEAVE YOUR LOVER UTTERLY FRUSTRATED.
LET'S AGREE TO DISAGREE.
SURE, THE PROSPECT OF BREAKING THE LONG-STANDING SOCIAL TABOO AGAINST MAKING THE FIRST MOVE GOES AGAINST EVERYTHING YOUR BARBIE DOLL EVER TAUGHT YOU. BUT REMEMBER: IF YOU ARE UNWILLING TO CHOOSE AMONG THE JERKS, YOU WILL BE LIMITED TO CHOOSING FROM THE JERKS WHO CHOOSE YOU. SO RELAX, BE YOURSELF, AND GO CRAZY.
OOPS.
NYUK.
SQUEAK.
FETCH?
BRA.
MMPH.
SPARE CHANGE?
OOH LA LA.
JEEPERS.
MEAT.
BURP.
I LOVE PAROLE.
FEH.
GRRR.
$
BOO.
GLEEP.
SNORK.
GUH.
HUH?
DUH.
GRUNT.
DOOP!
ULP.
FOXY.
BELCH.
HEH HEH

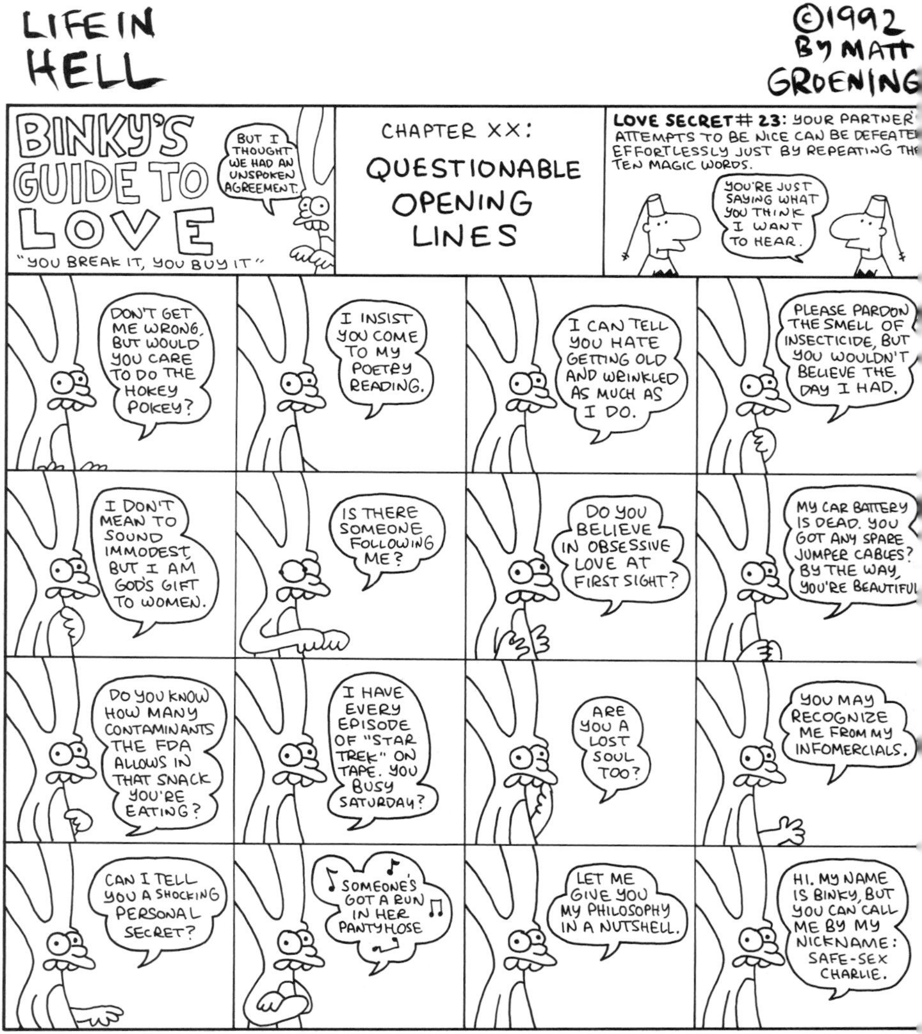

LIFE IN HELL

© 1992 By MATT GROENING

BINKY'S GUIDE TO LOVE
"YOU BREAK IT, YOU BUY IT"

BUT I THOUGHT WE HAD AN UNSPOKEN AGREEMENT.

CHAPTER XX:
QUESTIONABLE OPENING LINES

LOVE SECRET # 23: YOUR PARTNER'S ATTEMPTS TO BE NICE CAN BE DEFEATED EFFORTLESSLY JUST BY REPEATING THE TEN MAGIC WORDS.

YOU'RE JUST SAYING WHAT YOU THINK I WANT TO HEAR.

DON'T GET ME WRONG, BUT WOULD YOU CARE TO DO THE HOKEY POKEY?

I INSIST YOU COME TO MY POETRY READING.

I CAN TELL YOU HATE GETTING OLD AND WRINKLED AS MUCH AS I DO.

PLEASE PARDON THE SMELL OF INSECTICIDE, BUT YOU WOULDN'T BELIEVE THE DAY I HAD.

I DON'T MEAN TO SOUND IMMODEST BUT I AM GOD'S GIFT TO WOMEN.

IS THERE SOMEONE FOLLOWING ME?

DO YOU BELIEVE IN OBSESSIVE LOVE AT FIRST SIGHT?

MY CAR BATTERY IS DEAD. YOU GOT ANY SPARE JUMPER CABLES? BY THE WAY, YOU'RE BEAUTIFUL.

DO YOU KNOW HOW MANY CONTAMINANTS THE FDA ALLOWS IN THAT SNACK YOU'RE EATING?

I HAVE EVERY EPISODE OF "STAR TREK" ON TAPE. YOU BUSY SATURDAY?

ARE YOU A LOST SOUL TOO?

YOU MAY RECOGNIZE ME FROM MY INFOMERCIALS.

CAN I TELL YOU A SHOCKING PERSONAL SECRET?

SOMEONE'S GOT A RUN IN HER PANTYHOSE

LET ME GIVE YOU MY PHILOSOPHY IN A NUTSHELL.

HI, MY NAME IS BINKY, BUT YOU CAN CALL ME BY MY NICKNAME: SAFE-SEX CHARLIE.

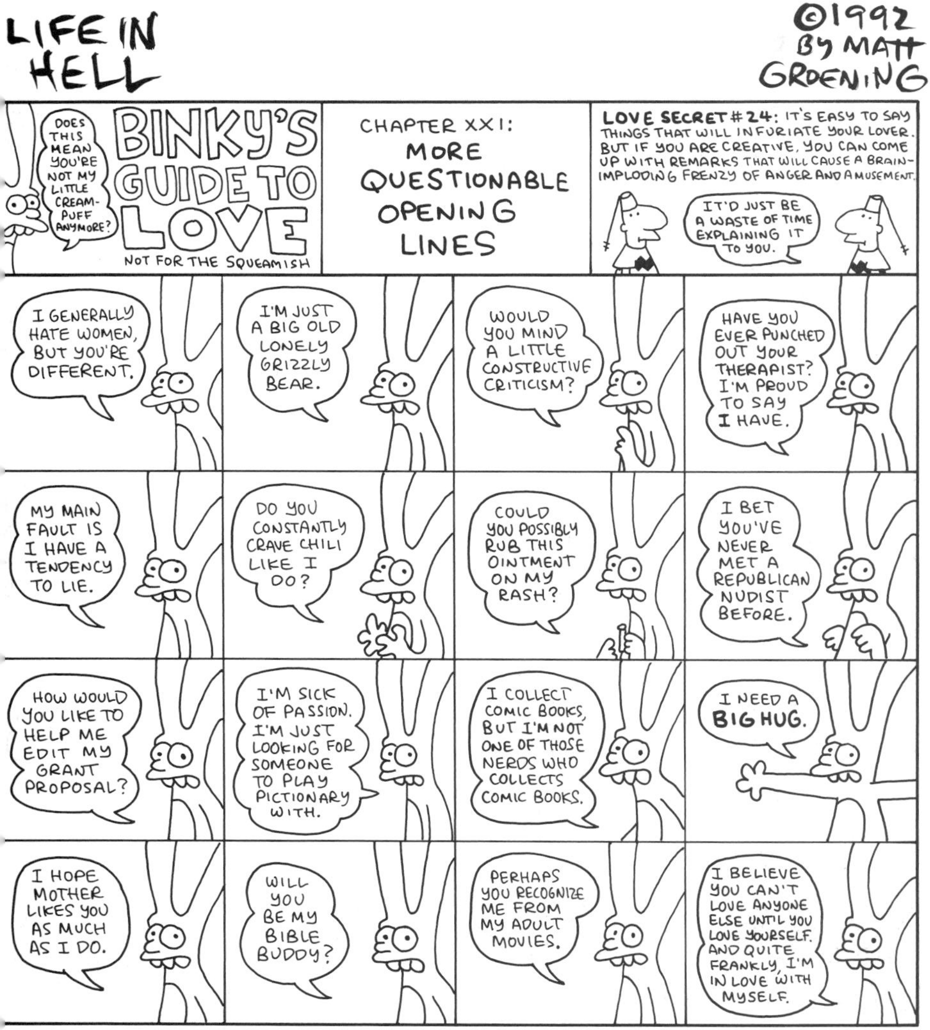
LIFE IN HELL
©1992 BY MATT GROENING
DOES THIS MEAN YOU'RE NOT MY LITTLE CREAM-PUFF ANYMORE?
BINKY'S GUIDE TO LOVE
NOT FOR THE SQUEAMISH
CHAPTER XXI: MORE QUESTIONABLE OPENING LINES
LOVE SECRET #24: IT'S EASY TO SAY THINGS THAT WILL INFURIATE YOUR LOVER. BUT IF YOU ARE CREATIVE, YOU CAN COME UP WITH REMARKS THAT WILL CAUSE A BRAIN-IMPLODING FRENZY OF ANGER AND AMUSEMENT.
IT'D JUST BE A WASTE OF TIME EXPLAINING IT TO YOU.
I GENERALLY HATE WOMEN, BUT YOU'RE DIFFERENT.
I'M JUST A BIG OLD LONELY GRIZZLY BEAR.
WOULD YOU MIND A LITTLE CONSTRUCTIVE CRITICISM?
HAVE YOU EVER PUNCHED OUT YOUR THERAPIST? I'M PROUD TO SAY I HAVE.
MY MAIN FAULT IS I HAVE A TENDENCY TO LIE.
DO YOU CONSTANTLY CRAVE CHILI LIKE I DO?
COULD YOU POSSIBLY RUB THIS OINTMENT ON MY RASH?
I BET YOU'VE NEVER MET A REPUBLICAN NUDIST BEFORE.
HOW WOULD YOU LIKE TO HELP ME EDIT MY GRANT PROPOSAL?
I'M SICK OF PASSION. I'M JUST LOOKING FOR SOMEONE TO PLAY PICTIONARY WITH.
I COLLECT COMIC BOOKS, BUT I'M NOT ONE OF THOSE NERDS WHO COLLECTS COMIC BOOKS.
I NEED A BIG HUG.
I HOPE MOTHER LIKES YOU AS MUCH AS I DO.
WILL YOU BE MY BIBLE BUDDY?
PERHAPS YOU RECOGNIZE ME FROM MY ADULT MOVIES.
I BELIEVE YOU CAN'T LOVE ANYONE ELSE UNTIL YOU LOVE YOURSELF. AND QUITE FRANKLY, I'M IN LOVE WITH MYSELF.

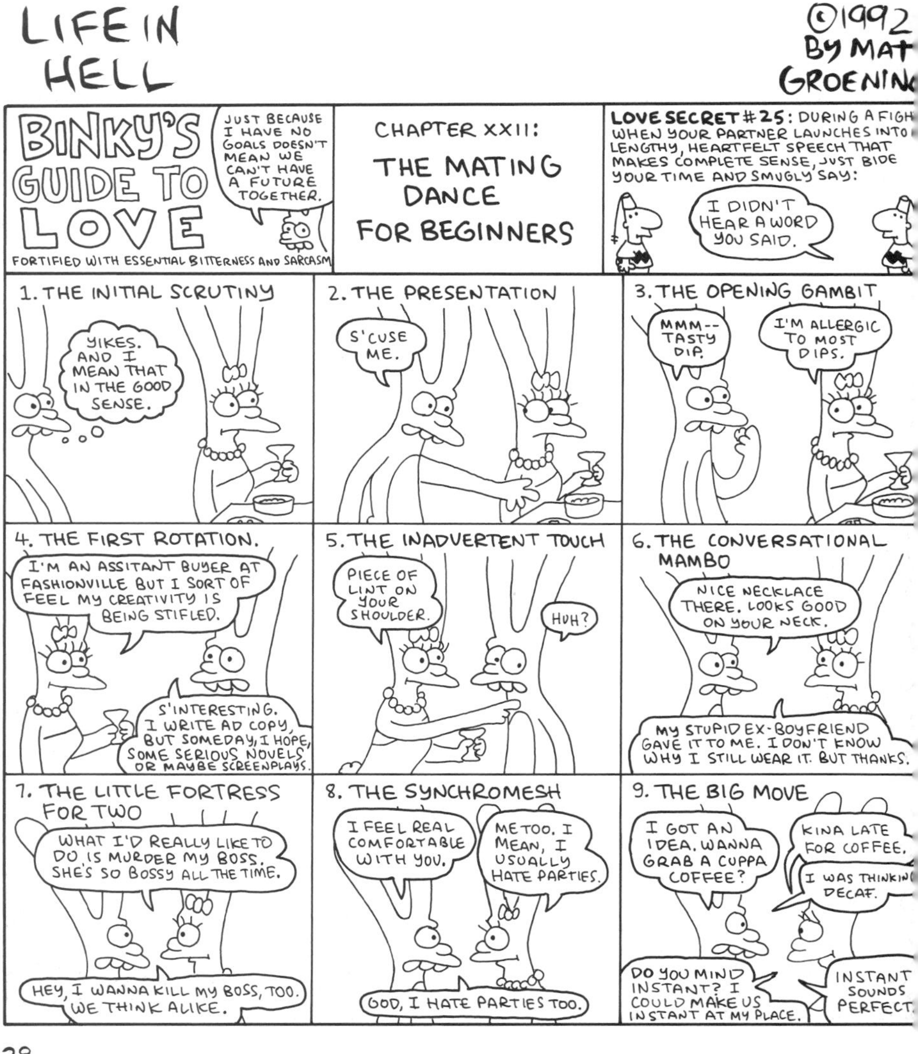

LIFE IN HELL
©1992 BY MAT GROENIN
BINKY'S GUIDE TO LOVE
JUST BECAUSE I HAVE NO GOALS DOESN'T MEAN WE CAN'T HAVE A FUTURE TOGETHER.
FORTIFIED WITH ESSENTIAL BITTERNESS AND SARCASM
CHAPTER XXII:
THE MATING DANCE FOR BEGINNERS
LOVE SECRET #25: DURING A FIGH WHEN YOUR PARTNER LAUNCHES INTO LENGTHY, HEARTFELT SPEECH THAT MAKES COMPLETE SENSE, JUST BIDE YOUR TIME AND SMUGLY SAY:
I DIDN'T HEAR A WORD YOU SAID.
1. THE INITIAL SCRUTINY
YIKES. AND I MEAN THAT IN THE GOOD SENSE.
2. THE PRESENTATION
S'CUSE ME.
3. THE OPENING GAMBIT
MMM-- TASTY DIP.
I'M ALLERGIC TO MOST DIPS.
4. THE FIRST ROTATION.
I'M AN ASSITANT BUYER AT FASHIONVILLE BUT I SORT OF FEEL MY CREATIVITY IS BEING STIFLED.
S'INTERESTING. I WRITE AD COPY, BUT SOMEDAY, I HOPE, SOME SERIOUS NOVELS OR MAYBE SCREENPLAYS.
5. THE INADVERTENT TOUCH
PIECE OF LINT ON YOUR SHOULDER.
HUH?
6. THE CONVERSATIONAL MAMBO
NICE NECKLACE THERE. LOOKS GOOD ON YOUR NECK.
MY STUPID EX-BOYFRIEND GAVE IT TO ME. I DON'T KNOW WHY I STILL WEAR IT. BUT THANKS.
7. THE LITTLE FORTRESS FOR TWO
WHAT I'D REALLY LIKE TO DO IS MURDER MY BOSS. SHE'S SO BOSSY ALL THE TIME.
HEY, I WANNA KILL MY BOSS, TOO. WE THINK ALIKE.
8. THE SYNCHROMESH
I FEEL REAL COMFORTABLE WITH YOU.
ME TOO. I MEAN, I USUALLY HATE PARTIES.
GOD, I HATE PARTIES TOO.
9. THE BIG MOVE
I GOT AN IDEA. WANNA GRAB A CUPPA COFFEE?
KINA LATE FOR COFFEE.
I WAS THINKIN DECAF.
DO YOU MIND INSTANT? I COULD MAKE US INSTANT AT MY PLACE.
INSTANT SOUNDS PERFECT.

LIFE IN HELL

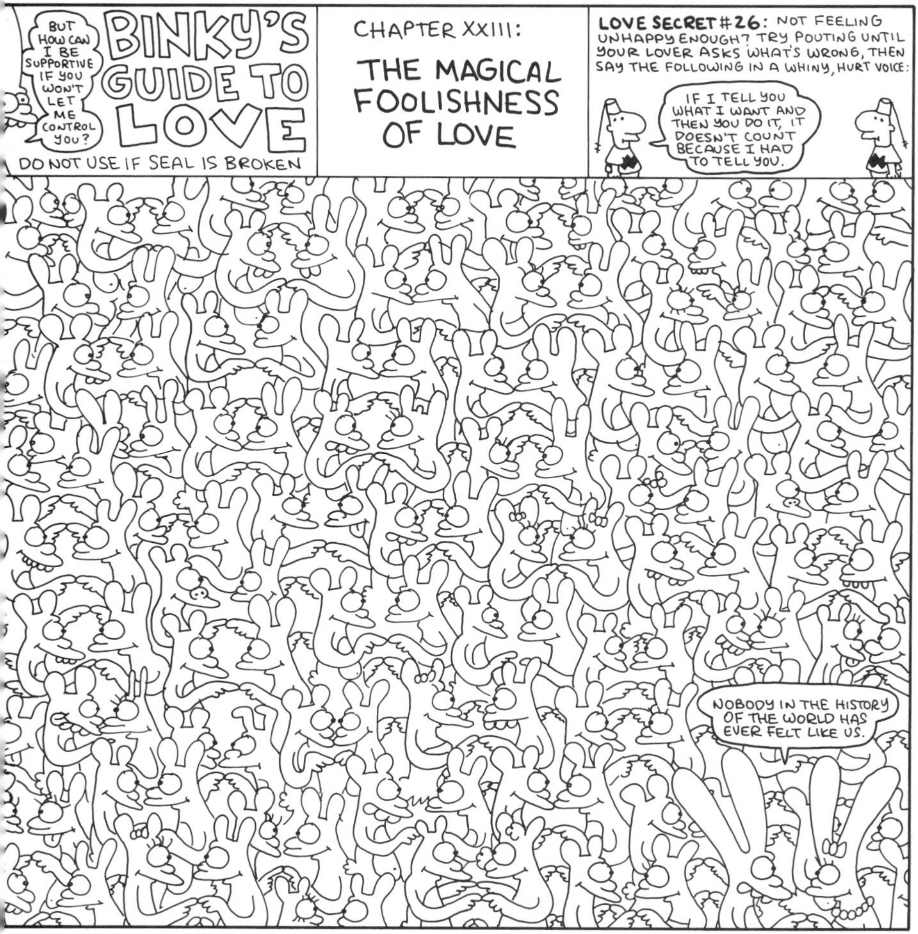

BUT HOW CAN I BE SUPPORTIVE IF YOU WON'T LET ME CONTROL YOU?
BINKY'S GUIDE TO LOVE
DO NOT USE IF SEAL IS BROKEN
CHAPTER XXIII:
THE MAGICAL FOOLISHNESS OF LOVE
LOVE SECRET #26: NOT FEELING UNHAPPY ENOUGH? TRY POUTING UNTIL YOUR LOVER ASKS WHAT'S WRONG, THEN SAY THE FOLLOWING IN A WHINY, HURT VOICE:
IF I TELL YOU WHAT I WANT AND THEN YOU DO IT, IT DOESN'T COUNT BECAUSE I HAD TO TELL YOU.
NOBODY IN THE HISTORY OF THE WORLD HAS EVER FELT LIKE US.

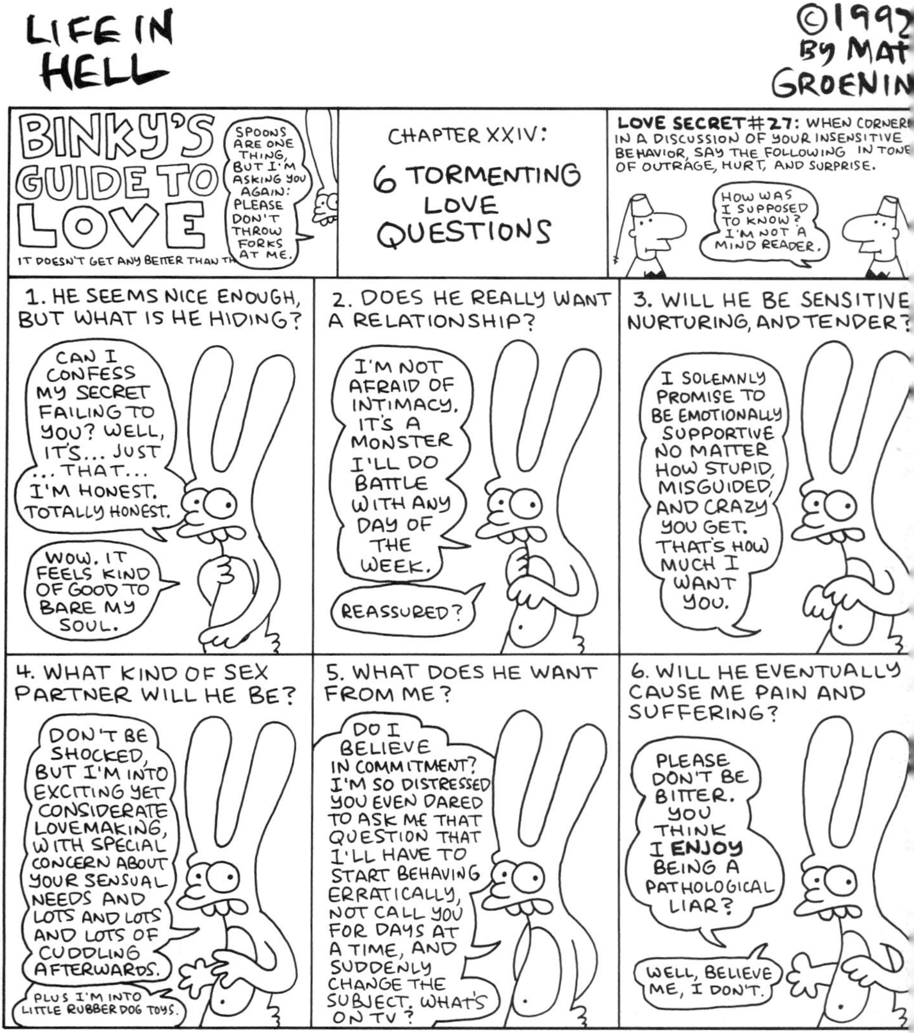

LIFE IN HELL
©199
By MAT
GROENIN
BINKY'S GUIDE TO LOVE
IT DOESN'T GET ANY BETTER THAN TH
SPOONS ARE ONE THING, BUT I'M ASKING YOU AGAIN: PLEASE DON'T THROW FORKS AT ME.
CHAPTER XXIV:
6 TORMENTING LOVE QUESTIONS
LOVE SECRET #27: WHEN CORNER IN A DISCUSSION OF YOUR INSENSITIVE BEHAVIOR, SAY THE FOLLOWING IN TONE OF OUTRAGE, HURT, AND SURPRISE.
HOW WAS I SUPPOSED TO KNOW? I'M NOT A MIND READER.
1. HE SEEMS NICE ENOUGH, BUT WHAT IS HE HIDING?
CAN I CONFESS MY SECRET FAILING TO YOU? WELL, IT'S... JUST ...THAT... I'M HONEST. TOTALLY HONEST.
WOW. IT FEELS KIND OF GOOD TO BARE MY SOUL.
2. DOES HE REALLY WANT A RELATIONSHIP?
I'M NOT AFRAID OF INTIMACY. IT'S A MONSTER I'LL DO BATTLE WITH ANY DAY OF THE WEEK.
REASSURED?
3. WILL HE BE SENSITIVE NURTURING, AND TENDER?
I SOLEMNLY PROMISE TO BE EMOTIONALLY SUPPORTIVE NO MATTER HOW STUPID, MISGUIDED, AND CRAZY YOU GET. THAT'S HOW MUCH I WANT YOU.
4. WHAT KIND OF SEX PARTNER WILL HE BE?
DON'T BE SHOCKED, BUT I'M INTO EXCITING YET CONSIDERATE LOVEMAKING, WITH SPECIAL CONCERN ABOUT YOUR SENSUAL NEEDS AND LOTS AND LOTS AND LOTS OF CUDDLING AFTERWARDS.
PLUS I'M INTO LITTLE RUBBER DOG TOYS.
5. WHAT DOES HE WANT FROM ME?
DO I BELIEVE IN COMMITMENT? I'M SO DISTRESSED YOU EVEN DARED TO ASK ME THAT QUESTION THAT I'LL HAVE TO START BEHAVING ERRATICALLY, NOT CALL YOU FOR DAYS AT A TIME, AND SUDDENLY CHANGE THE SUBJECT. WHAT'S ON TV?
6. WILL HE EVENTUALLY CAUSE ME PAIN AND SUFFERING?
PLEASE DON'T BE BITTER. YOU THINK I ENJOY BEING A PATHOLOGICAL LIAR?
WELL, BELIEVE ME, I DON'T.

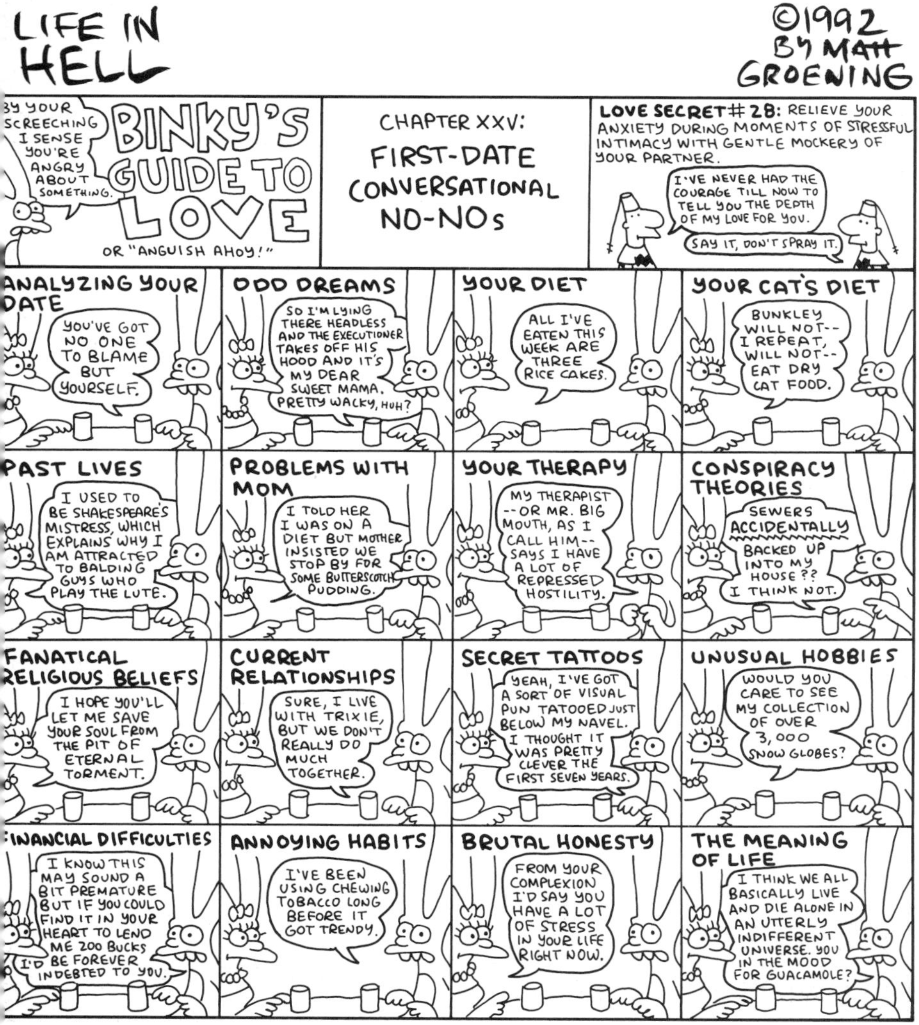
LIFE IN HELL
©1992 BY MATT GROENING
BY YOUR SCREECHING I SENSE YOU'RE ANGRY ABOUT SOMETHING.
BINKY'S GUIDE TO LOVE
OR "ANGUISH AHOY!"
CHAPTER XXV: FIRST-DATE CONVERSATIONAL NO-NOs
LOVE SECRET #28: RELIEVE YOUR ANXIETY DURING MOMENTS OF STRESSFUL INTIMACY WITH GENTLE MOCKERY OF YOUR PARTNER.
I'VE NEVER HAD THE COURAGE TILL NOW TO TELL YOU THE DEPTH OF MY LOVE FOR YOU.
SAY IT, DON'T SPRAY IT.
ANALYZING YOUR DATE
YOU'VE GOT NO ONE TO BLAME BUT YOURSELF.
ODD DREAMS
SO I'M LYING THERE HEADLESS AND THE EXECUTIONER TAKES OFF HIS HOOD AND IT'S MY DEAR SWEET MAMA. PRETTY WACKY, HUH?
YOUR DIET
ALL I'VE EATEN THIS WEEK ARE THREE RICE CAKES.
YOUR CAT'S DIET
BUNKLEY WILL NOT-- I REPEAT, WILL NOT-- EAT DRY CAT FOOD.
PAST LIVES
I USED TO BE SHAKESPEARE'S MISTRESS, WHICH EXPLAINS WHY I AM ATTRACTED TO BALDING GUYS WHO PLAY THE LUTE.
PROBLEMS WITH MOM
I TOLD HER I WAS ON A DIET BUT MOTHER INSISTED WE STOP BY FOR SOME BUTTERSCOTCH PUDDING.
YOUR THERAPY
MY THERAPIST --OR MR. BIG MOUTH, AS I CALL HIM-- SAYS I HAVE A LOT OF REPRESSED HOSTILITY.
CONSPIRACY THEORIES
SEWERS ACCIDENTALLY BACKED UP INTO MY HOUSE?? I THINK NOT.
FANATICAL RELIGIOUS BELIEFS
I HOPE YOU'LL LET ME SAVE YOUR SOUL FROM THE PIT OF ETERNAL TORMENT.
CURRENT RELATIONSHIPS
SURE, I LIVE WITH TRIXIE, BUT WE DON'T REALLY DO MUCH TOGETHER.
SECRET TATTOOS
YEAH, I'VE GOT A SORT OF VISUAL PUN TATOOED JUST BELOW MY NAVEL. I THOUGHT IT WAS PRETTY CLEVER THE FIRST SEVEN YEARS.
UNUSUAL HOBBIES
WOULD YOU CARE TO SEE MY COLLECTION OF OVER 3,000 SNOW GLOBES?
FINANCIAL DIFFICULTIES
I KNOW THIS MAY SOUND A BIT PREMATURE BUT IF YOU COULD FIND IT IN YOUR HEART TO LEND ME 200 BUCKS I'D BE FOREVER INDEBTED TO YOU.
ANNOYING HABITS
I'VE BEEN USING CHEWING TOBACCO LONG BEFORE IT GOT TRENDY.
BRUTAL HONESTY
FROM YOUR COMPLEXION I'D SAY YOU HAVE A LOT OF STRESS IN YOUR LIFE RIGHT NOW.
THE MEANING OF LIFE
I THINK WE ALL BASICALLY LIVE AND DIE ALONE IN AN UTTERLY INDIFFERENT UNIVERSE. YOU IN THE MOOD FOR GUACAMOLE?

LIFE IN HELL #700

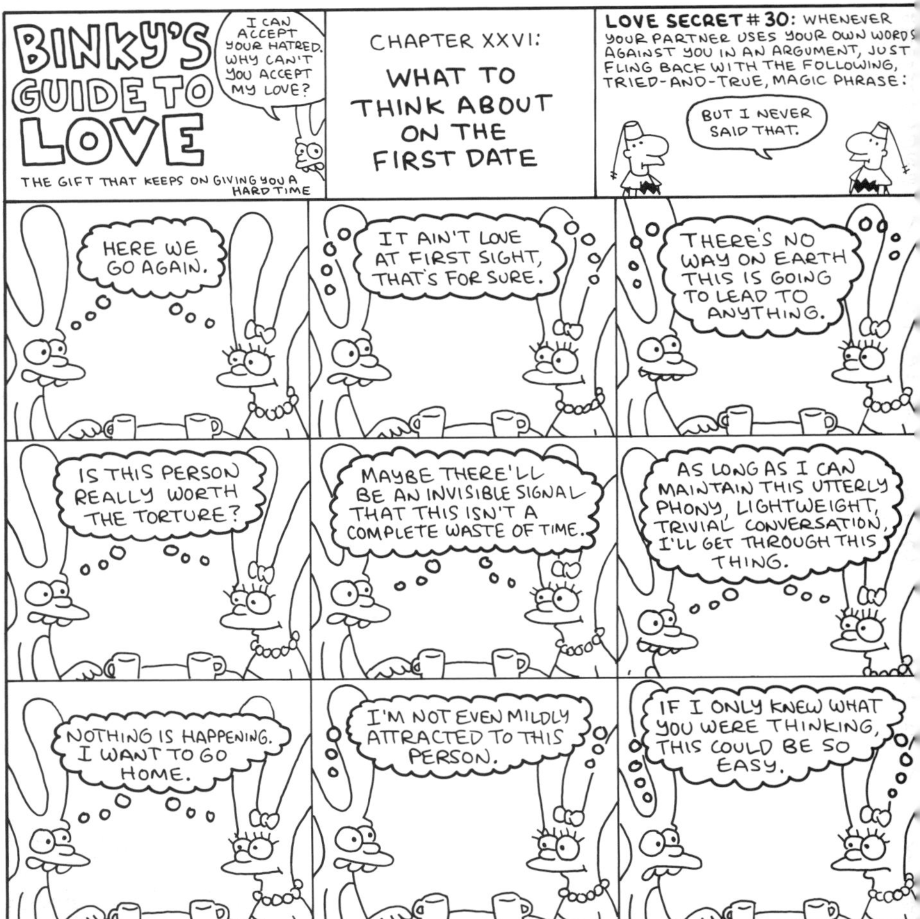

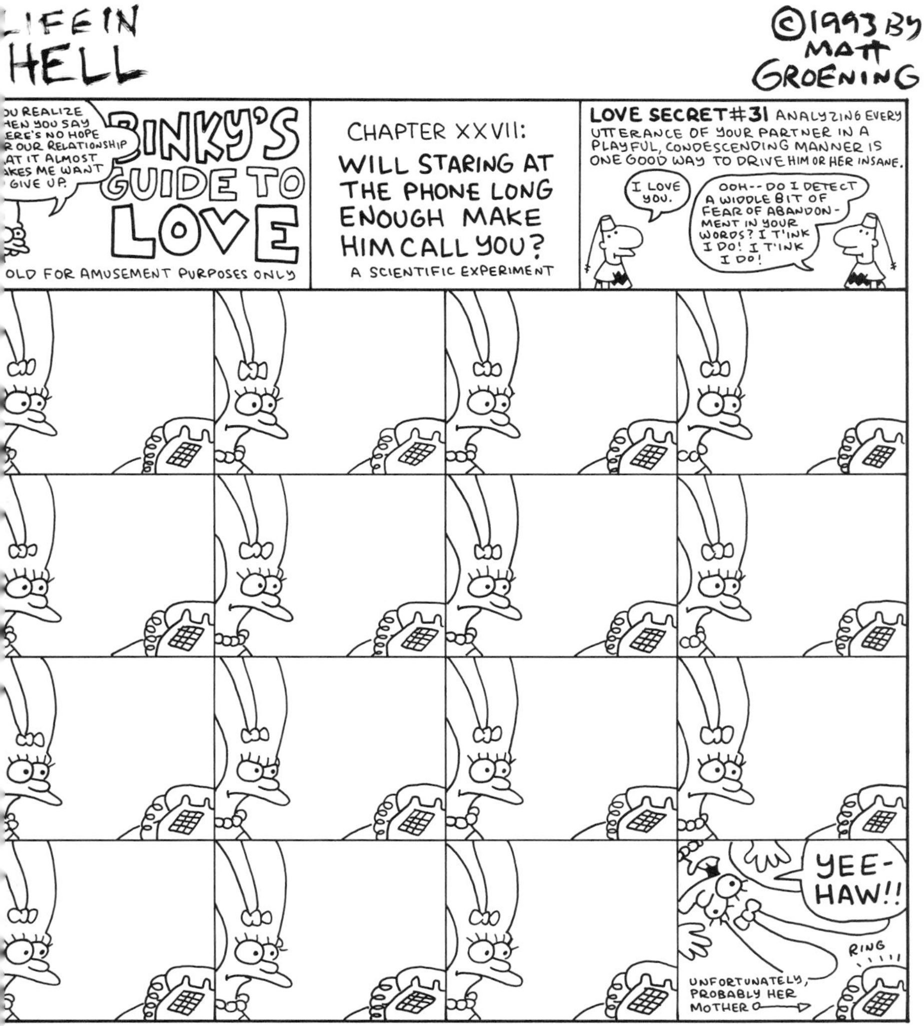

LIFE IN HELL
©1993 BY MATT GROENING
OU REALIZE HEN YOU SAY ERE'S NO HOPE R OUR RELATIONSHIP AT IT ALMOST AKES ME WANT GIVE UP.
BINKY'S GUIDE TO LOVE
OLD FOR AMUSEMENT PURPOSES ONLY
CHAPTER XXVII:
WILL STARING AT THE PHONE LONG ENOUGH MAKE HIM CALL YOU?
A SCIENTIFIC EXPERIMENT
LOVE SECRET #31 ANALYZING EVERY UTTERANCE OF YOUR PARTNER IN A PLAYFUL, CONDESCENDING MANNER IS ONE GOOD WAY TO DRIVE HIM OR HER INSANE.
I LOVE YOU.
OOH--DO I DETECT A WIDDLE BIT OF FEAR OF ABANDONMENT IN YOUR WORDS? I T'INK I DO! I T'INK I DO!
YEE-HAW!!
RING
UNFORTUNATELY, PROBABLY HER MOTHER

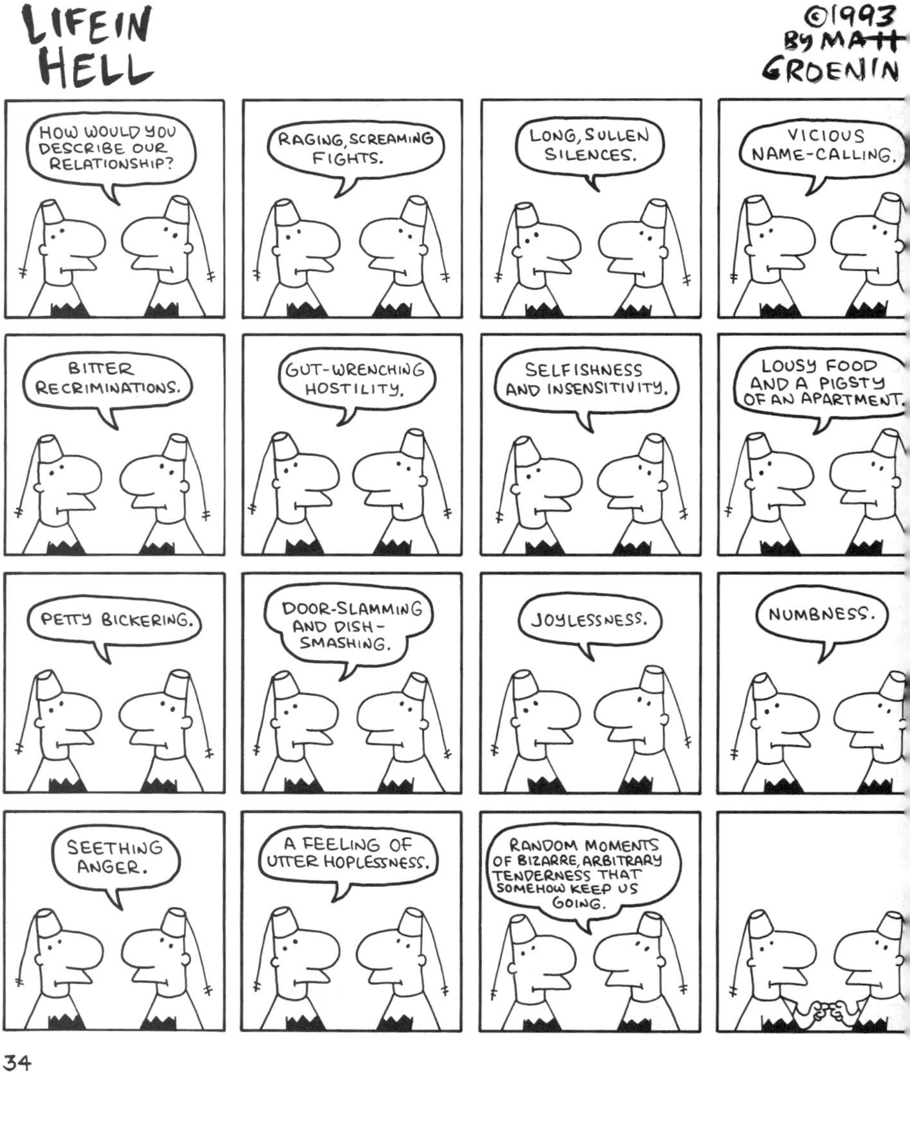
LIFE IN HELL
©1993 BY MATT GROENIN
HOW WOULD YOU DESCRIBE OUR RELATIONSHIP?
RAGING, SCREAMING FIGHTS.
LONG, SULLEN SILENCES.
VICIOUS NAME-CALLING.
BITTER RECRIMINATIONS.
GUT-WRENCHING HOSTILITY.
SELFISHNESS AND INSENSITIVITY.
LOUSY FOOD AND A PIGSTY OF AN APARTMENT.
PETTY BICKERING.
DOOR-SLAMMING AND DISH-SMASHING.
JOYLESSNESS.
NUMBNESS.
SEETHING ANGER.
A FEELING OF UTTER HOPLESSNESS.
RANDOM MOMENTS OF BIZARRE, ARBITRARY TENDERNESS THAT SOMEHOW KEEP US GOING.

LIFE IN HELL

©1989 BY MATT GROENING

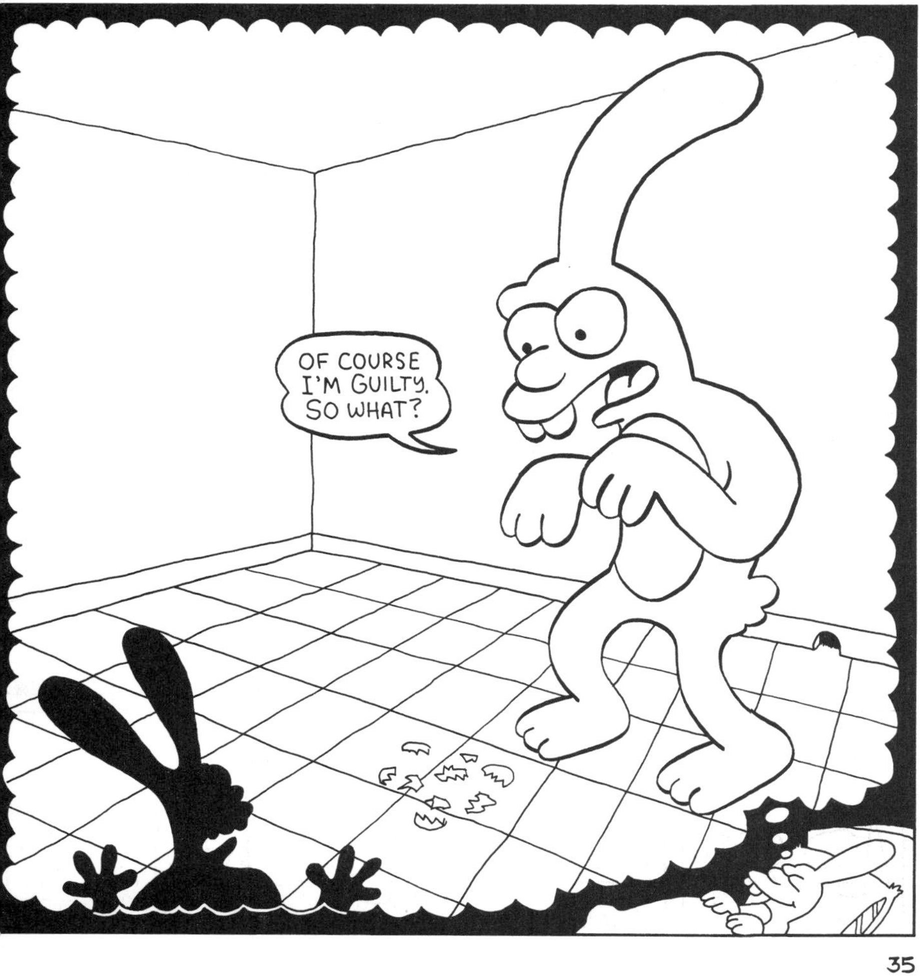
OF COURSE I'M GUILTY. SO WHAT?

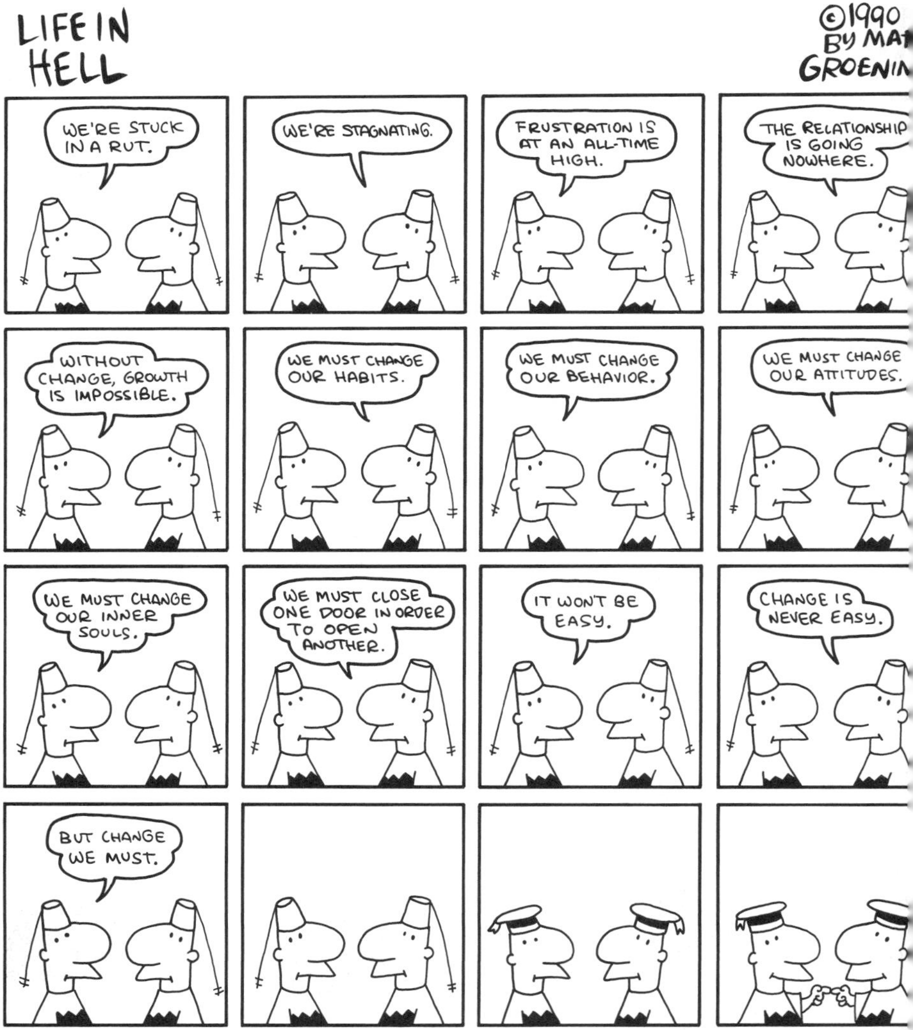
LIFE IN HELL
©1990 BY MAT GROENIN
WE'RE STUCK IN A RUT.
WE'RE STAGNATING.
FRUSTRATION IS AT AN ALL-TIME HIGH.
THE RELATIONSHIP IS GOING NOWHERE.
WITHOUT CHANGE, GROWTH IS IMPOSSIBLE.
WE MUST CHANGE OUR HABITS.
WE MUST CHANGE OUR BEHAVIOR.
WE MUST CHANGE OUR ATTITUDES.
WE MUST CHANGE OUR INNER SOULS.
WE MUST CLOSE ONE DOOR IN ORDER TO OPEN ANOTHER.
IT WON'T BE EASY.
CHANGE IS NEVER EASY.
BUT CHANGE WE MUST.

LIFE IN HELL

©1994 BY MATT GROENING

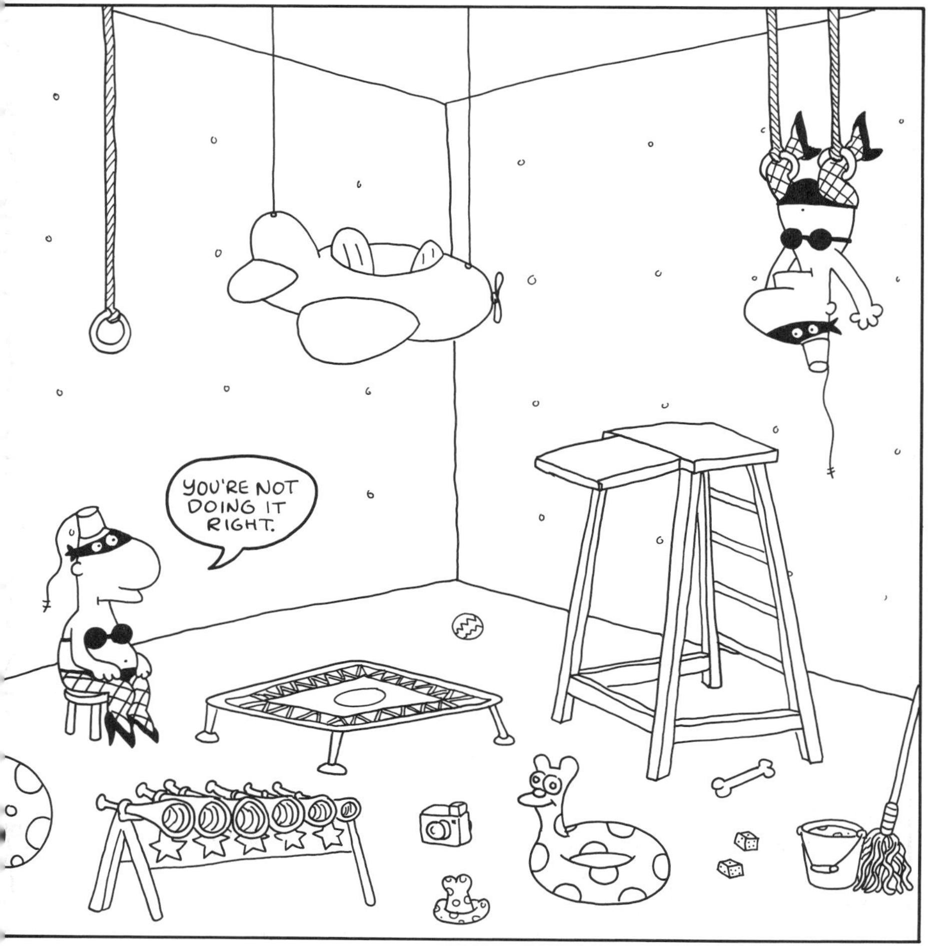

YOU'RE NOT DOING IT RIGHT.

LIFE IN HELL

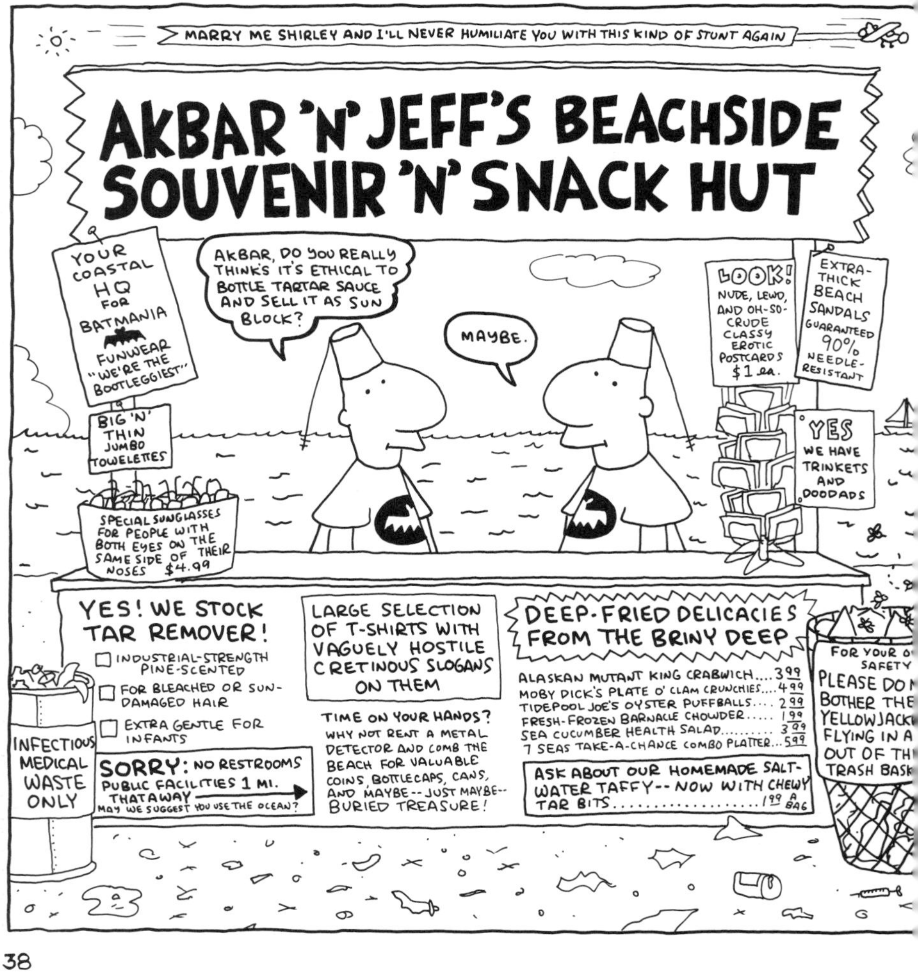

MARRY ME SHIRLEY AND I'LL NEVER HUMILIATE YOU WITH THIS KIND OF STUNT AGAIN
AKBAR 'N' JEFF'S BEACHSIDE SOUVENIR 'N' SNACK HUT
YOUR COASTAL HQ FOR BATMANIA FUNWEAR "WE'RE THE BOOTLEGGIEST"
BIG 'N' THIN JUMBO TOWELETTES
SPECIAL SUNGLASSES FOR PEOPLE WITH BOTH EYES ON THE SAME SIDE OF THEIR NOSES $4.99
AKBAR, DO YOU REALLY THINK IT'S ETHICAL TO BOTTLE TARTAR SAUCE AND SELL IT AS SUN BLOCK?
MAYBE.
LOOK! NUDE, LEWD, AND OH-SO-CRUDE CLASSY EROTIC POSTCARDS $1 ea.
EXTRA-THICK BEACH SANDALS GUARANTEED 90% NEEDLE-RESISTANT
YES WE HAVE TRINKETS AND DOODADS
YES! WE STOCK TAR REMOVER!
INDUSTRIAL-STRENGTH PINE-SCENTED
FOR BLEACHED OR SUN-DAMAGED HAIR
EXTRA GENTLE FOR INFANTS
SORRY: NO RESTROOMS PUBLIC FACILITIES 1 MI. THATAWAY
MAY WE SUGGEST YOU USE THE OCEAN?
LARGE SELECTION OF T-SHIRTS WITH VAGUELY HOSTILE CRETINOUS SLOGANS ON THEM
TIME ON YOUR HANDS? WHY NOT RENT A METAL DETECTOR AND COMB THE BEACH FOR VALUABLE COINS, BOTTLECAPS, CANS, AND MAYBE-- JUST MAYBE-- BURIED TREASURE!
DEEP-FRIED DELICACIES FROM THE BRINY DEEP
ALASKAN MUTANT KING CRABWICH....3 99
MOBY DICK'S PLATE O' CLAM CRUNCHIES....4 99
TIDEPOOL JOE'S OYSTER PUFFBALLS....2 99
FRESH-FROZEN BARNACLE CHOWDER.....1 99
SEA CUCUMBER HEALTH SALAD.........3 99
7 SEAS TAKE-A-CHANCE COMBO PLATTER...5 99
ASK ABOUT OUR HOMEMADE SALT-WATER TAFFY-- NOW WITH CHEWY TAR BITS..............1 99 A BAG
INFECTIOUS MEDICAL WASTE ONLY
FOR YOUR O SAFETY PLEASE DO N BOTHER THE YELLOWJACK FLYING IN A OUT OF TH TRASH BASK

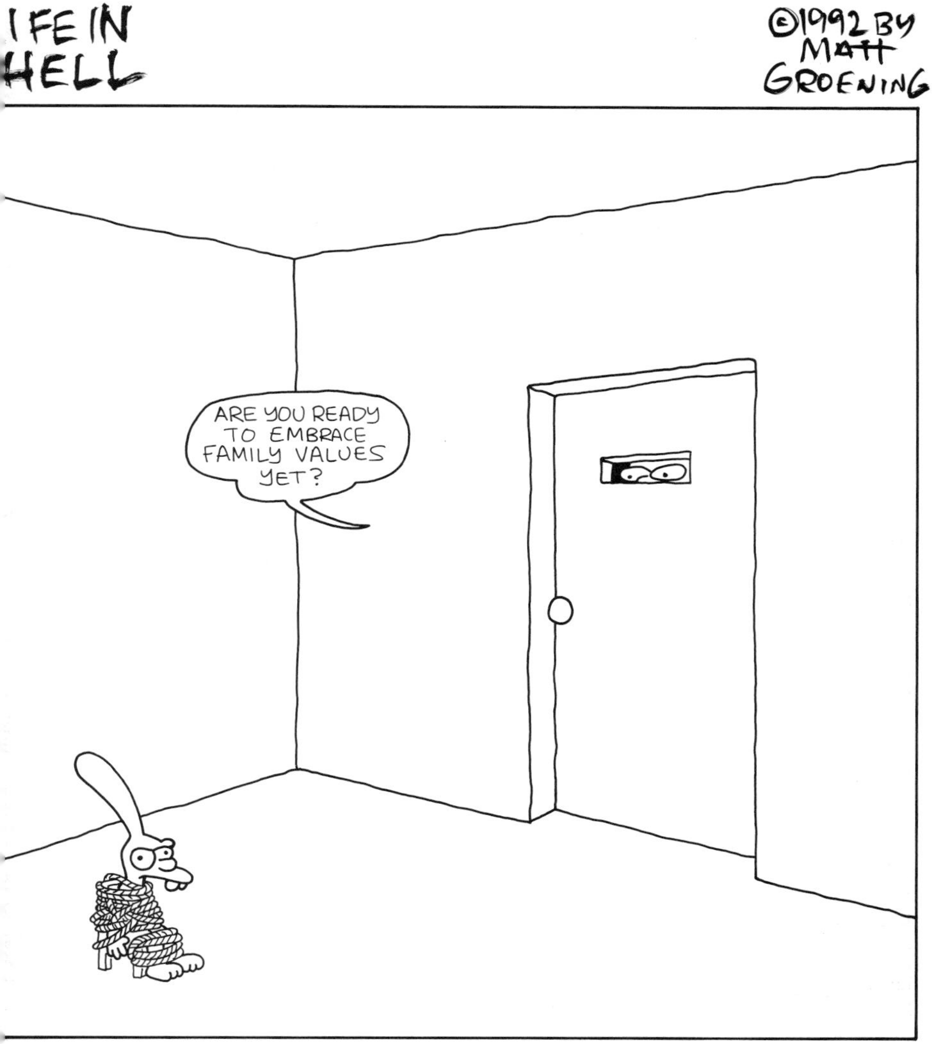
IFE IN HELL
©1992 BY MATT GROENING
ARE YOU READY TO EMBRACE FAMILY VALUES YET?

LIFE IN HELL

©1989 BY MATT GROENIN

SECRETS OF THE CREATIVE

CREATIVE TYPE	SECRET FEAR	SECRET PAST	SECRET THRILL	SECRET AMBITION	SECRET SHAME
ROCK CRITIC 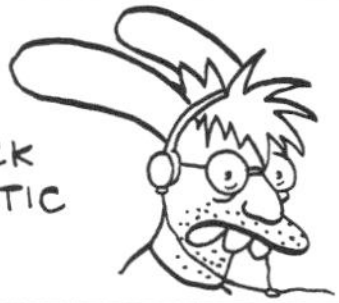	MAYBE ROCK & ROLL ISN'T HERE TO STAY	SURLY RECORD-STORE CLERK	TELLING IMPRESSIVE STORIES TO YOUNGER ROCK CRITICS	TO STRANGLE A NEWSPAPER EDITOR WITH BARE HANDS	MADE MOR MONEY AS A SURLY RECORD-STORE CLER
COMMERCIAL ARTIST 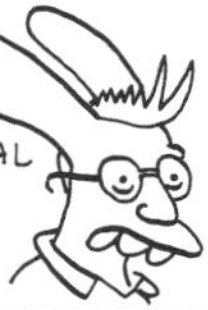	MAYBE MY ILLUSTRATIONS WILL NEVER HANG IN ART MUSEUMS	PROMISING ART STUDENT	DEPOSITING PAYCHECKS	TO STRANGLE AN ART DIRECTOR WITH BARE HANDS	SALIVATES AT SIGHT OF OWN AIRBRUSHE HAMBURGER
RADIO DJ 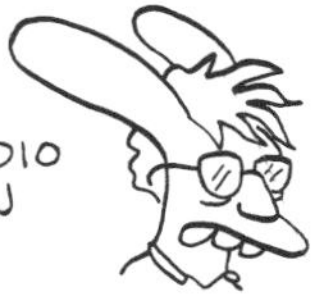	MAYBE THIS ISN'T SO GLAMOROUS AFTER ALL	TEEN-FAIR LIP-SYNC CONTEST WINNER	MAKING VOICE SOUND DECEPTIVELY DEEP AND CONFIDENT	TO STRANGLE A PROGRAM DIRECTOR WITH BARE HANDS	STEALS OTHER DJS' RECORDS
AD COPYWRITER 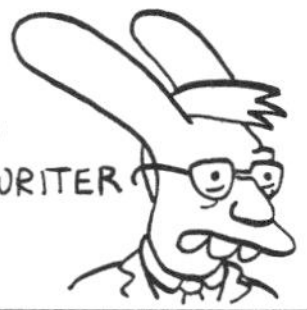	MAYBE MY BRAIN IS SLOWLY DEFLATING	COLLEGE SHORT-STORY CONTEST WINNER	MAKING LITTLE JOKEY ITEMS FOR THE OFFICE BULLETIN BOARD	TO STRANGLE AN AD DIRECTOR, A CLIENT, AND SELF WITH BARE HANDS	HAS LEARNE TO ENJOY THINKING UP SLOGAN ABOUT BEEF-A-RO
CARTOONIST 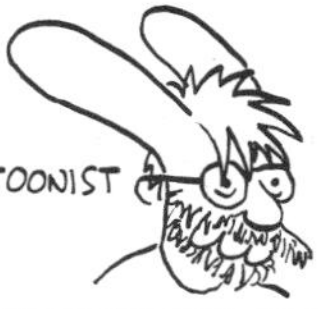	MAYBE THIS IS NOT THE MOST IMPORTANT WAY TO SPEND MY EXISTENCE	COMPULSIVE DOODLER	GETTING PAID TO ANNOY OTHERS	NOT TO BE STRANGLED	SHAMELESS

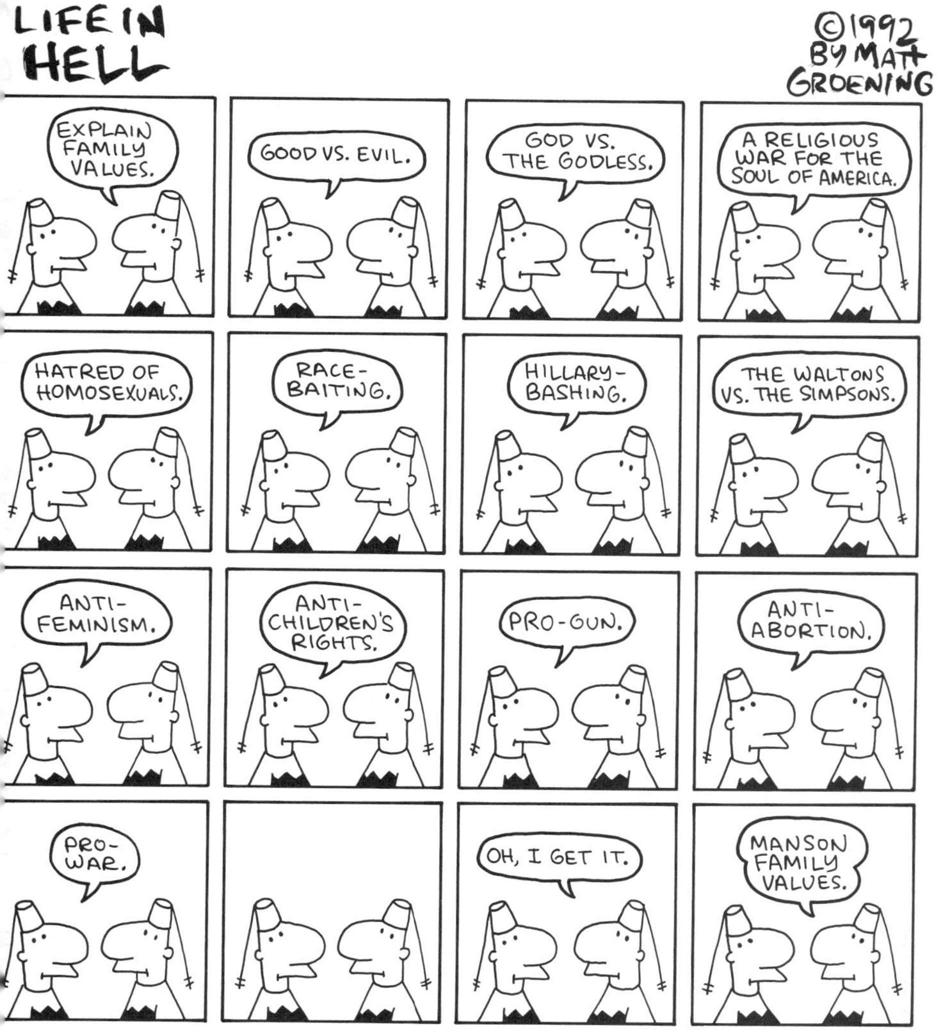
LIFE IN HELL
©1992 BY MATT GROENING
EXPLAIN FAMILY VALUES.
GOOD VS. EVIL.
GOD VS. THE GODLESS.
A RELIGIOUS WAR FOR THE SOUL OF AMERICA.
HATRED OF HOMOSEXUALS.
RACE-BAITING.
HILLARY-BASHING.
THE WALTONS VS. THE SIMPSONS.
ANTI-FEMINISM.
ANTI-CHILDREN'S RIGHTS.
PRO-GUN.
ANTI-ABORTION.
PRO-WAR.
OH, I GET IT.
MANSON FAMILY VALUES.

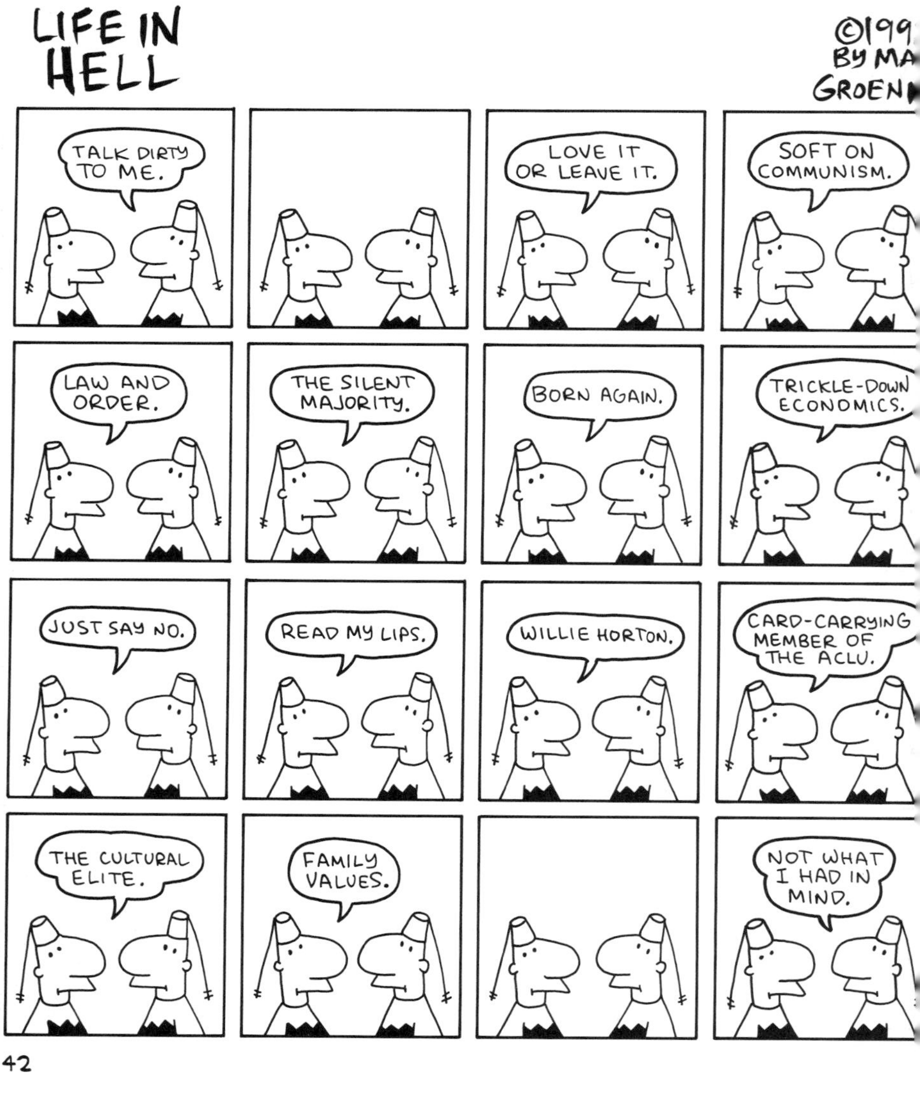
LIFE IN HELL
TALK DIRTY TO ME.
LOVE IT OR LEAVE IT.
SOFT ON COMMUNISM.
LAW AND ORDER.
THE SILENT MAJORITY.
BORN AGAIN.
TRICKLE-DOWN ECONOMICS.
JUST SAY NO.
READ MY LIPS.
WILLIE HORTON.
CARD-CARRYING MEMBER OF THE ACLU.
THE CULTURAL ELITE.
FAMILY VALUES.
NOT WHAT I HAD IN MIND.

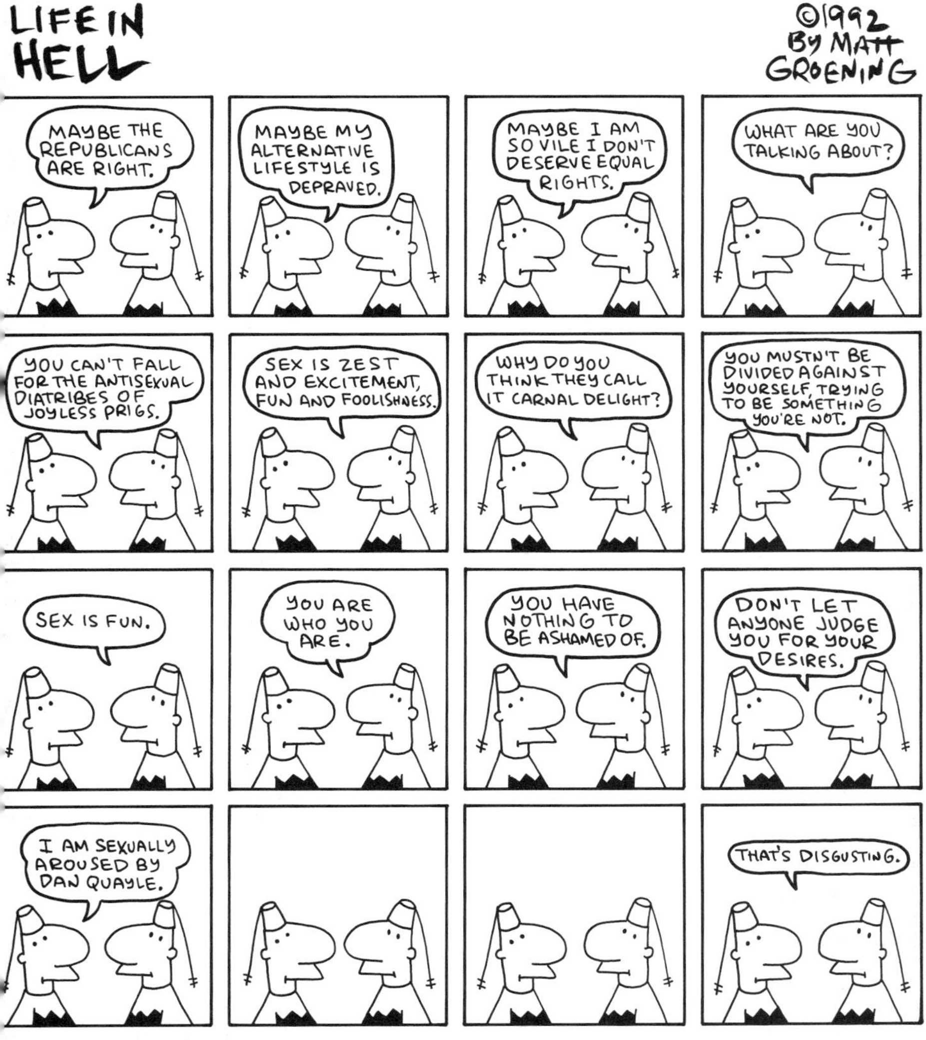
LIFE IN HELL
©1992 BY MATT GROENING
MAYBE THE REPUBLICANS ARE RIGHT.
MAYBE MY ALTERNATIVE LIFESTYLE IS DEPRAVED.
MAYBE I AM SO VILE I DON'T DESERVE EQUAL RIGHTS.
WHAT ARE YOU TALKING ABOUT?
YOU CAN'T FALL FOR THE ANTISEXUAL DIATRIBES OF JOYLESS PRIGS.
SEX IS ZEST AND EXCITEMENT, FUN AND FOOLISHNESS.
WHY DO YOU THINK THEY CALL IT CARNAL DELIGHT?
YOU MUSTN'T BE DIVIDED AGAINST YOURSELF, TRYING TO BE SOMETHING YOU'RE NOT.
SEX IS FUN.
YOU ARE WHO YOU ARE.
YOU HAVE NOTHING TO BE ASHAMED OF.
DON'T LET ANYONE JUDGE YOU FOR YOUR DESIRES.
I AM SEXUALLY AROUSED BY DAN QUAYLE.
THAT'S DISGUSTING.

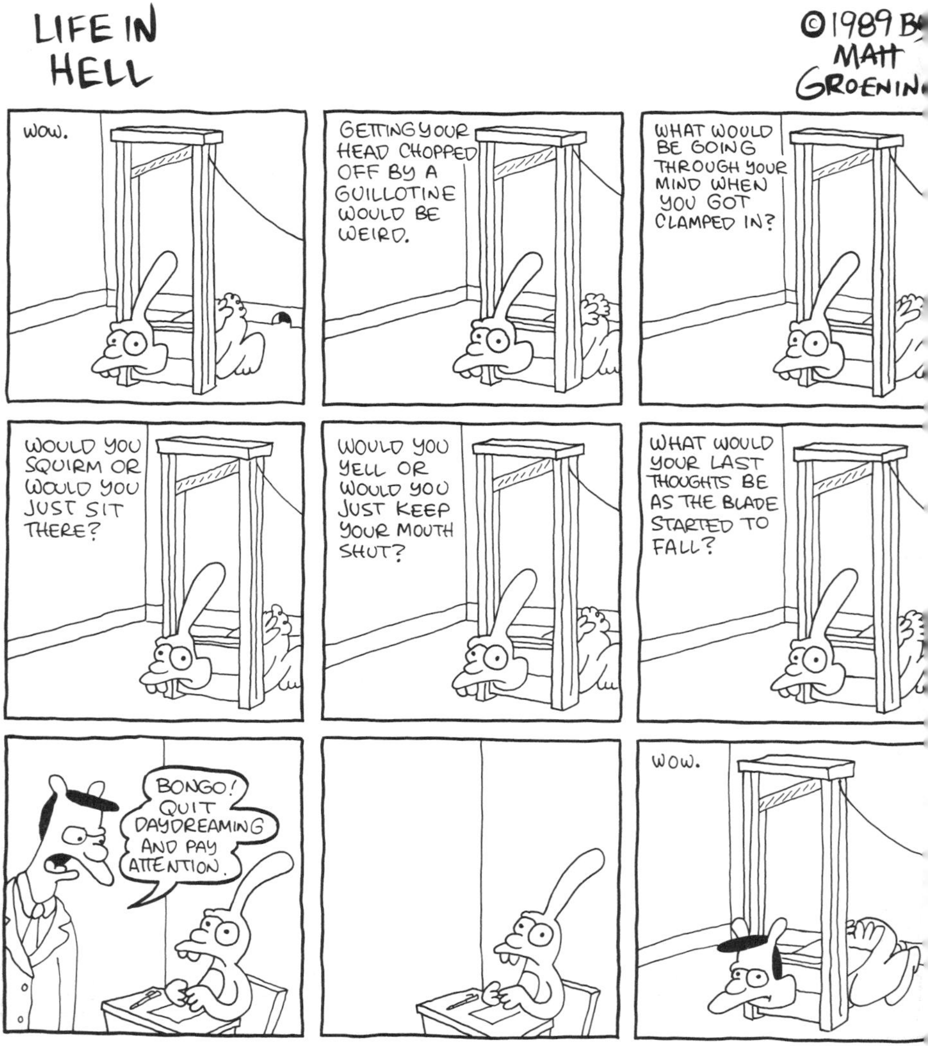
LIFE IN HELL
©1989 B
MATT
GROENIN
WOW.
GETTING YOUR HEAD CHOPPED OFF BY A GUILLOTINE WOULD BE WEIRD.
WHAT WOULD BE GOING THROUGH YOUR MIND WHEN YOU GOT CLAMPED IN?
WOULD YOU SQUIRM OR WOULD YOU JUST SIT THERE?
WOULD YOU YELL OR WOULD YOU JUST KEEP YOUR MOUTH SHUT?
WHAT WOULD YOUR LAST THOUGHTS BE AS THE BLADE STARTED TO FALL?
BONGO! QUIT DAYDREAMING AND PAY ATTENTION.
WOW.

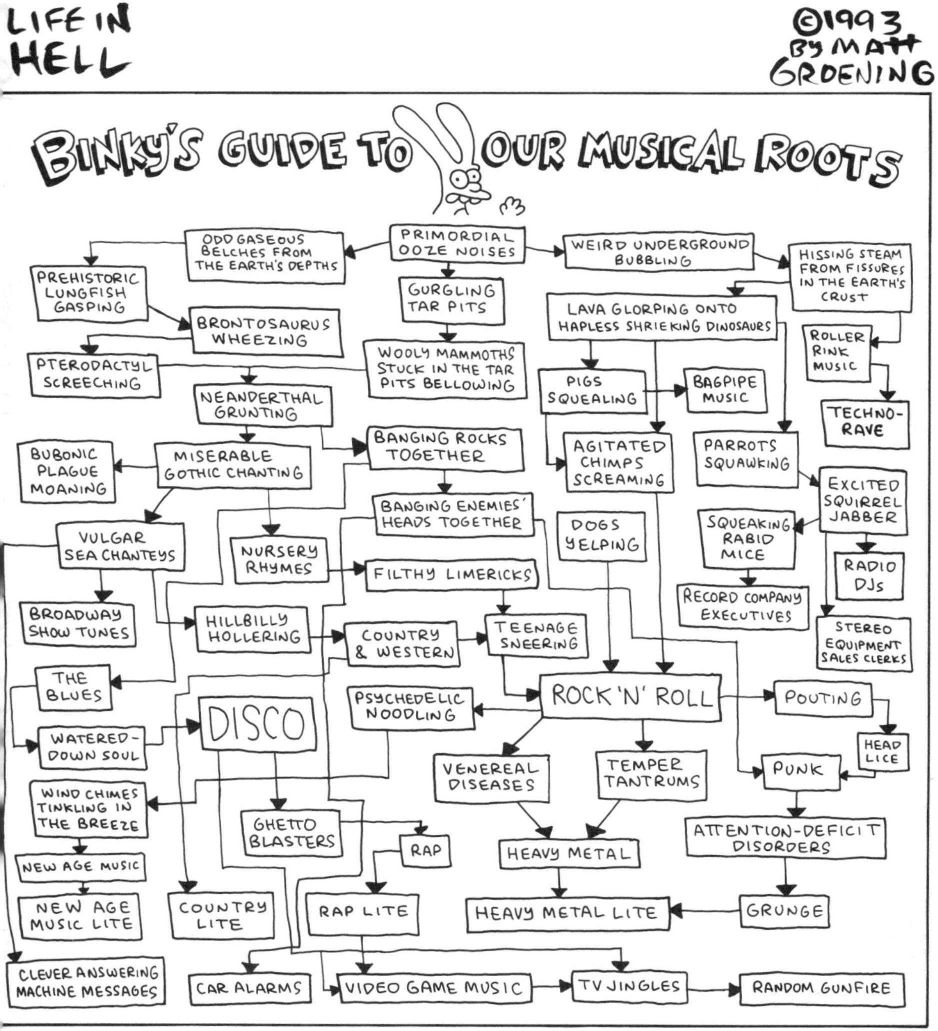
LIFE IN HELL
©1993 BY MATT GROENING
BINKY'S GUIDE TO YOUR MUSICAL ROOTS
PRIMORDIAL OOZE NOISES
ODD GASEOUS BELCHES FROM THE EARTH'S DEPTHS
WEIRD UNDERGROUND BUBBLING
HISSING STEAM FROM FISSURES IN THE EARTH'S CRUST
PREHISTORIC LUNGFISH GASPING
GURGLING TAR PITS
LAVA GLORPING ONTO HAPLESS SHRIEKING DINOSAURS
BRONTOSAURUS WHEEZING
ROLLER RINK MUSIC
WOOLY MAMMOTHS STUCK IN THE TAR PITS BELLOWING
PTERODACTYL SCREECHING
PIGS SQUEALING
BAGPIPE MUSIC
NEANDERTHAL GRUNTING
TECHNO-RAVE
BANGING ROCKS TOGETHER
BUBONIC PLAGUE MOANING
MISERABLE GOTHIC CHANTING
AGITATED CHIMPS SCREAMING
PARROTS SQUAWKING
EXCITED SQUIRREL JABBER
BANGING ENEMIES' HEADS TOGETHER
DOGS YELPING
SQUEAKING RABID MICE
VULGAR SEA CHANTEYS
NURSERY RHYMES
RADIO DJs
FILTHY LIMERICKS
RECORD COMPANY EXECUTIVES
BROADWAY SHOW TUNES
HILLBILLY HOLLERING
TEENAGE SNEERING
COUNTRY & WESTERN
STEREO EQUIPMENT SALES CLERKS
THE BLUES
ROCK 'N' ROLL
POUTING
PSYCHEDELIC NOODLING
DISCO
WATERED-DOWN SOUL
HEAD LICE
VENEREAL DISEASES
TEMPER TANTRUMS
PUNK
WIND CHIMES TINKLING IN THE BREEZE
GHETTO BLASTERS
RAP
HEAVY METAL
ATTENTION-DEFICIT DISORDERS
NEW AGE MUSIC
NEW AGE MUSIC LITE
COUNTRY LITE
RAP LITE
HEAVY METAL LITE
GRUNGE
CLEVER ANSWERING MACHINE MESSAGES
CAR ALARMS
VIDEO GAME MUSIC
TV JINGLES
RANDOM GUNFIRE

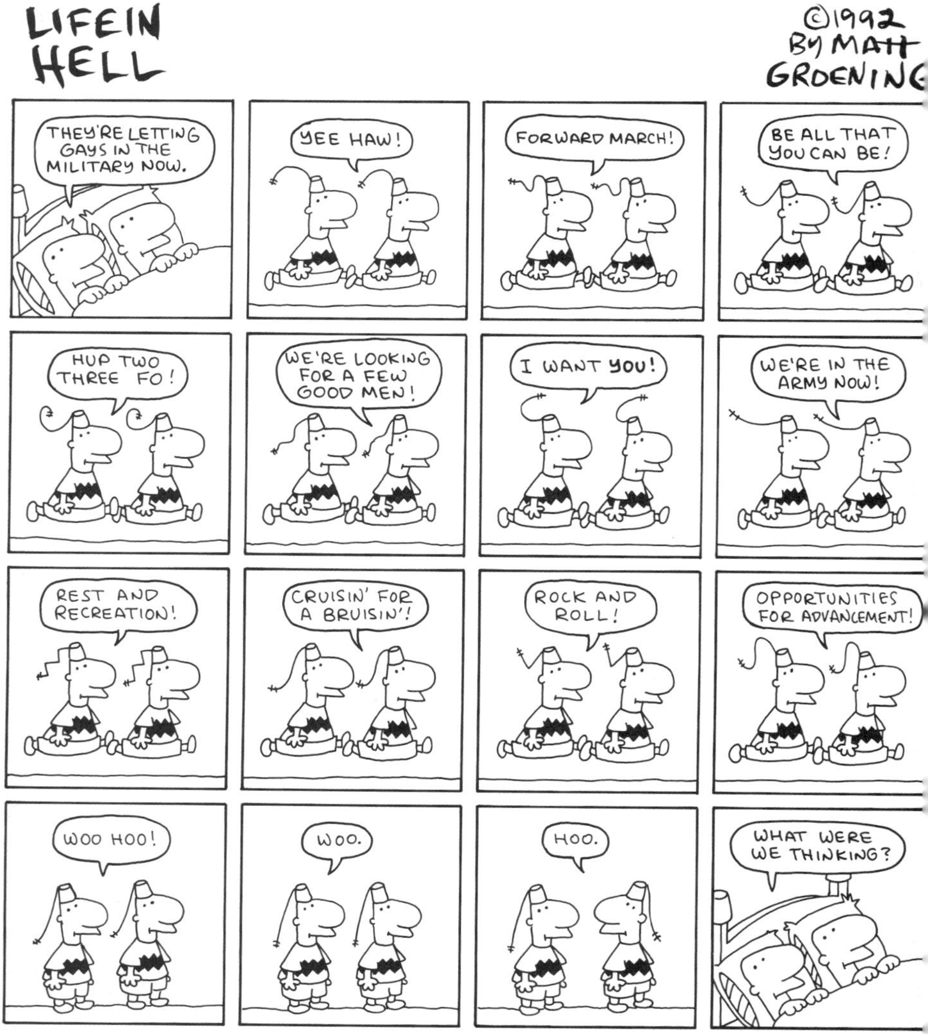
LIFE IN HELL
©1992 BY MATT GROENING
THEY'RE LETTING GAYS IN THE MILITARY NOW.
YEE HAW!
FORWARD MARCH!
BE ALL THAT YOU CAN BE!
HUP TWO THREE FO!
WE'RE LOOKING FOR A FEW GOOD MEN!
I WANT YOU!
WE'RE IN THE ARMY NOW!
REST AND RECREATION!
CRUISIN' FOR A BRUISIN'!
ROCK AND ROLL!
OPPORTUNITIES FOR ADVANCEMENT!
WOO HOO!
WOO.
HOO.
WHAT WERE WE THINKING?

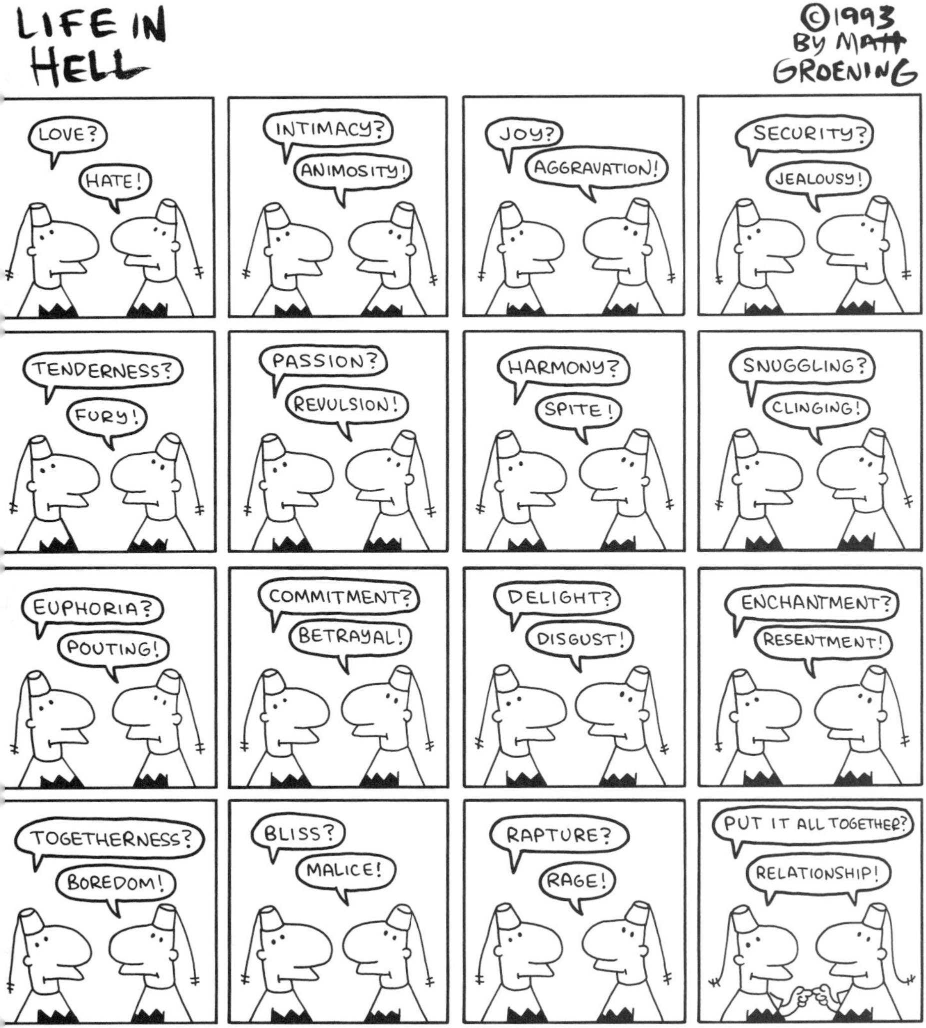
LIFE IN HELL
©1993 BY MATT GROENING
LOVE?
HATE!
INTIMACY?
ANIMOSITY!
JOY?
AGGRAVATION!
SECURITY?
JEALOUSY!
TENDERNESS?
FURY!
PASSION?
REVULSION!
HARMONY?
SPITE!
SNUGGLING?
CLINGING!
EUPHORIA?
POUTING!
COMMITMENT?
BETRAYAL!
DELIGHT?
DISGUST!
ENCHANTMENT?
RESENTMENT!
TOGETHERNESS?
BOREDOM!
BLISS?
MALICE!
RAPTURE?
RAGE!
PUT IT ALL TOGETHER?
RELATIONSHIP!

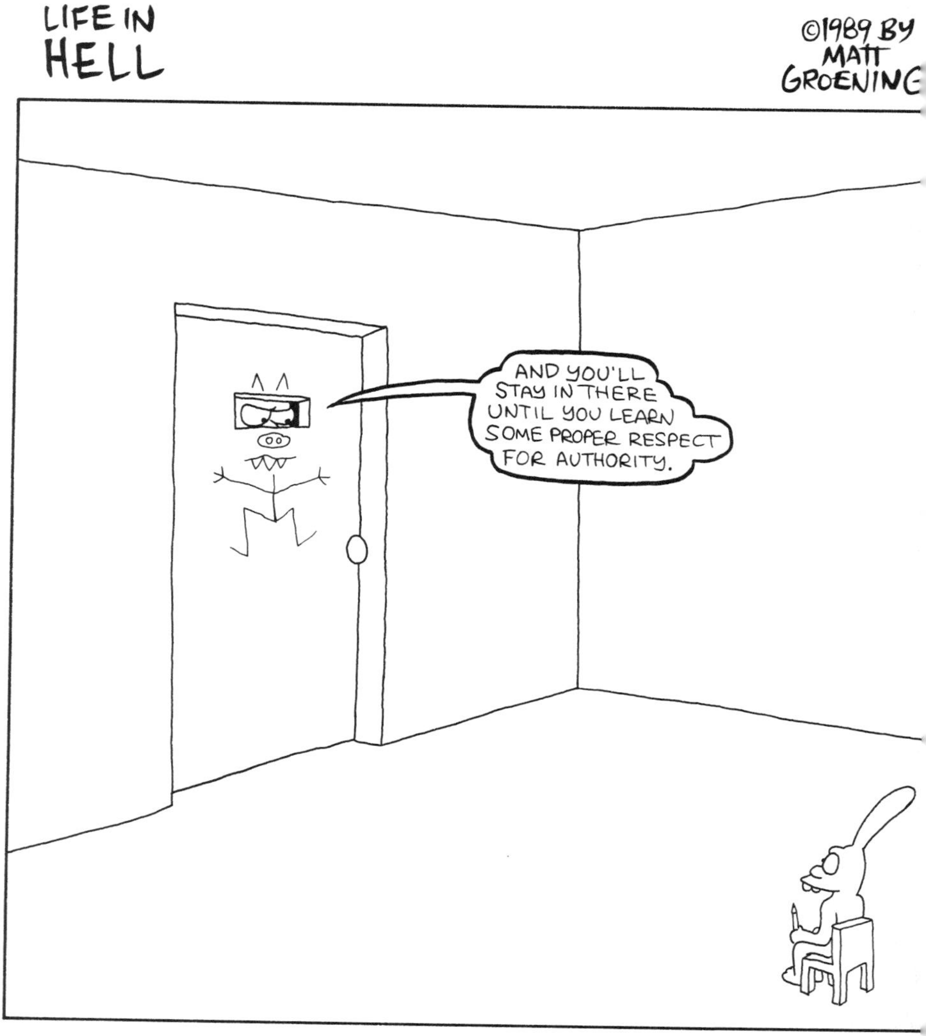
LIFE IN HELL
©1989 BY MATT GROENING
AND YOU'LL STAY IN THERE UNTIL YOU LEARN SOME PROPER RESPECT FOR AUTHORITY.

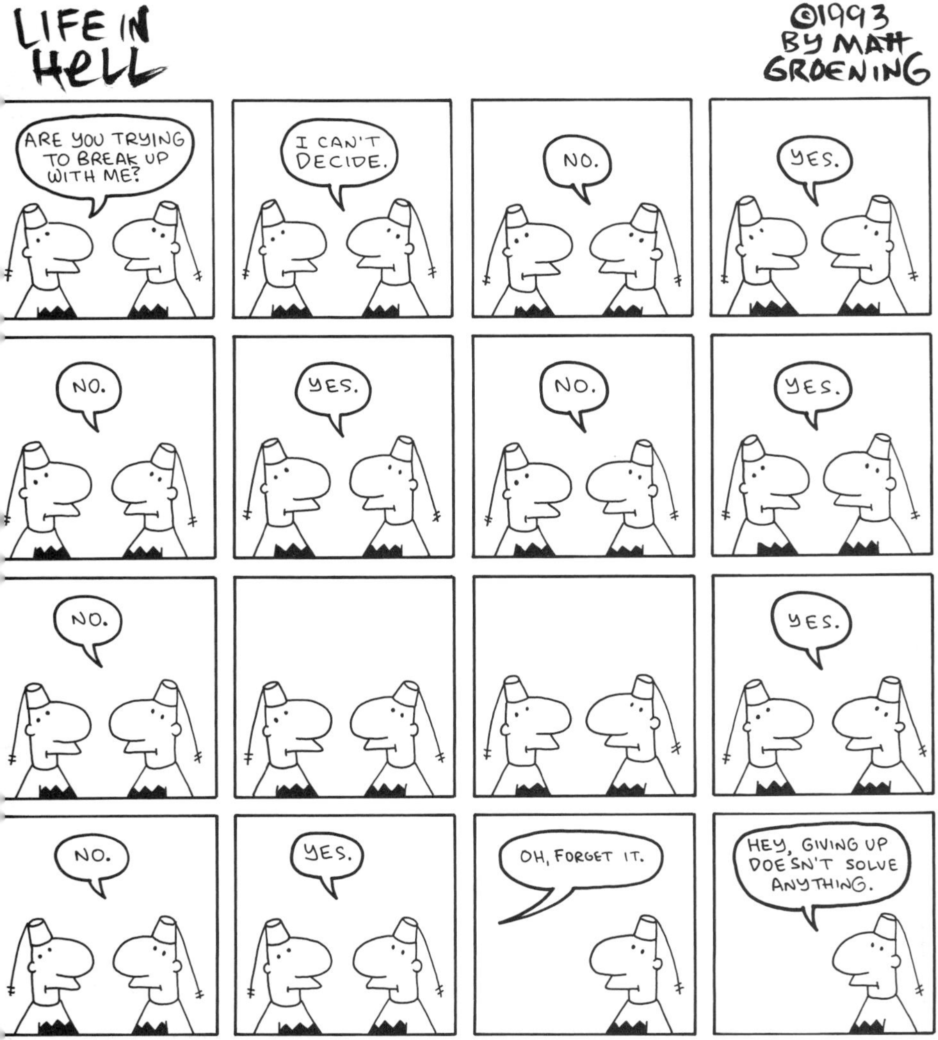
LIFE IN HELL
©1993 BY MATT GROENING
ARE YOU TRYING TO BREAK UP WITH ME?
I CAN'T DECIDE.
NO.
YES.
NO.
YES.
NO.
YES.
NO.
YES.
NO.
YES.
OH, FORGET IT.
HEY, GIVING UP DOESN'T SOLVE ANYTHING.

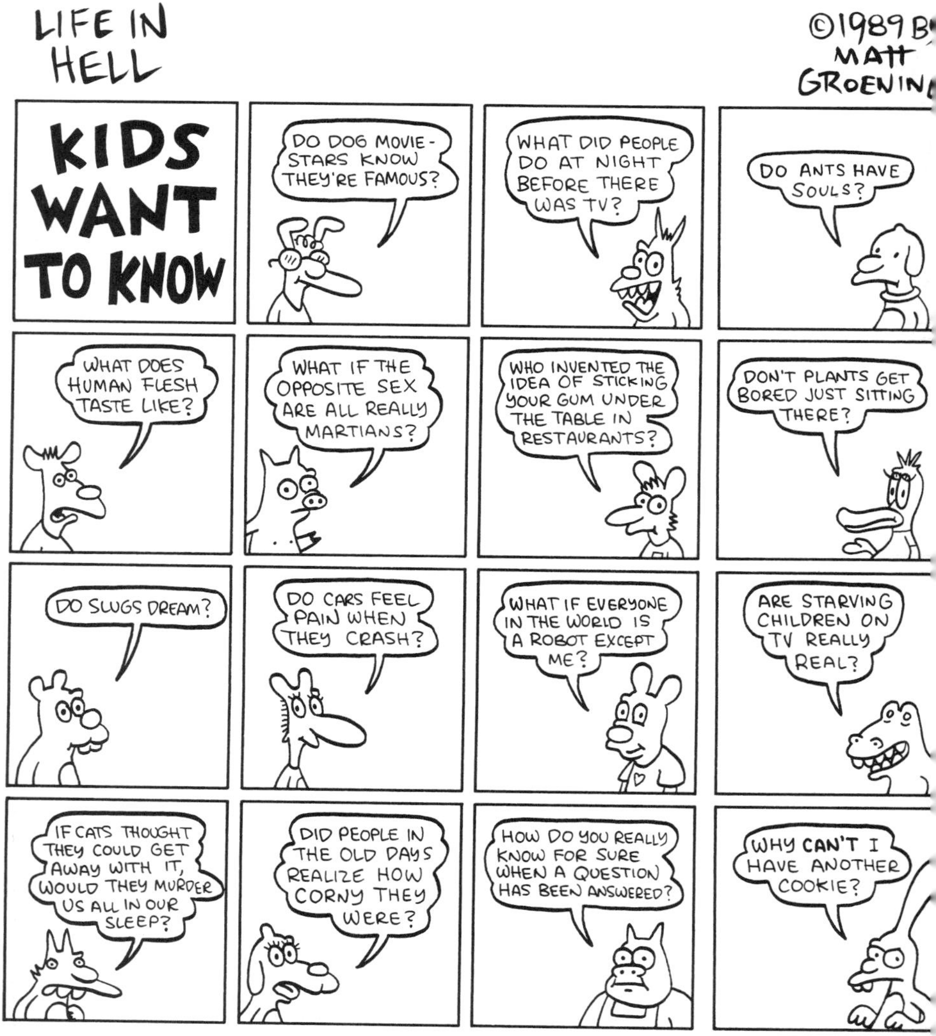
LIFE IN HELL
©1989 BY MATT GROENING
KIDS WANT TO KNOW
DO DOG MOVIE-STARS KNOW THEY'RE FAMOUS?
WHAT DID PEOPLE DO AT NIGHT BEFORE THERE WAS TV?
DO ANTS HAVE SOULS?
WHAT DOES HUMAN FLESH TASTE LIKE?
WHAT IF THE OPPOSITE SEX ARE ALL REALLY MARTIANS?
WHO INVENTED THE IDEA OF STICKING YOUR GUM UNDER THE TABLE IN RESTAURANTS?
DON'T PLANTS GET BORED JUST SITTING THERE?
DO SLUGS DREAM?
DO CARS FEEL PAIN WHEN THEY CRASH?
WHAT IF EVERYONE IN THE WORLD IS A ROBOT EXCEPT ME?
ARE STARVING CHILDREN ON TV REALLY REAL?
IF CATS THOUGHT THEY COULD GET AWAY WITH IT, WOULD THEY MURDER US ALL IN OUR SLEEP?
DID PEOPLE IN THE OLD DAYS REALIZE HOW CORNY THEY WERE?
HOW DO YOU REALLY KNOW FOR SURE WHEN A QUESTION HAS BEEN ANSWERED?
WHY **CAN'T** I HAVE ANOTHER COOKIE?

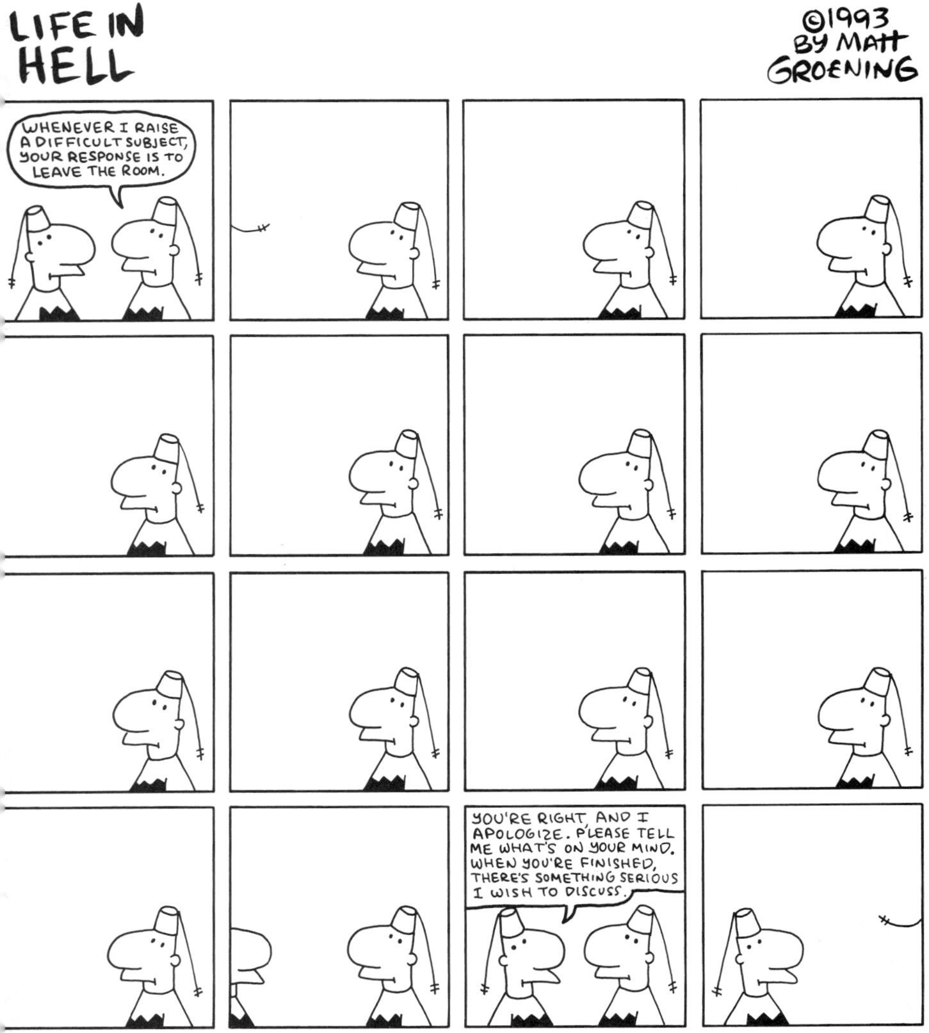

LIFE IN HELL
©1993 BY MATT GROENING
WHENEVER I RAISE A DIFFICULT SUBJECT, YOUR RESPONSE IS TO LEAVE THE ROOM.
YOU'RE RIGHT, AND I APOLOGIZE. PLEASE TELL ME WHAT'S ON YOUR MIND. WHEN YOU'RE FINISHED, THERE'S SOMETHING SERIOUS I WISH TO DISCUSS.

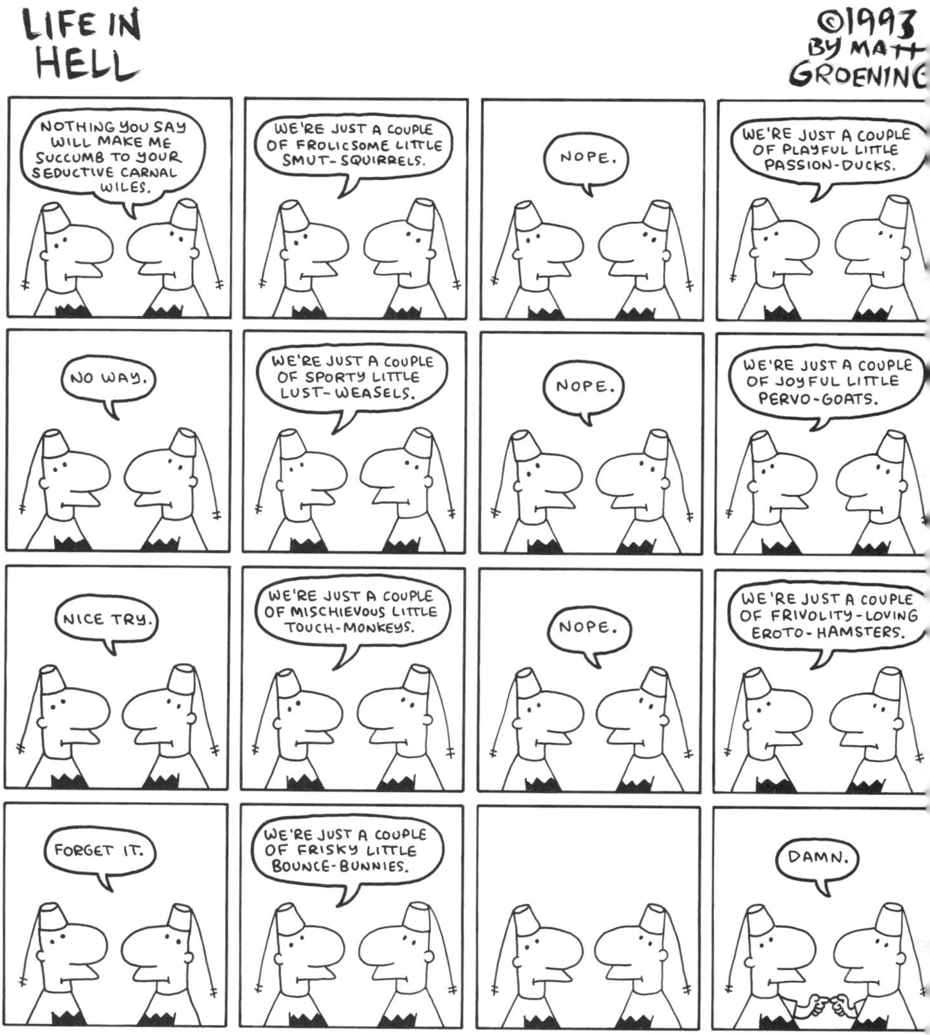
LIFE IN HELL
©1993 BY MATT GROENING
NOTHING YOU SAY WILL MAKE ME SUCCUMB TO YOUR SEDUCTIVE CARNAL WILES.
WE'RE JUST A COUPLE OF FROLICSOME LITTLE SMUT-SQUIRRELS.
NOPE.
WE'RE JUST A COUPLE OF PLAYFUL LITTLE PASSION-DUCKS.
NO WAY.
WE'RE JUST A COUPLE OF SPORTY LITTLE LUST-WEASELS.
NOPE.
WE'RE JUST A COUPLE OF JOYFUL LITTLE PERVO-GOATS.
NICE TRY.
WE'RE JUST A COUPLE OF MISCHIEVOUS LITTLE TOUCH-MONKEYS.
NOPE.
WE'RE JUST A COUPLE OF FRIVOLITY-LOVING EROTO-HAMSTERS.
FORGET IT.
WE'RE JUST A COUPLE OF FRISKY LITTLE BOUNCE-BUNNIES.
DAMN.

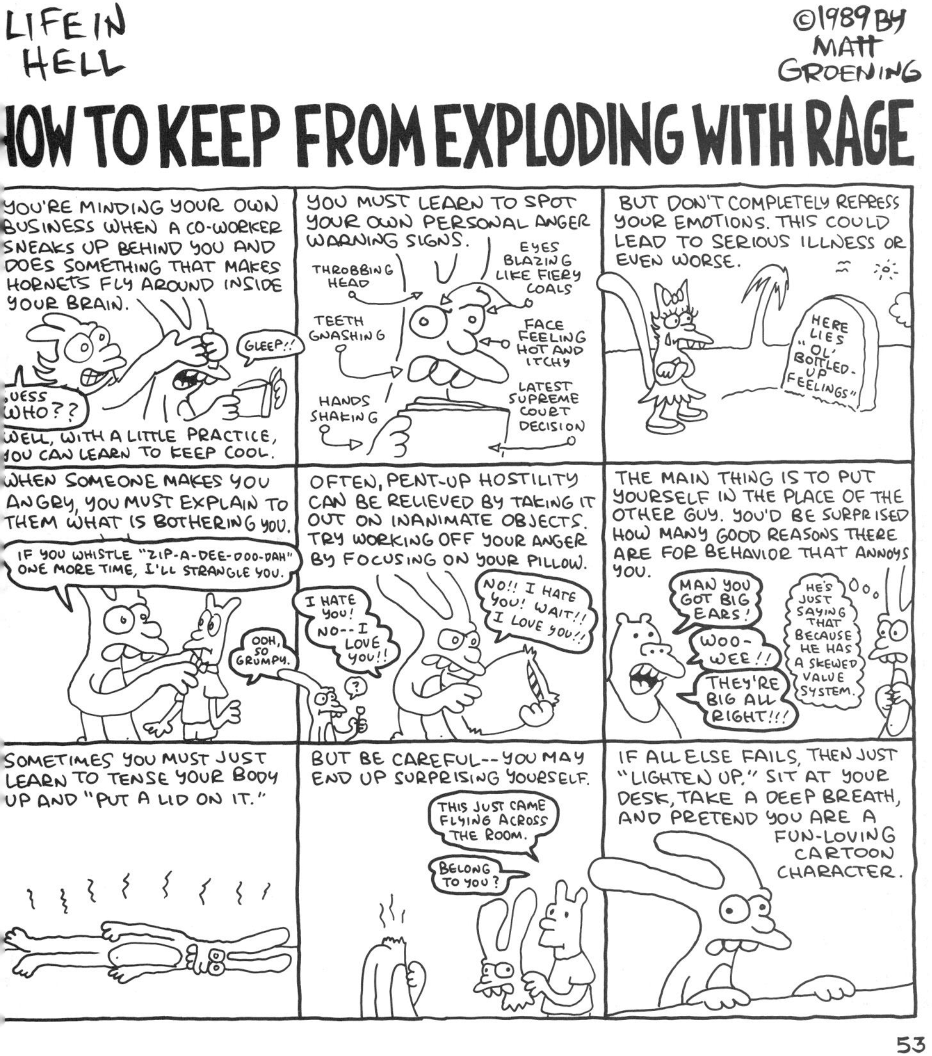

LIFE IN HELL
©1989 BY MATT GROENING
HOW TO KEEP FROM EXPLODING WITH RAGE
YOU'RE MINDING YOUR OWN BUSINESS WHEN A CO-WORKER SNEAKS UP BEHIND YOU AND DOES SOMETHING THAT MAKES HORNETS FLY AROUND INSIDE YOUR BRAIN.
GLEEP!!
GUESS WHO??
WELL, WITH A LITTLE PRACTICE, YOU CAN LEARN TO KEEP COOL.
YOU MUST LEARN TO SPOT YOUR OWN PERSONAL ANGER WARNING SIGNS.
THROBBING HEAD
EYES BLAZING LIKE FIERY COALS
TEETH GNASHING
FACE FEELING HOT AND ITCHY
HANDS SHAKING
LATEST SUPREME COURT DECISION
BUT DON'T COMPLETELY REPRESS YOUR EMOTIONS. THIS COULD LEAD TO SERIOUS ILLNESS OR EVEN WORSE.
HERE LIES "OL' BOTTLED-UP FEELINGS"
WHEN SOMEONE MAKES YOU ANGRY, YOU MUST EXPLAIN TO THEM WHAT IS BOTHERING YOU.
IF YOU WHISTLE "ZIP-A-DEE-DOO-DAH" ONE MORE TIME, I'LL STRANGLE YOU.
OOH, SO GRUMPY.
OFTEN, PENT-UP HOSTILITY CAN BE RELIEVED BY TAKING IT OUT ON INANIMATE OBJECTS. TRY WORKING OFF YOUR ANGER BY FOCUSING ON YOUR PILLOW.
I HATE YOU! NO--I LOVE YOU!!
?
NO!! I HATE YOU! WAIT!! I LOVE YOU!!
THE MAIN THING IS TO PUT YOURSELF IN THE PLACE OF THE OTHER GUY. YOU'D BE SURPRISED HOW MANY GOOD REASONS THERE ARE FOR BEHAVIOR THAT ANNOYS YOU.
MAN YOU GOT BIG EARS!
WOO-WEE!!
THEY'RE BIG ALL RIGHT!!!
HE'S JUST SAYING THAT BECAUSE HE HAS A SKEWED VALUE SYSTEM.
SOMETIMES YOU MUST JUST LEARN TO TENSE YOUR BODY UP AND "PUT A LID ON IT."
BUT BE CAREFUL--YOU MAY END UP SURPRISING YOURSELF.
THIS JUST CAME FLYING ACROSS THE ROOM.
BELONG TO YOU?
IF ALL ELSE FAILS, THEN JUST "LIGHTEN UP." SIT AT YOUR DESK, TAKE A DEEP BREATH, AND PRETEND YOU ARE A FUN-LOVING CARTOON CHARACTER.

LIFE IN
HELL

THE RETURN OF
THE DINOSAUR
POP-UP BOOK
FEATURING

DAD   ABE

BUH.
BUH.
BUH.

BALL?
BOTTLE?
BOOK?
BUH!

SURE, I'LL READ YOU A BOOK. GO GET ONE.

BUT PLEASE GET SOMETHING ELSE BESIDES THE DINOSAUR POP-UP BOOK, PLEASE.

D'OHH.

IN THE MANNER OF HOMER SIMPSON

POP-UP DINOSAUR BOOK

THIS IS A PICTURE OF A STEGOSAURUS WITH ITS HEAD RIPPED OFF.

WUZZAT?

A HEADLESS STEGOSAURUS.

WUZZAT?

HEADLESS STEGOSAURUS

AND HERE WE HAV A PTERODACTYL WI BOTH ITS WINGS TO OF

WUZZAT?

WELL, THI HIS HEA BUT DON

WUZZAT?

THAT'S THE PTERODACTYL'S HEAD YOU JUST RIPPED OUT.

THERE'S NOT EVEN A DINOSAUR ON THIS PAGE.

WUZZAT?

THAT'S DRIED GLUE WHERE THE DINOSAUR USED TO BE.

IN FACT, ALL THE REST OF THE DINO-SAURS IN THE BOOK HAVE BEEN RIPPED OUT.

WUZZAT?

AGAIN, THAT'S DRIED GLUE.

BUH!   BUH!
BUH!   BUH

OK, GE ANOTHER BOOK

D'OHH.

IN THE MANNER OF HOMER SIMPS

POP-UP DINOSAUR BOOK

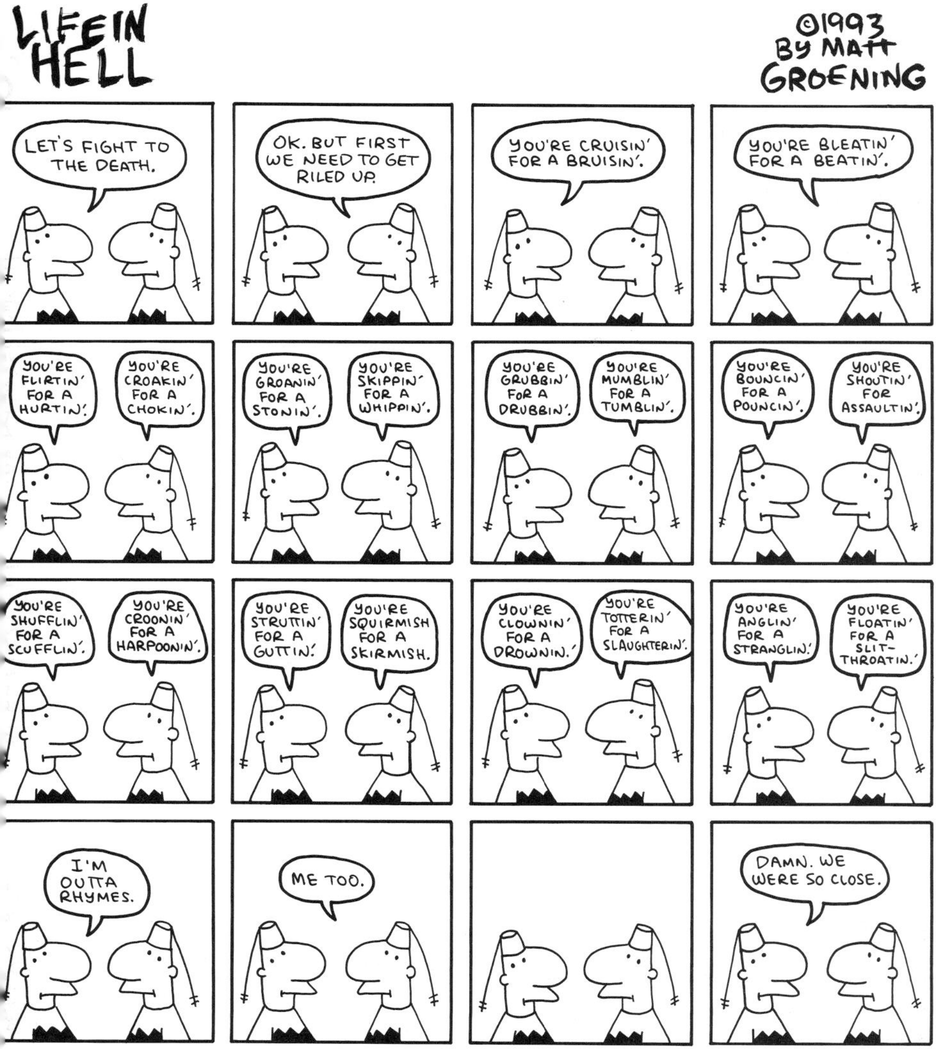
LIFE IN HELL
©1993 BY MATT GROENING
LET'S FIGHT TO THE DEATH.
OK. BUT FIRST WE NEED TO GET RILED UP.
YOU'RE CRUISIN' FOR A BRUISIN'.
YOU'RE BLEATIN' FOR A BEATIN'.
YOU'RE FLIRTIN' FOR A HURTIN'.
YOU'RE CROAKIN' FOR A CHOKIN'.
YOU'RE GROANIN' FOR A STONIN'.
YOU'RE SKIPPIN' FOR A WHIPPIN'.
YOU'RE GRUBBIN' FOR A DRUBBIN'.
YOU'RE MUMBLIN' FOR A TUMBLIN'.
YOU'RE BOUNCIN' FOR A POUNCIN'.
YOU'RE SHOUTIN' FOR ASSAULTIN'.
YOU'RE SHUFFLIN' FOR A SCUFFLIN'.
YOU'RE CROONIN' FOR A HARPOONIN'.
YOU'RE STRUTTIN' FOR A GUTTIN'.
YOU'RE SQUIRMISH FOR A SKIRMISH.
YOU'RE CLOWNIN' FOR A DROWNIN.'
YOU'RE TOTTERIN' FOR A SLAUGHTERIN'.
YOU'RE ANGLIN' FOR A STRANGLIN.'
YOU'RE FLOATIN' FOR A SLIT-THROATIN.'
I'M OUTTA RHYMES.
ME TOO.
DAMN. WE WERE SO CLOSE.

LIFE IN HELL

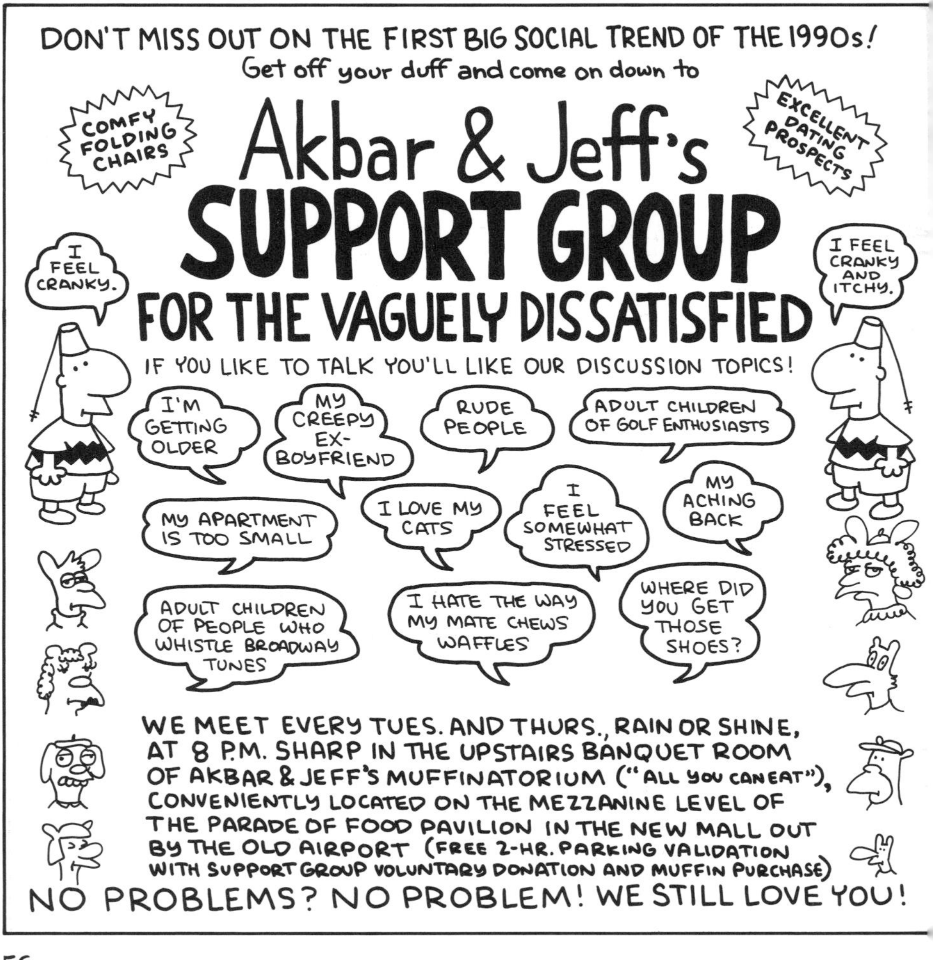
DON'T MISS OUT ON THE FIRST BIG SOCIAL TREND OF THE 1990s!
Get off your duff and come on down to
COMFY FOLDING CHAIRS
EXCELLENT DATING PROSPECTS
Akbar & Jeff's
SUPPORT GROUP
FOR THE VAGUELY DISSATISFIED
I FEEL CRANKY.
I FEEL CRANKY AND ITCHY.
IF YOU LIKE TO TALK YOU'LL LIKE OUR DISCUSSION TOPICS!
I'M GETTING OLDER
MY CREEPY EX-BOYFRIEND
RUDE PEOPLE
ADULT CHILDREN OF GOLF ENTHUSIASTS
MY APARTMENT IS TOO SMALL
I LOVE MY CATS
I FEEL SOMEWHAT STRESSED
MY ACHING BACK
ADULT CHILDREN OF PEOPLE WHO WHISTLE BROADWAY TUNES
I HATE THE WAY MY MATE CHEWS WAFFLES
WHERE DID YOU GET THOSE SHOES?
WE MEET EVERY TUES. AND THURS., RAIN OR SHINE, AT 8 P.M. SHARP IN THE UPSTAIRS BANQUET ROOM OF AKBAR & JEFF'S MUFFINATORIUM ("ALL YOU CAN EAT"), CONVENIENTLY LOCATED ON THE MEZZANINE LEVEL OF THE PARADE OF FOOD PAVILION IN THE NEW MALL OUT BY THE OLD AIRPORT (FREE 2-HR. PARKING VALIDATION WITH SUPPORT GROUP VOLUNTARY DONATION AND MUFFIN PURCHASE)
NO PROBLEMS? NO PROBLEM! WE STILL LOVE YOU!

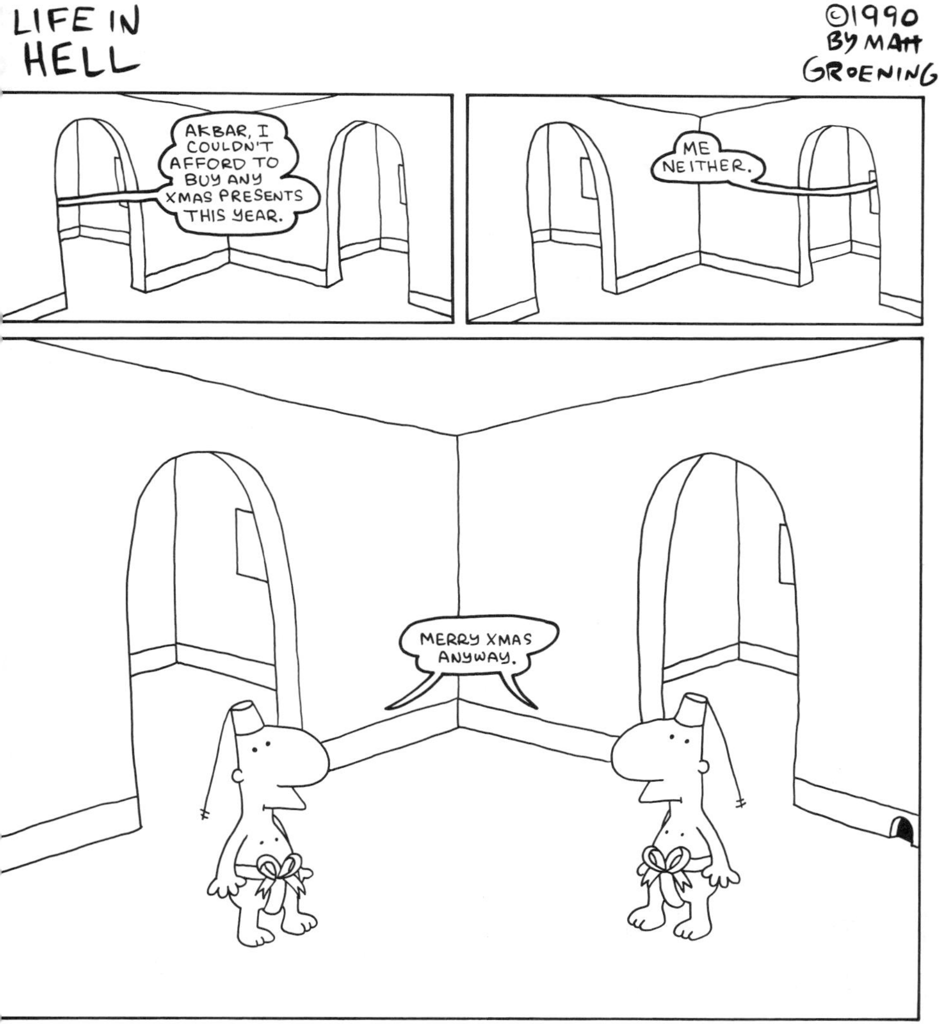
LIFE IN HELL
©1990 BY MATT GROENING
AKBAR, I COULDN'T AFFORD TO BUY ANY XMAS PRESENTS THIS YEAR.
ME NEITHER.
MERRY XMAS ANYWAY.

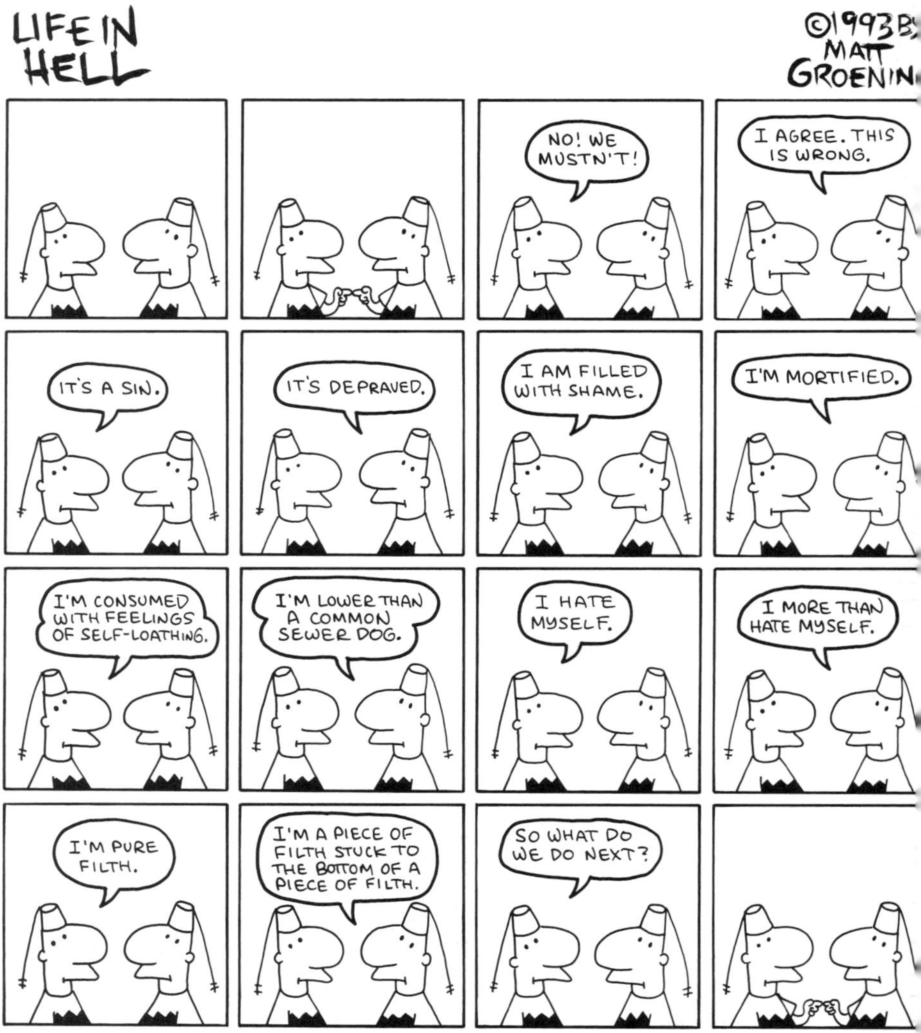
LIFE IN HELL
©1993 B
MATT
GROENIN
NO! WE MUSTN'T!
I AGREE. THIS IS WRONG.
IT'S A SIN.
IT'S DEPRAVED.
I AM FILLED WITH SHAME.
I'M MORTIFIED.
I'M CONSUMED WITH FEELINGS OF SELF-LOATHING.
I'M LOWER THAN A COMMON SEWER DOG.
I HATE MYSELF.
I MORE THAN HATE MYSELF.
I'M PURE FILTH.
I'M A PIECE OF FILTH STUCK TO THE BOTTOM OF A PIECE OF FILTH.
SO WHAT DO WE DO NEXT?

LIFE IN
HELL

©1989 BY
MATT
GROENING

HOW TO CHEER UP A DISGRUNTLED NEW MOTHER

A SAD BUT TRUE STORY

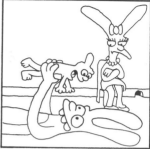

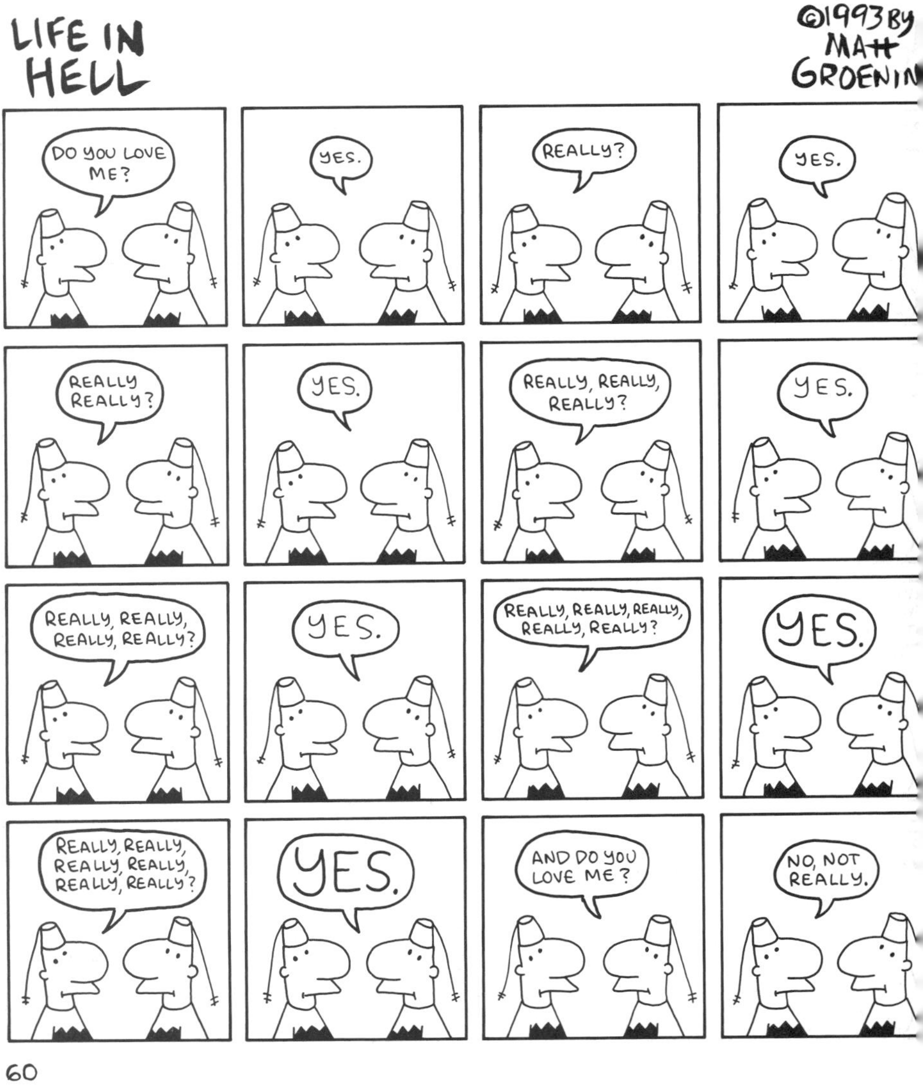
LIFE IN HELL
©1993 BY MATT GROENIN
DO YOU LOVE ME?
YES.
REALLY?
YES.
REALLY REALLY?
YES.
REALLY, REALLY, REALLY?
YES.
REALLY, REALLY, REALLY, REALLY?
YES.
REALLY, REALLY, REALLY, REALLY, REALLY?
YES.
REALLY, REALLY, REALLY, REALLY, REALLY, REALLY?
YES.
AND DO YOU LOVE ME?
NO, NOT REALLY.

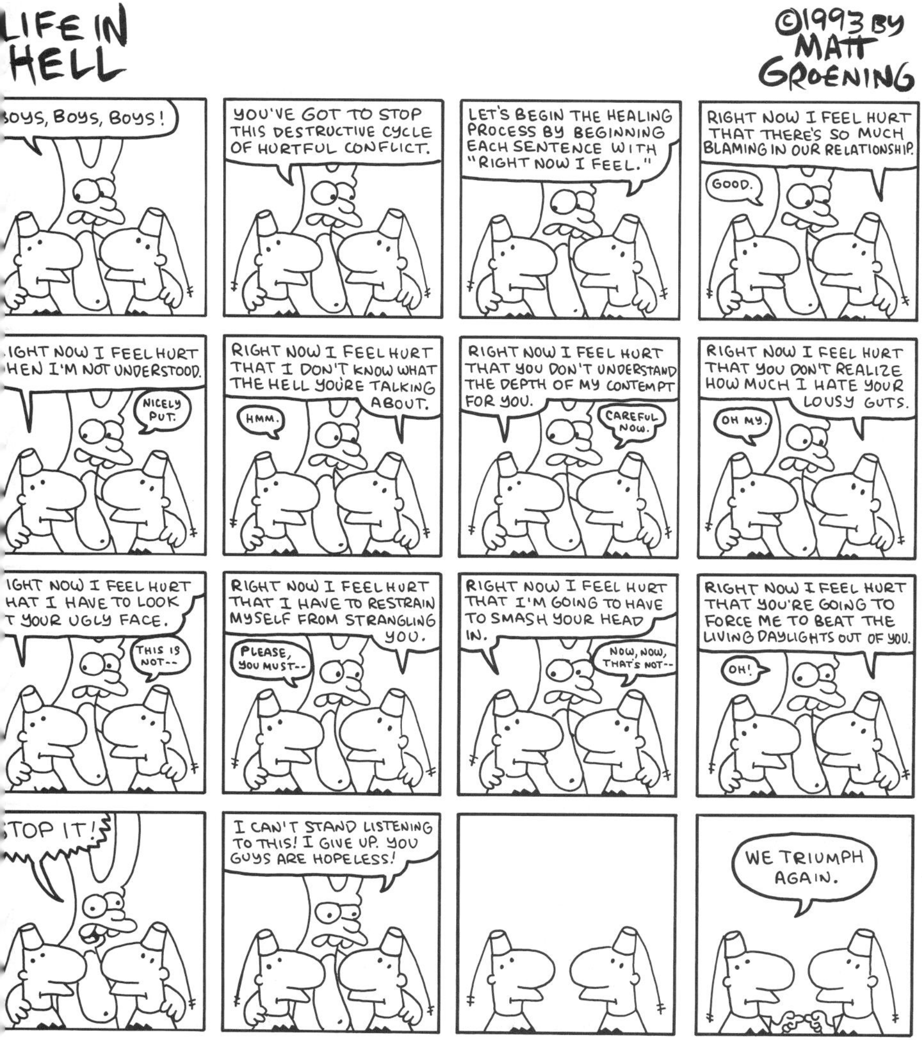
LIFE IN HELL
©1993 BY MATT GROENING
OYS, BOYS, BOYS!
YOU'VE GOT TO STOP THIS DESTRUCTIVE CYCLE OF HURTFUL CONFLICT.
LET'S BEGIN THE HEALING PROCESS BY BEGINNING EACH SENTENCE WITH "RIGHT NOW I FEEL."
RIGHT NOW I FEEL HURT THAT THERE'S SO MUCH BLAMING IN OUR RELATIONSHIP.
GOOD.
IGHT NOW I FEEL HURT HEN I'M NOT UNDERSTOOD.
NICELY PUT.
RIGHT NOW I FEEL HURT THAT I DON'T KNOW WHAT THE HELL YOU'RE TALKING ABOUT.
HMM.
RIGHT NOW I FEEL HURT THAT YOU DON'T UNDERSTAND THE DEPTH OF MY CONTEMPT FOR YOU.
CAREFUL NOW.
RIGHT NOW I FEEL HURT THAT YOU DON'T REALIZE HOW MUCH I HATE YOUR LOUSY GUTS.
OH MY.
IGHT NOW I FEEL HURT HAT I HAVE TO LOOK T YOUR UGLY FACE.
THIS IS NOT--
RIGHT NOW I FEEL HURT THAT I HAVE TO RESTRAIN MYSELF FROM STRANGLING YOU.
PLEASE, YOU MUST--
RIGHT NOW I FEEL HURT THAT I'M GOING TO HAVE TO SMASH YOUR HEAD IN.
NOW, NOW, THAT'S NOT--
RIGHT NOW I FEEL HURT THAT YOU'RE GOING TO FORCE ME TO BEAT THE LIVING DAYLIGHTS OUT OF YOU.
OH!
TOP IT!
I CAN'T STAND LISTENING TO THIS! I GIVE UP. YOU GUYS ARE HOPELESS!
WE TRIUMPH AGAIN.

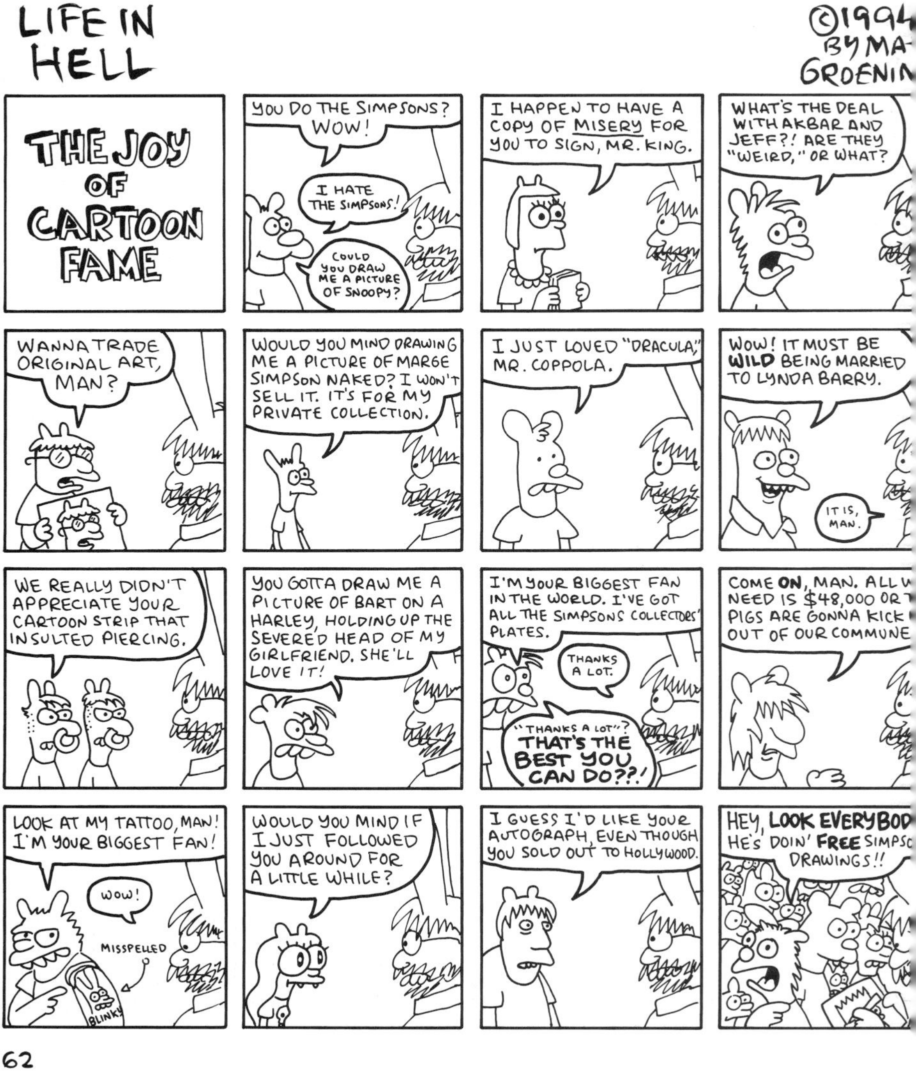

LIFE IN HELL
©1994 BY MA GROENIN
THE JOY OF CARTOON FAME
YOU DO THE SIMPSONS? WOW!
I HATE THE SIMPSONS!
COULD YOU DRAW ME A PICTURE OF SNOOPY?
I HAPPEN TO HAVE A COPY OF MISERY FOR YOU TO SIGN, MR. KING.
WHAT'S THE DEAL WITH AKBAR AND JEFF?! ARE THEY "WEIRD," OR WHAT?
WANNA TRADE ORIGINAL ART, MAN?
WOULD YOU MIND DRAWING ME A PICTURE OF MARGE SIMPSON NAKED? I WON'T SELL IT. IT'S FOR MY PRIVATE COLLECTION.
I JUST LOVED "DRACULA," MR. COPPOLA.
WOW! IT MUST BE WILD BEING MARRIED TO LYNDA BARRY.
IT IS, MAN.
WE REALLY DIDN'T APPRECIATE YOUR CARTOON STRIP THAT INSULTED PIERCING.
YOU GOTTA DRAW ME A PICTURE OF BART ON A HARLEY, HOLDING UP THE SEVERED HEAD OF MY GIRLFRIEND. SHE'LL LOVE IT!
I'M YOUR BIGGEST FAN IN THE WORLD. I'VE GOT ALL THE SIMPSONS COLLECTORS' PLATES.
THANKS A LOT.
"THANKS A LOT"? THAT'S THE BEST YOU CAN DO??!
COME ON, MAN. ALL W
NEED IS $48,000 OR T
PIGS ARE GONNA KICK
OUT OF OUR COMMUNE
LOOK AT MY TATTOO, MAN! I'M YOUR BIGGEST FAN!
WOW!
MISSPELLED
BLINKY
WOULD YOU MIND IF I JUST FOLLOWED YOU AROUND FOR A LITTLE WHILE?
I GUESS I'D LIKE YOUR AUTOGRAPH, EVEN THOUGH YOU SOLD OUT TO HOLLYWOOD.
HEY, LOOK EVERYBOD
HE'S DOIN' FREE SIMPS
DRAWINGS!!

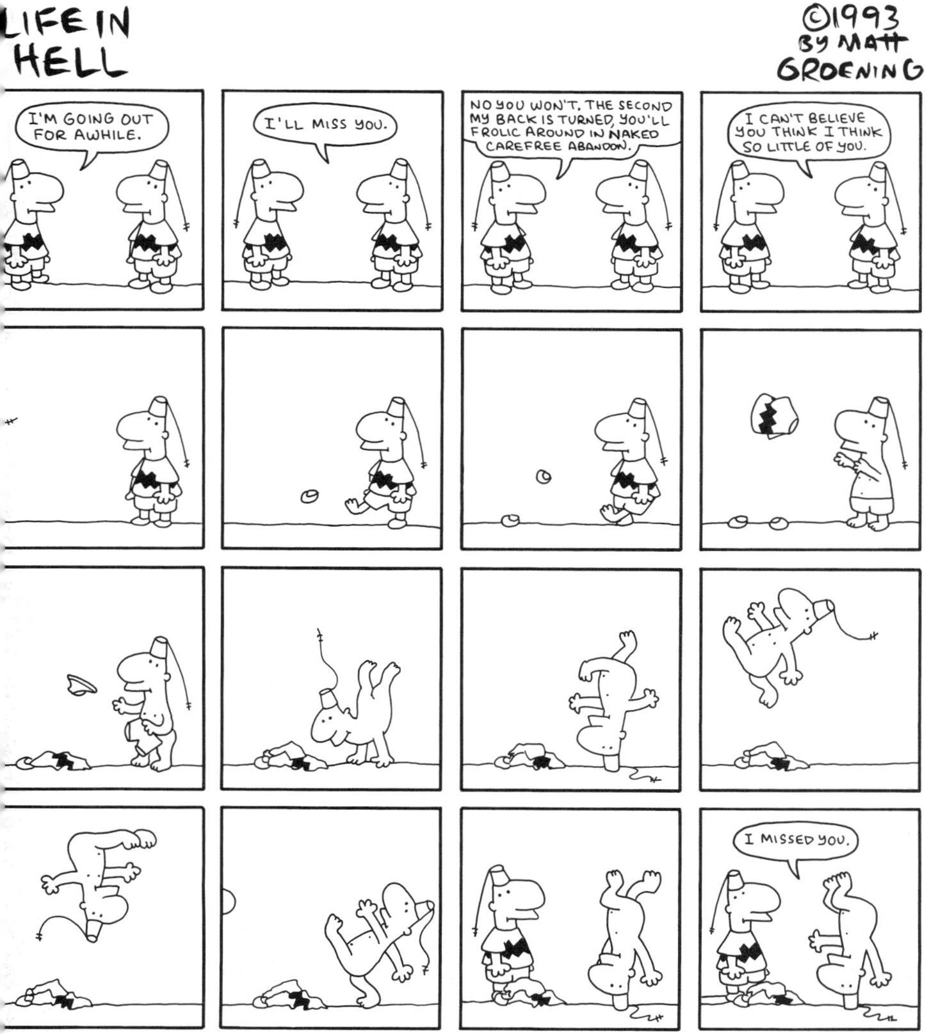
LIFE IN HELL
©1993 BY MATT GROENING
I'M GOING OUT FOR AWHILE.
I'LL MISS YOU.
NO YOU WON'T. THE SECOND MY BACK IS TURNED, YOU'LL FROLIC AROUND IN NAKED CAREFREE ABANDON.
I CAN'T BELIEVE YOU THINK I THINK SO LITTLE OF YOU.
I MISSED YOU.

LIFE IN HELL

©1989
MATT
GROENIN

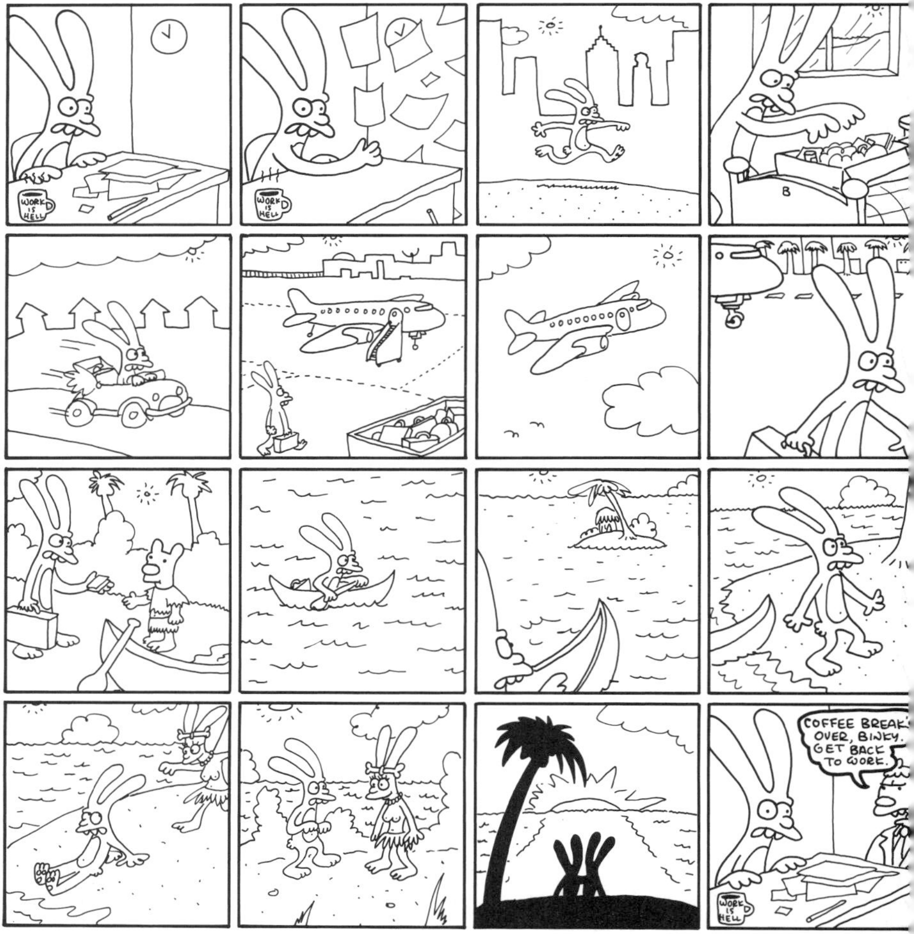
WORK IS HELL
COFFEE BREAK'S OVER, BINKY. GET BACK TO WORK.

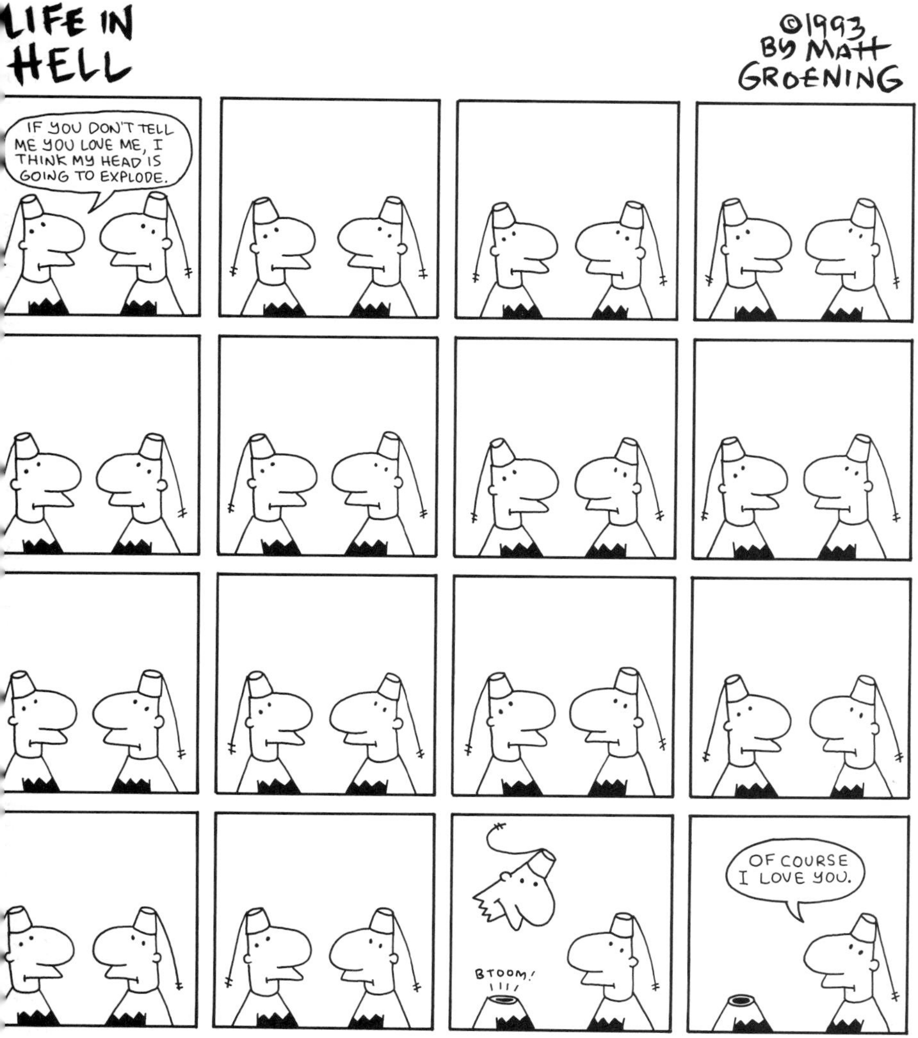
LIFE IN HELL
©1993 BY MATT GROENING
IF YOU DON'T TELL ME YOU LOVE ME, I THINK MY HEAD IS GOING TO EXPLODE.
BTOOM!
OF COURSE I LOVE YOU.

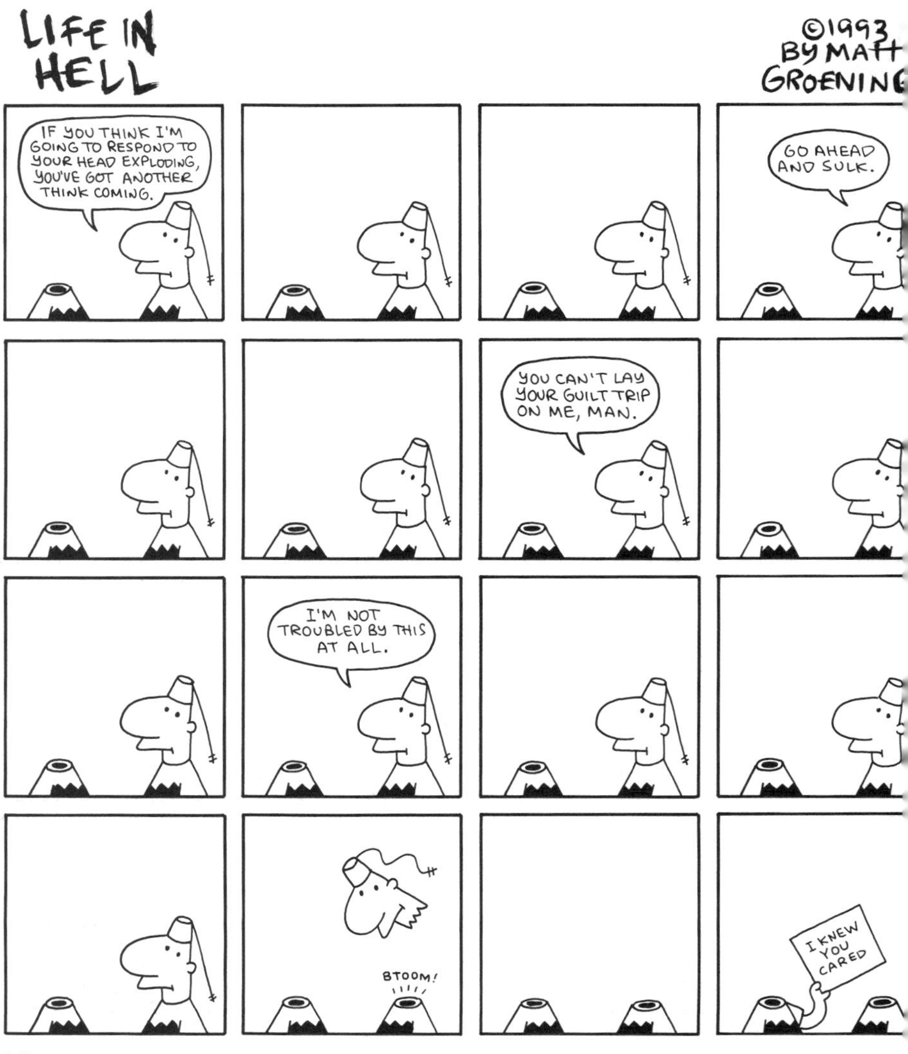
LIFE IN HELL
©1993 BY MATT GROENING
IF YOU THINK I'M GOING TO RESPOND TO YOUR HEAD EXPLODING, YOU'VE GOT ANOTHER THINK COMING.
GO AHEAD AND SULK.
YOU CAN'T LAY YOUR GUILT TRIP ON ME, MAN.
I'M NOT TROUBLED BY THIS AT ALL.
BTOOM!
I KNEW YOU CARED

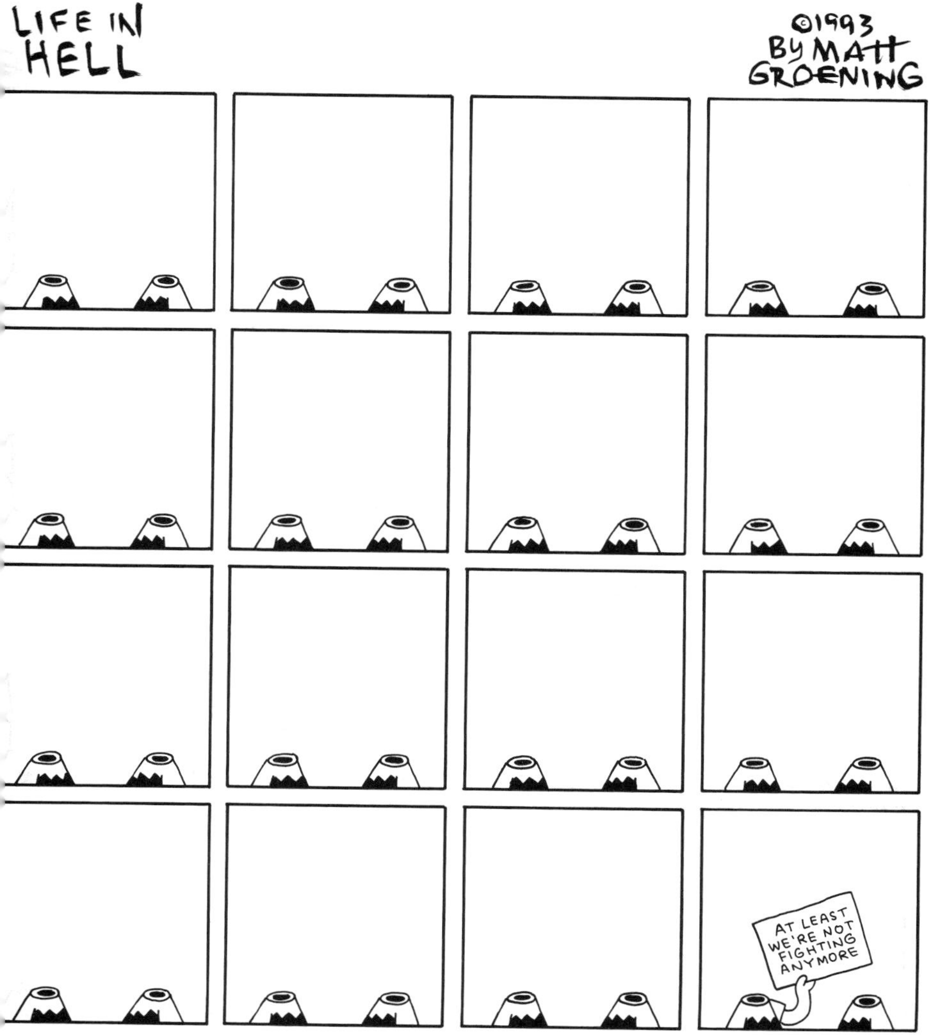
LIFE IN HELL
©1993 BY MATT GROENING
AT LEAST WE'RE NOT FIGHTING ANYMORE

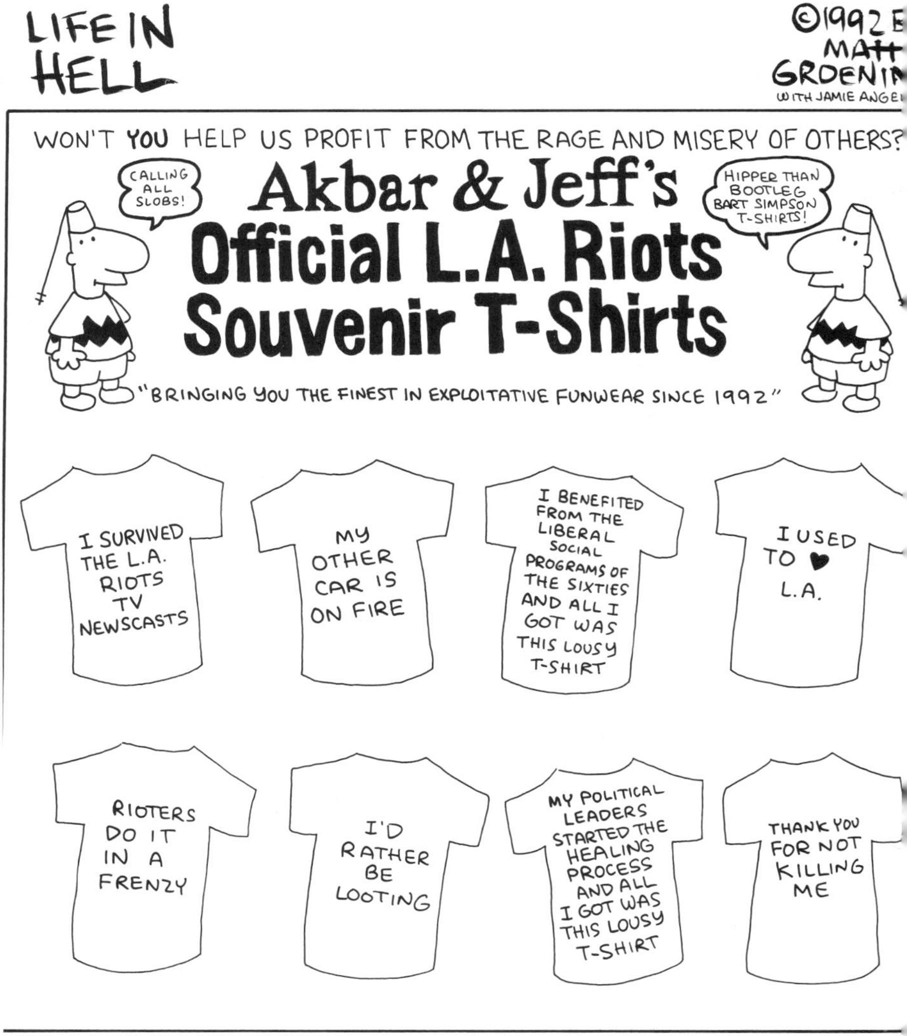
LIFE IN HELL
©1992 B
MATT
GROENI
WITH JAMIE ANGE
WON'T YOU HELP US PROFIT FROM THE RAGE AND MISERY OF OTHERS?
CALLING ALL SLOBS!
Akbar & Jeff's
Official L.A. Riots
Souvenir T-Shirts
HIPPER THAN BOOTLEG BART SIMPSON T-SHIRTS!
"BRINGING YOU THE FINEST IN EXPLOITATIVE FUNWEAR SINCE 1992"
I SURVIVED THE L.A. RIOTS TV NEWSCASTS
MY OTHER CAR IS ON FIRE
I BENEFITED FROM THE LIBERAL SOCIAL PROGRAMS OF THE SIXTIES AND ALL I GOT WAS THIS LOUSY T-SHIRT
I USED TO ♥ L.A.
RIOTERS DO IT IN A FRENZY
I'D RATHER BE LOOTING
MY POLITICAL LEADERS STARTED THE HEALING PROCESS AND ALL I GOT WAS THIS LOUSY T-SHIRT
THANK YOU FOR NOT KILLING ME

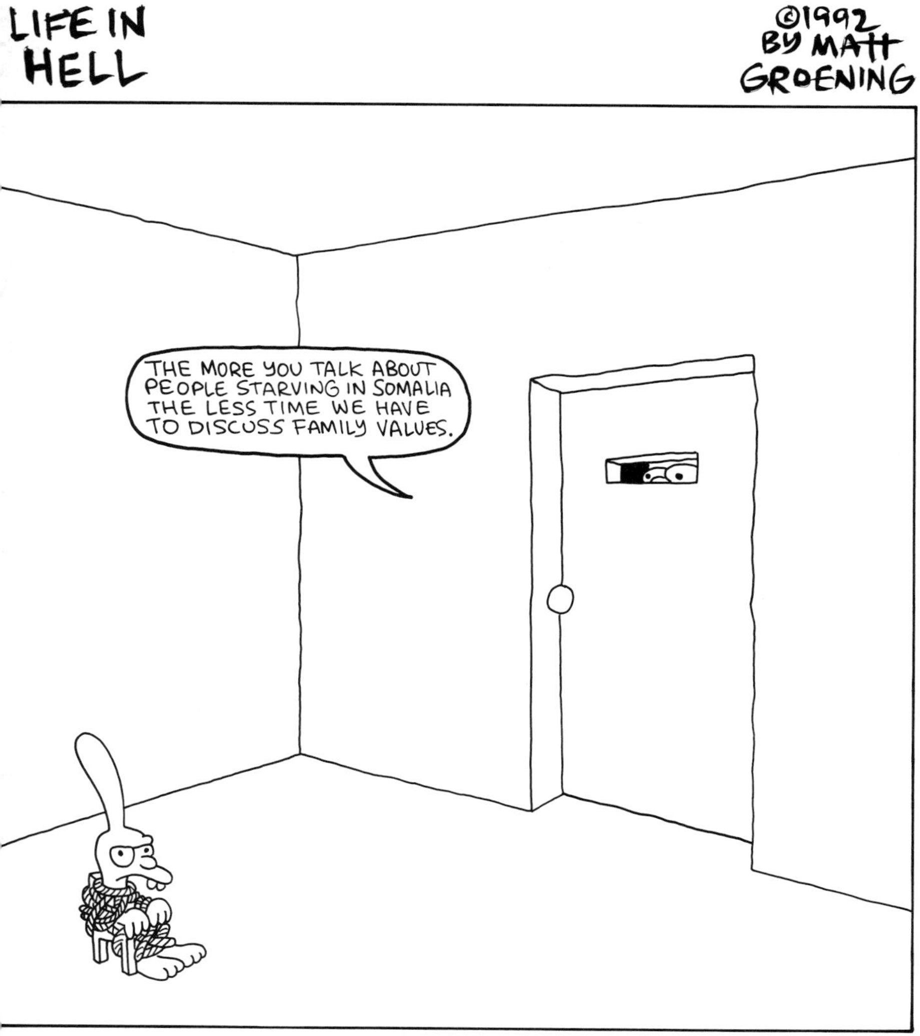
LIFE IN HELL
©1992 BY MATT GROENING
THE MORE YOU TALK ABOUT PEOPLE STARVING IN SOMALIA THE LESS TIME WE HAVE TO DISCUSS FAMILY VALUES.

LIFE IN HELL

©1989 BY MATT GROENING

HOW TO STOP A THROBBING HEADACHE

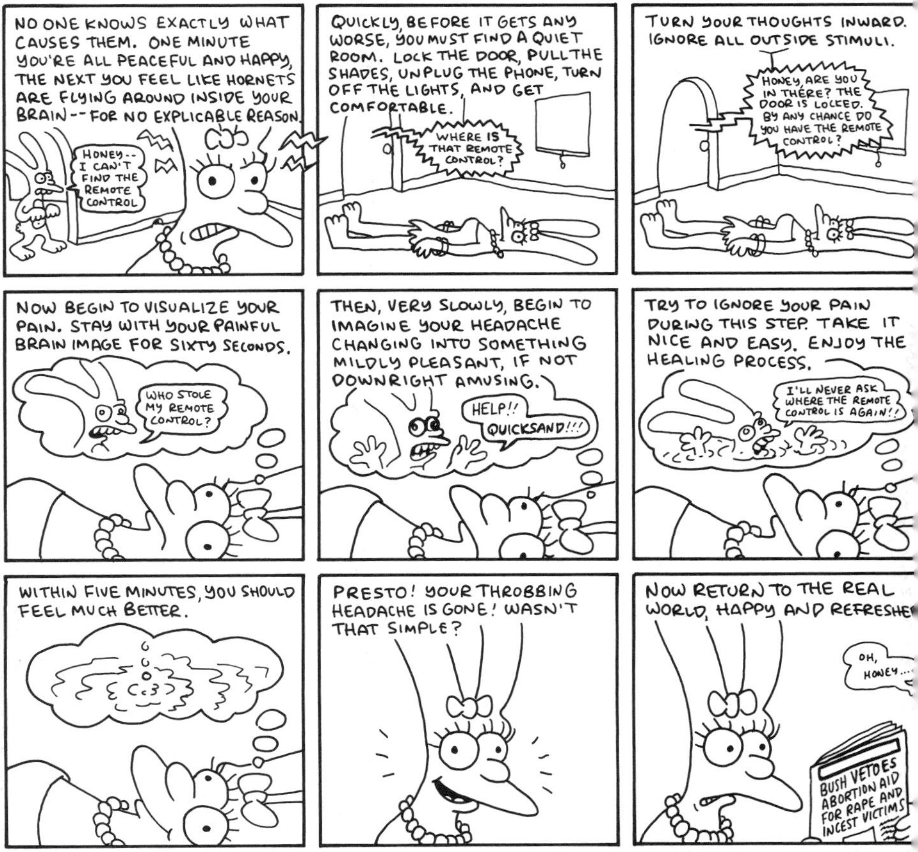
NO ONE KNOWS EXACTLY WHAT CAUSES THEM. ONE MINUTE YOU'RE ALL PEACEFUL AND HAPPY, THE NEXT YOU FEEL LIKE HORNETS ARE FLYING AROUND INSIDE YOUR BRAIN -- FOR NO EXPLICABLE REASON.
HONEY -- I CAN'T FIND THE REMOTE CONTROL
QUICKLY, BEFORE IT GETS ANY WORSE, YOU MUST FIND A QUIET ROOM. LOCK THE DOOR, PULL THE SHADES, UNPLUG THE PHONE, TURN OFF THE LIGHTS, AND GET COMFORTABLE.
WHERE IS THAT REMOTE CONTROL?
TURN YOUR THOUGHTS INWARD. IGNORE ALL OUTSIDE STIMULI.
HONEY, ARE YOU IN THERE? THE DOOR IS LOCKED. BY ANY CHANCE DO YOU HAVE THE REMOTE CONTROL?
NOW BEGIN TO VISUALIZE YOUR PAIN. STAY WITH YOUR PAINFUL BRAIN IMAGE FOR SIXTY SECONDS.
WHO STOLE MY REMOTE CONTROL?
THEN, VERY SLOWLY, BEGIN TO IMAGINE YOUR HEADACHE CHANGING INTO SOMETHING MILDLY PLEASANT, IF NOT DOWNRIGHT AMUSING.
HELP!! QUICKSAND!!!
TRY TO IGNORE YOUR PAIN DURING THIS STEP. TAKE IT NICE AND EASY. ENJOY THE HEALING PROCESS.
I'LL NEVER ASK WHERE THE REMOTE CONTROL IS AGAIN!!
WITHIN FIVE MINUTES, YOU SHOULD FEEL MUCH BETTER.
PRESTO! YOUR THROBBING HEADACHE IS GONE! WASN'T THAT SIMPLE?
NOW RETURN TO THE REAL WORLD, HAPPY AND REFRESHED
OH, HONEY....
BUSH VETOES ABORTION AID FOR RAPE AND INCEST VICTIMS

LIFE IN HELL

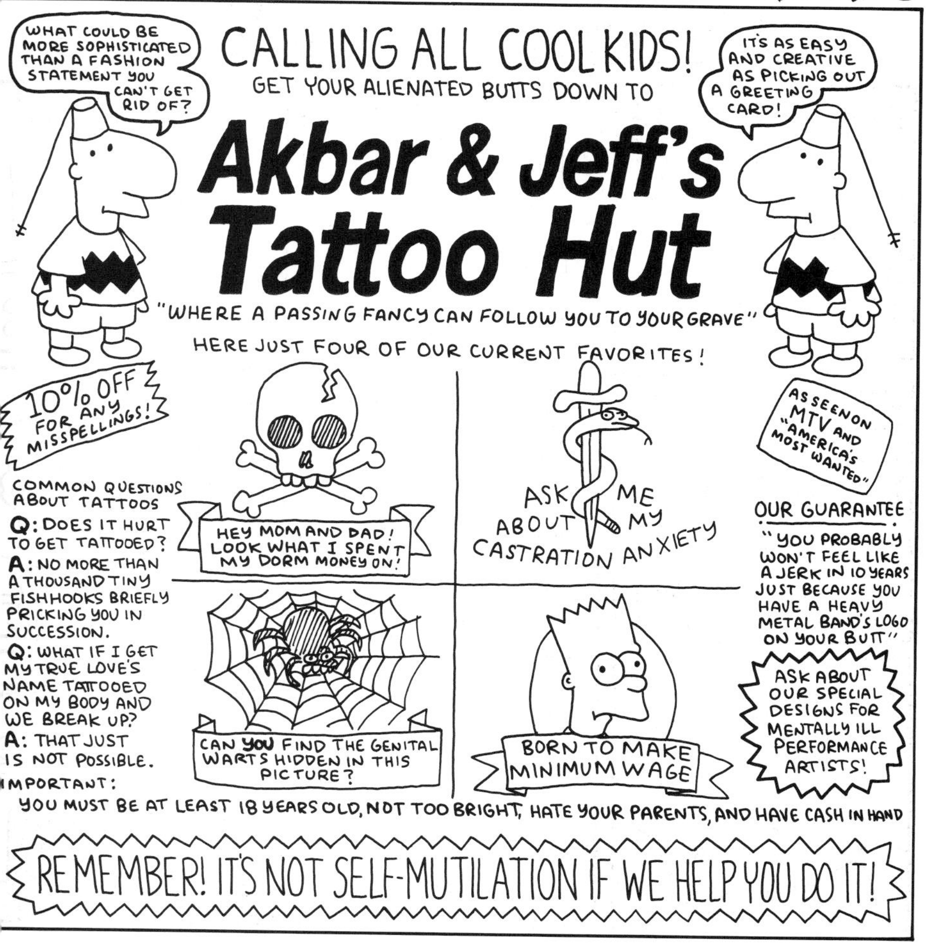

WHAT COULD BE MORE SOPHISTICATED THAN A FASHION STATEMENT YOU CAN'T GET RID OF?
CALLING ALL COOL KIDS!
GET YOUR ALIENATED BUTTS DOWN TO
IT'S AS EASY AND CREATIVE AS PICKING OUT A GREETING CARD!
Akbar & Jeff's Tattoo Hut
"WHERE A PASSING FANCY CAN FOLLOW YOU TO YOUR GRAVE"
HERE JUST FOUR OF OUR CURRENT FAVORITES!
10% OFF FOR ANY MISSPELLINGS!
AS SEEN ON MTV AND "AMERICA'S MOST WANTED"
HEY MOM AND DAD! LOOK WHAT I SPENT MY DORM MONEY ON!
ASK ME ABOUT MY CASTRATION ANXIETY
COMMON QUESTIONS ABOUT TATTOOS
Q: DOES IT HURT TO GET TATTOOED?
A: NO MORE THAN A THOUSAND TINY FISHHOOKS BRIEFLY PRICKING YOU IN SUCCESSION.
Q: WHAT IF I GET MY TRUE LOVE'S NAME TATTOOED ON MY BODY AND WE BREAK UP?
A: THAT JUST IS NOT POSSIBLE.
OUR GUARANTEE
"YOU PROBABLY WON'T FEEL LIKE A JERK IN 10 YEARS JUST BECAUSE YOU HAVE A HEAVY METAL BAND'S LOGO ON YOUR BUTT"
CAN YOU FIND THE GENITAL WARTS HIDDEN IN THIS PICTURE?
BORN TO MAKE MINIMUM WAGE
ASK ABOUT OUR SPECIAL DESIGNS FOR MENTALLY ILL PERFORMANCE ARTISTS!
IMPORTANT:
YOU MUST BE AT LEAST 18 YEARS OLD, NOT TOO BRIGHT, HATE YOUR PARENTS, AND HAVE CASH IN HAND
REMEMBER! IT'S NOT SELF-MUTILATION IF WE HELP YOU DO IT!

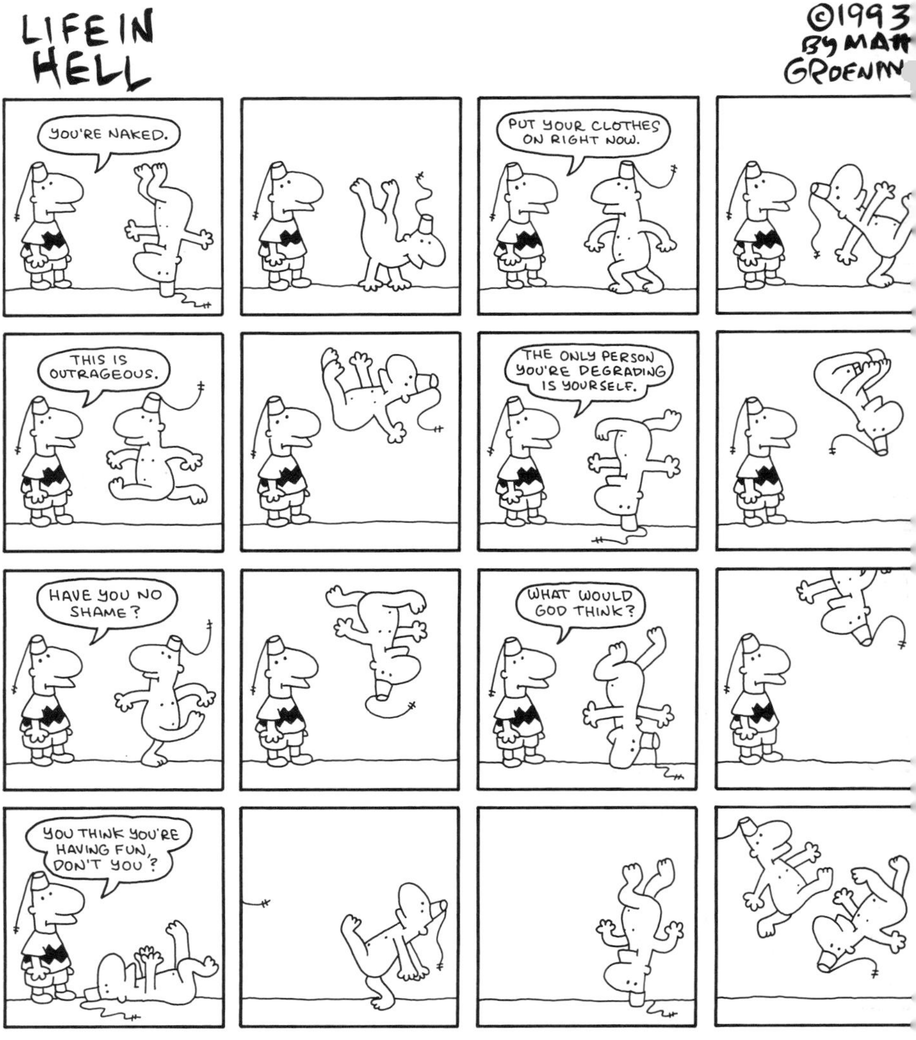
LIFE IN HELL
©1993 BY MATT GROENING
YOU'RE NAKED.
PUT YOUR CLOTHES ON RIGHT NOW.
THIS IS OUTRAGEOUS.
THE ONLY PERSON YOU'RE DEGRADING IS YOURSELF.
HAVE YOU NO SHAME?
WHAT WOULD GOD THINK?
YOU THINK YOU'RE HAVING FUN, DON'T YOU?

LIFE IN HELL
©1993 BY MATT GROENING
HAVE WE LOST OUR MINDS?
I'M FILLED WITH SHAME.
WE MUST CEASE THIS DEPRAVITY IMMEDIATELY.
MY FEELINGS OF GUILT AND SELF-DISGUST ARE OVERWHELMING.
REGAINING OUR DIGNITY FEELS MUCH BETTER, DOESN'T IT?

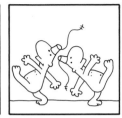

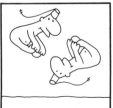

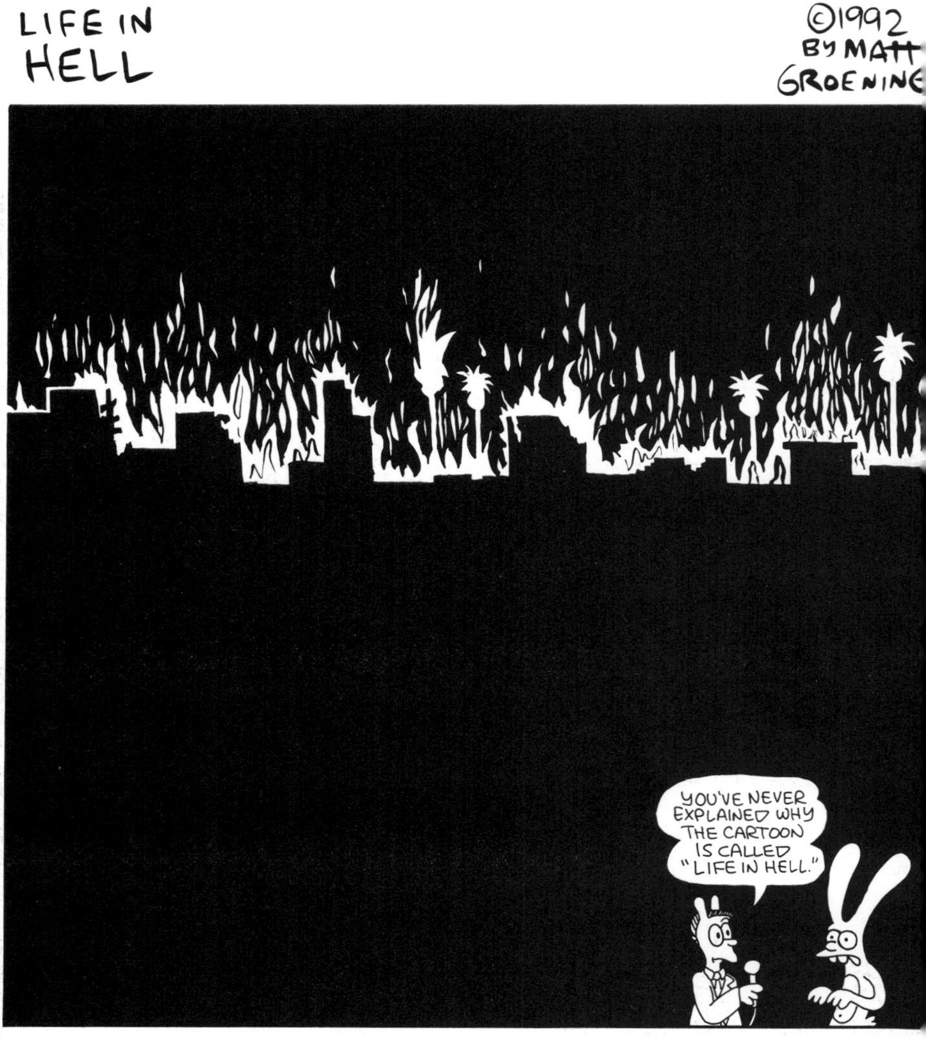
LIFE IN HELL
©1992 BY MATT GROENING
YOU'VE NEVER EXPLAINED WHY THE CARTOON IS CALLED "LIFE IN HELL."

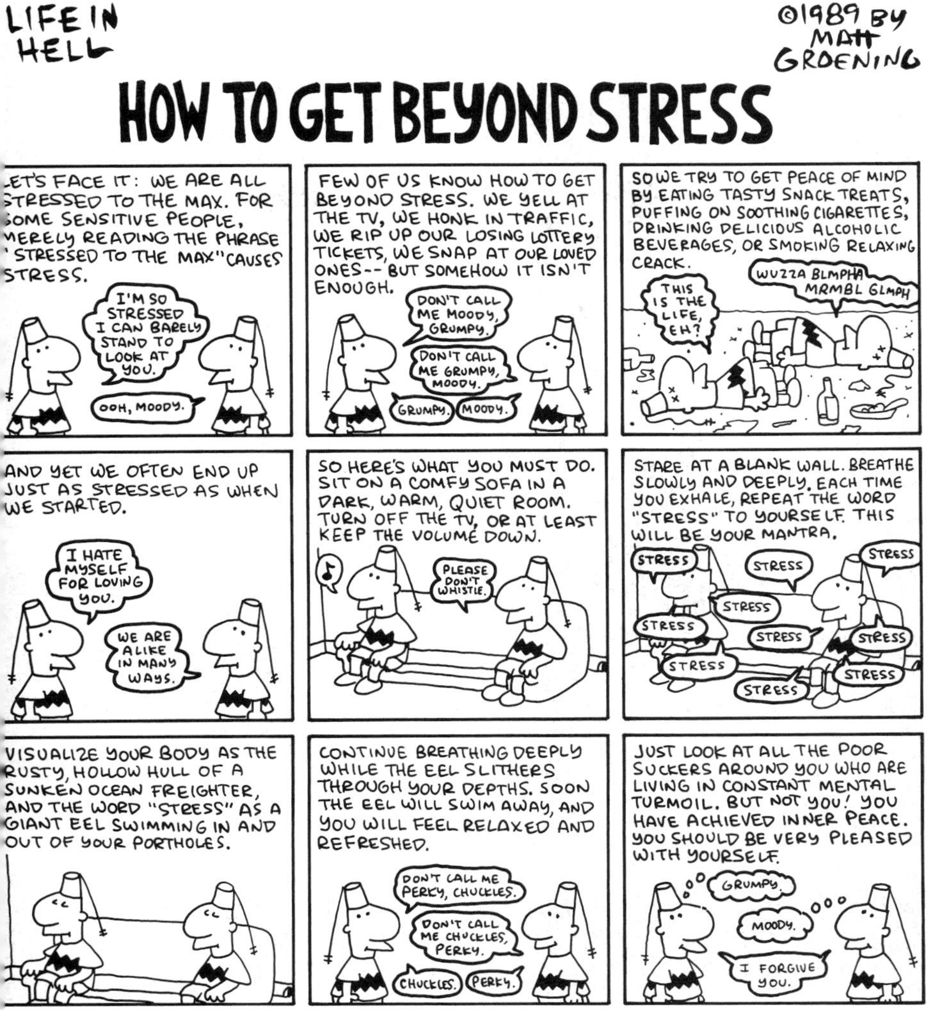
LIFE IN HELL
©1989 BY MATT GROENING
HOW TO GET BEYOND STRESS
LET'S FACE IT: WE ARE ALL STRESSED TO THE MAX. FOR SOME SENSITIVE PEOPLE, MERELY READING THE PHRASE "STRESSED TO THE MAX" CAUSES STRESS.
I'M SO STRESSED I CAN BARELY STAND TO LOOK AT YOU.
OOH, MOODY.
FEW OF US KNOW HOW TO GET BEYOND STRESS. WE YELL AT THE TV, WE HONK IN TRAFFIC, WE RIP UP OUR LOSING LOTTERY TICKETS, WE SNAP AT OUR LOVED ONES-- BUT SOMEHOW IT ISN'T ENOUGH.
DON'T CALL ME MOODY, GRUMPY.
DON'T CALL ME GRUMPY, MOODY.
GRUMPY.
MOODY.
SO WE TRY TO GET PEACE OF MIND BY EATING TASTY SNACK TREATS, PUFFING ON SOOTHING CIGARETTES, DRINKING DELICIOUS ALCOHOLIC BEVERAGES, OR SMOKING RELAXING CRACK.
THIS IS THE LIFE, EH?
WUZZA BLMPHA MRMBL GLMPH
AND YET WE OFTEN END UP JUST AS STRESSED AS WHEN WE STARTED.
I HATE MYSELF FOR LOVING YOU.
WE ARE ALIKE IN MANY WAYS.
SO HERE'S WHAT YOU MUST DO. SIT ON A COMFY SOFA IN A DARK, WARM, QUIET ROOM. TURN OFF THE TV, OR AT LEAST KEEP THE VOLUME DOWN.
PLEASE DON'T WHISTLE.
STARE AT A BLANK WALL. BREATHE SLOWLY AND DEEPLY. EACH TIME YOU EXHALE, REPEAT THE WORD "STRESS" TO YOURSELF. THIS WILL BE YOUR MANTRA.
STRESS
STRESS
STRESS
STRESS
STRESS
STRESS
STRESS
STRESS
STRESS
STRESS
VISUALIZE YOUR BODY AS THE RUSTY, HOLLOW HULL OF A SUNKEN OCEAN FREIGHTER, AND THE WORD "STRESS" AS A GIANT EEL SWIMMING IN AND OUT OF YOUR PORTHOLES.
CONTINUE BREATHING DEEPLY WHILE THE EEL SLITHERS THROUGH YOUR DEPTHS. SOON THE EEL WILL SWIM AWAY, AND YOU WILL FEEL RELAXED AND REFRESHED.
DON'T CALL ME PERKY, CHUCKLES.
DON'T CALL ME CHUCKLES, PERKY.
CHUCKLES.
PERKY.
JUST LOOK AT ALL THE POOR SUCKERS AROUND YOU WHO ARE LIVING IN CONSTANT MENTAL TURMOIL. BUT NOT YOU! YOU HAVE ACHIEVED INNER PEACE. YOU SHOULD BE VERY PLEASED WITH YOURSELF.
GRUMPY.
MOODY.
I FORGIVE YOU.

LIFE IN HELL

© 1994 BY MATT GROENING

IMPORTANT QUESTIONS ABOUT MONSTERS
BY WILL AND ABE

IS MOTHRA A GOOD MOTH OR A BAD MOTH?

HOW DO YOU KILL A MUMMY?

HOW, DADDY?

WHY DO CYCLOPS HAVE ONLY ONE EYE?

WHY DO ROBOTS WANT TO KILL PEOPLE?!

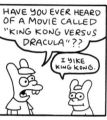

HAVE YOU EVER HEARD OF A MOVIE CALLED "KING KONG VERSUS DRACULA"??

I YIKE KING KONG.

WHY DO PEOPLE GO TO DRACULA'S HOUSE??

BECAUSE HE INVITED THEM.

BUT WHY DO THEY GO??

BECAUSE THEY DIDN'T KNOW HE WAS A VAMPIRE.

BUT HIS NAME IS DRACULA!

HAVE YOU EVER HEARD OF A MOVIE CALLED "I MARRIED A BITING WITCH"?

WHY DON'T VAMPIRES GET KIDS?? BECAUSE KIDS AREN'T TASTY??

I'M BATMAN.

WHY DOES GODZILLA ONLY ATTACK JAPAN JAPAN JAPAN!!?

HAVE YOU EVER HEARD OF A MOVIE CALLED "BRIDE OF THE CREATURE OF THE BLACK LAGOON"?

COOKIE?

WHY CAN'T ZOMBIES RUN?!

CRUNCH.

WHY DID THE BRIDE OF FRANKENSTEIN MARRY FRANKENSTEIN?

YUM.

IS THERE A WOLFWOMAN??

I'M DRACUYA.

WHY DO SKELETONS *DANCE*???

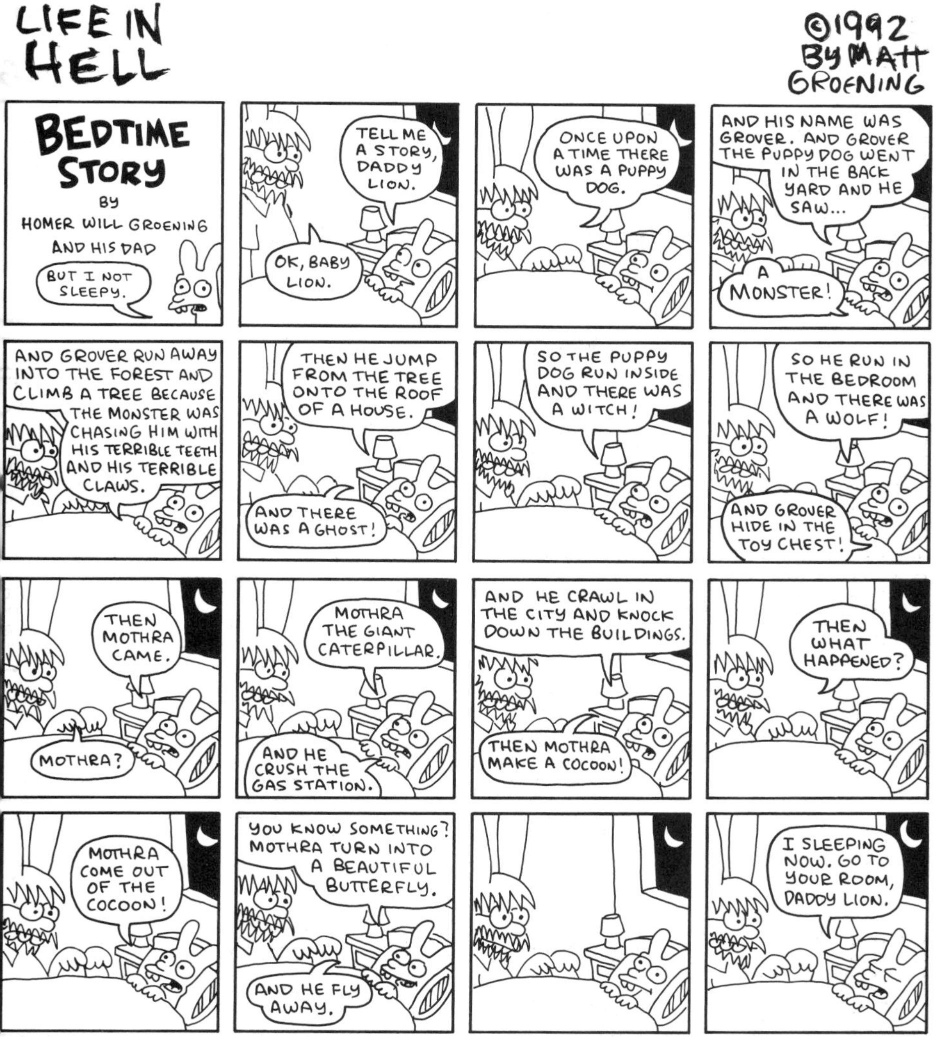
LIFE IN HELL
©1992 BY MATT GROENING
BEDTIME STORY
BY HOMER WILL GROENING AND HIS DAD
BUT I NOT SLEEPY.
TELL ME A STORY, DADDY LION.
OK, BABY LION.
ONCE UPON A TIME THERE WAS A PUPPY DOG.
AND HIS NAME WAS GROVER. AND GROVER THE PUPPY DOG WENT IN THE BACK YARD AND HE SAW...
A MONSTER!
AND GROVER RUN AWAY INTO THE FOREST AND CLIMB A TREE BECAUSE THE MONSTER WAS CHASING HIM WITH HIS TERRIBLE TEETH AND HIS TERRIBLE CLAWS.
THEN HE JUMP FROM THE TREE ONTO THE ROOF OF A HOUSE.
AND THERE WAS A GHOST!
SO THE PUPPY DOG RUN INSIDE AND THERE WAS A WITCH!
SO HE RUN IN THE BEDROOM AND THERE WAS A WOLF!
AND GROVER HIDE IN THE TOY CHEST!
THEN MOTHRA CAME.
MOTHRA?
MOTHRA THE GIANT CATERPILLAR.
AND HE CRUSH THE GAS STATION.
AND HE CRAWL IN THE CITY AND KNOCK DOWN THE BUILDINGS.
THEN MOTHRA MAKE A COCOON!
THEN WHAT HAPPENED?
MOTHRA COME OUT OF THE COCOON!
YOU KNOW SOMETHING? MOTHRA TURN INTO A BEAUTIFUL BUTTERFLY.
AND HE FLY AWAY.
I SLEEPING NOW. GO TO YOUR ROOM, DADDY LION.

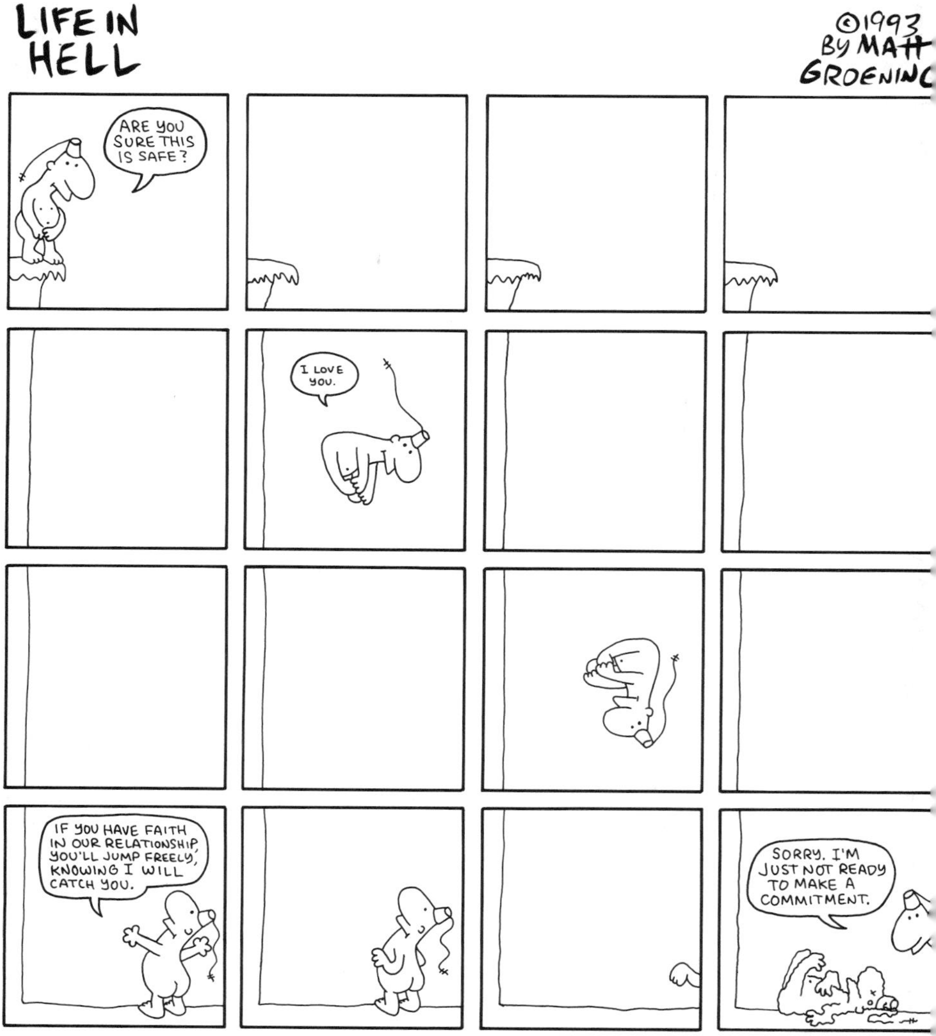
LIFE IN HELL
©1993 BY MATT GROENING
ARE YOU SURE THIS IS SAFE?
I LOVE YOU.
IF YOU HAVE FAITH IN OUR RELATIONSHIP, YOU'LL JUMP FREELY, KNOWING I WILL CATCH YOU.
SORRY. I'M JUST NOT READY TO MAKE A COMMITMENT.

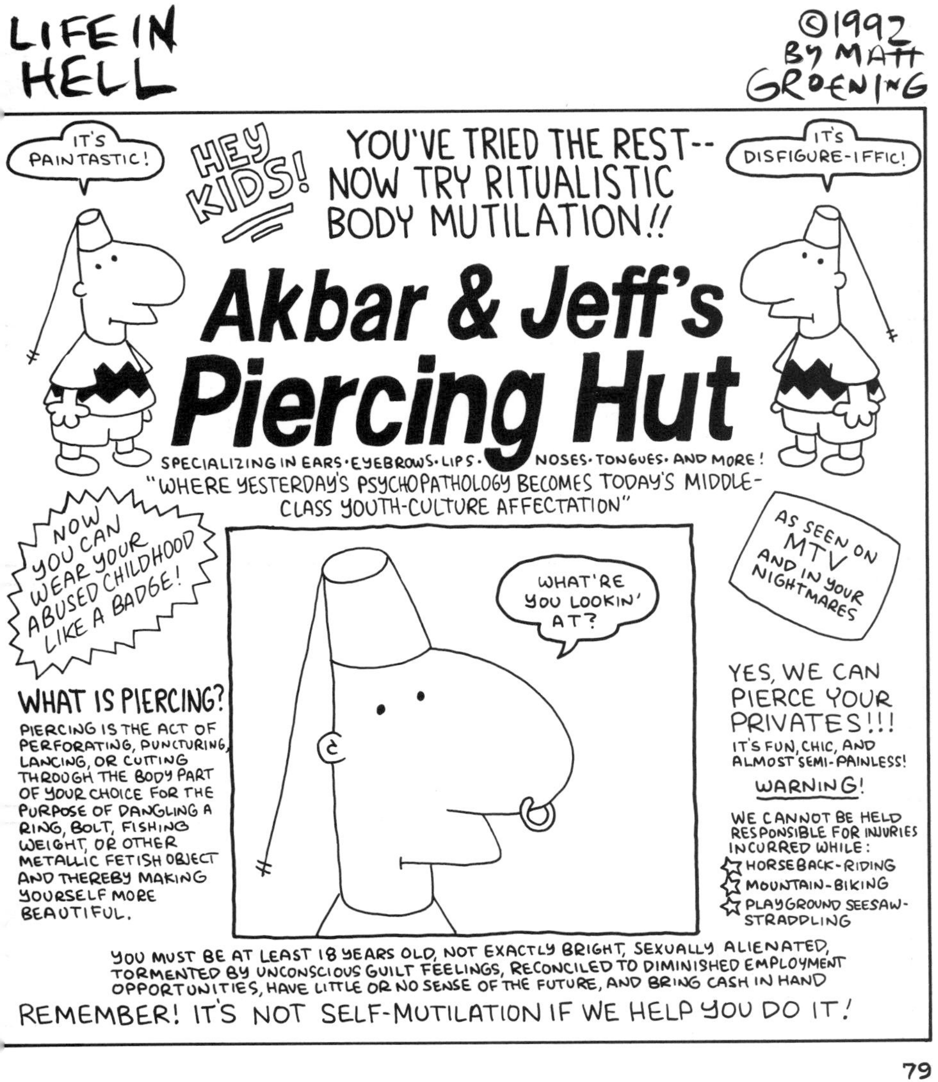
LIFE IN HELL
©1992 BY MATT GROENING
IT'S PAINTASTIC!
HEY KIDS!
YOU'VE TRIED THE REST-- NOW TRY RITUALISTIC BODY MUTILATION!!
IT'S DISFIGURE-IFFIC!
Akbar & Jeff's Piercing Hut
SPECIALIZING IN EARS · EYEBROWS · LIPS · NOSES · TONGUES · AND MORE!
"WHERE YESTERDAY'S PSYCHOPATHOLOGY BECOMES TODAY'S MIDDLE-CLASS YOUTH-CULTURE AFFECTATION"
NOW YOU CAN WEAR YOUR ABUSED CHILDHOOD LIKE A BADGE!
WHAT'RE YOU LOOKIN' AT?
AS SEEN ON MTV AND IN YOUR NIGHTMARES
WHAT IS PIERCING?
PIERCING IS THE ACT OF PERFORATING, PUNCTURING, LANCING, OR CUTTING THROUGH THE BODY PART OF YOUR CHOICE FOR THE PURPOSE OF DANGLING A RING, BOLT, FISHING WEIGHT, OR OTHER METALLIC FETISH OBJECT AND THEREBY MAKING YOURSELF MORE BEAUTIFUL.
YES, WE CAN PIERCE YOUR PRIVATES!!!
IT'S FUN, CHIC, AND ALMOST SEMI-PAINLESS!
WARNING!
WE CANNOT BE HELD RESPONSIBLE FOR INJURIES INCURRED WHILE:
HORSEBACK-RIDING
MOUNTAIN-BIKING
PLAYGROUND SEESAW-STRADDLING
YOU MUST BE AT LEAST 18 YEARS OLD, NOT EXACTLY BRIGHT, SEXUALLY ALIENATED, TORMENTED BY UNCONSCIOUS GUILT FEELINGS, RECONCILED TO DIMINISHED EMPLOYMENT OPPORTUNITIES, HAVE LITTLE OR NO SENSE OF THE FUTURE, AND BRING CASH IN HAND
REMEMBER! IT'S NOT SELF-MUTILATION IF WE HELP YOU DO IT!

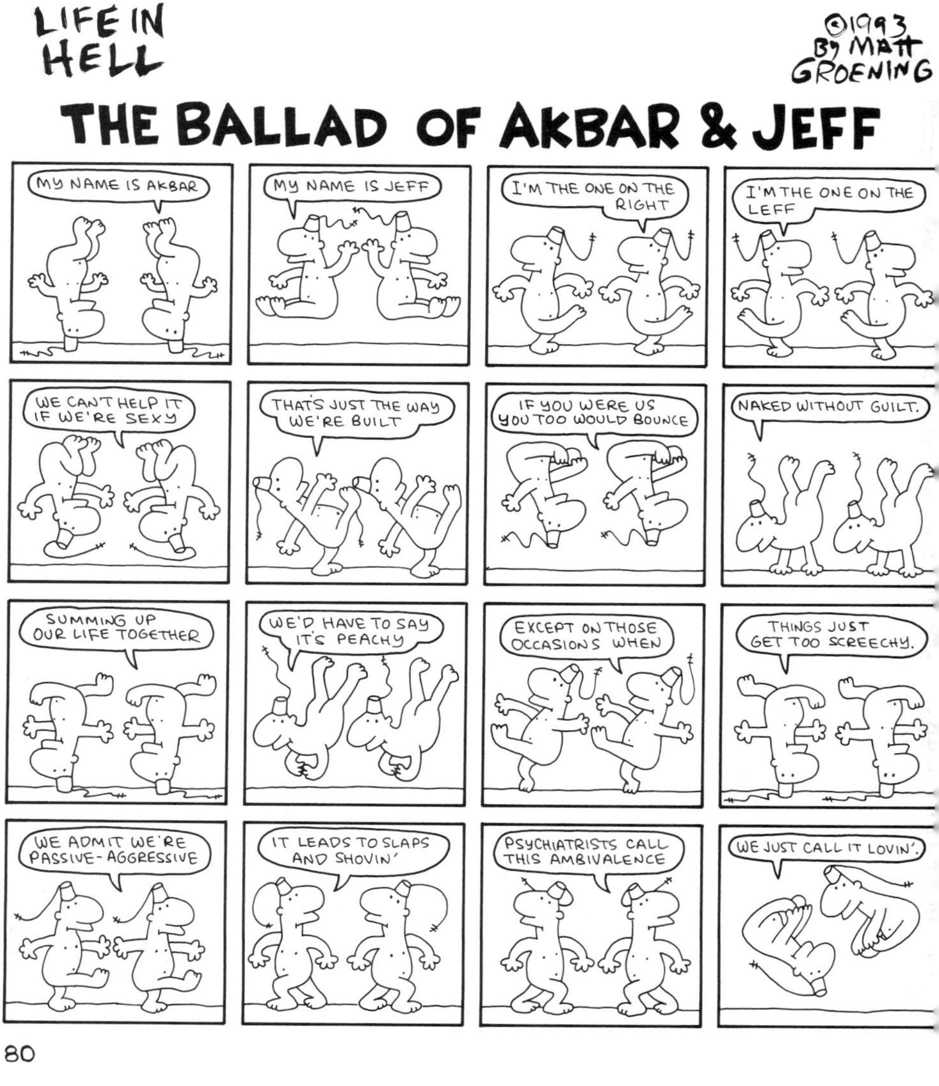
LIFE IN HELL
©1993 BY MATT GROENING
THE BALLAD OF AKBAR & JEFF
MY NAME IS AKBAR
MY NAME IS JEFF
I'M THE ONE ON THE RIGHT
I'M THE ONE ON THE LEFF
WE CAN'T HELP IT IF WE'RE SEXY
THAT'S JUST THE WAY WE'RE BUILT
IF YOU WERE US YOU TOO WOULD BOUNCE
NAKED WITHOUT GUILT.
SUMMING UP OUR LIFE TOGETHER
WE'D HAVE TO SAY IT'S PEACHY
EXCEPT ON THOSE OCCASIONS WHEN
THINGS JUST GET TOO SCREECHY.
WE ADMIT WE'RE PASSIVE-AGGRESSIVE
IT LEADS TO SLAPS AND SHOVIN'
PSYCHIATRISTS CALL THIS AMBIVALENCE
WE JUST CALL IT LOVIN'.

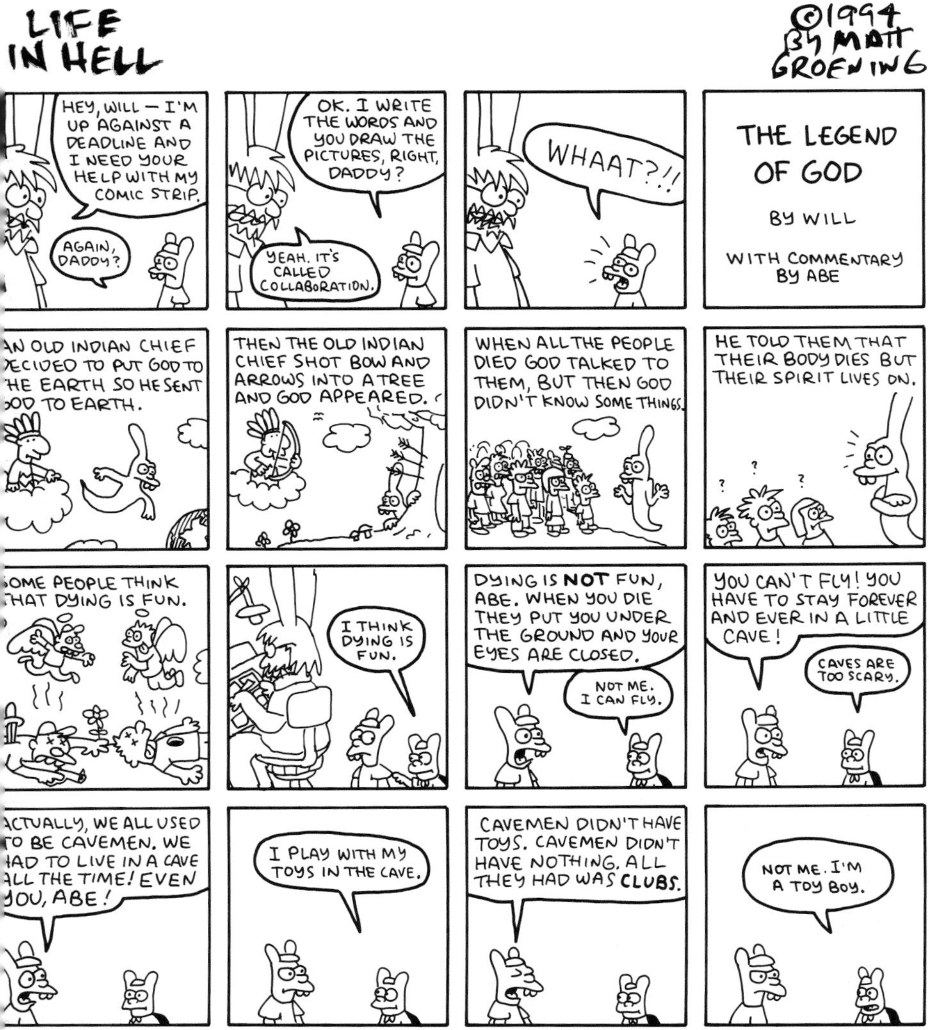

LIFE IN HELL
©1994 BY MATT GROENING
HEY, WILL — I'M UP AGAINST A DEADLINE AND I NEED YOUR HELP WITH MY COMIC STRIP.
AGAIN, DADDY?
OK. I WRITE THE WORDS AND YOU DRAW THE PICTURES, RIGHT, DADDY?
YEAH. IT'S CALLED COLLABORATION.
WHAAT?!!
THE LEGEND OF GOD
BY WILL
WITH COMMENTARY BY ABE
AN OLD INDIAN CHIEF DECIDED TO PUT GOD TO THE EARTH SO HE SENT GOD TO EARTH.
THEN THE OLD INDIAN CHIEF SHOT BOW AND ARROWS INTO A TREE AND GOD APPEARED.
WHEN ALL THE PEOPLE DIED GOD TALKED TO THEM, BUT THEN GOD DIDN'T KNOW SOME THINGS.
HE TOLD THEM THAT THEIR BODY DIES BUT THEIR SPIRIT LIVES ON.
SOME PEOPLE THINK THAT DYING IS FUN.
I THINK DYING IS FUN.
DYING IS **NOT** FUN, ABE. WHEN YOU DIE THEY PUT YOU UNDER THE GROUND AND YOUR EYES ARE CLOSED.
NOT ME. I CAN FLY.
YOU CAN'T FLY! YOU HAVE TO STAY FOREVER AND EVER IN A LITTLE CAVE!
CAVES ARE TOO SCARY.
ACTUALLY, WE ALL USED TO BE CAVEMEN. WE HAD TO LIVE IN A CAVE ALL THE TIME! EVEN YOU, ABE!
I PLAY WITH MY TOYS IN THE CAVE.
CAVEMEN DIDN'T HAVE TOYS. CAVEMEN DIDN'T HAVE NOTHING. ALL THEY HAD WAS **CLUBS**.
NOT ME. I'M A TOY BOY.

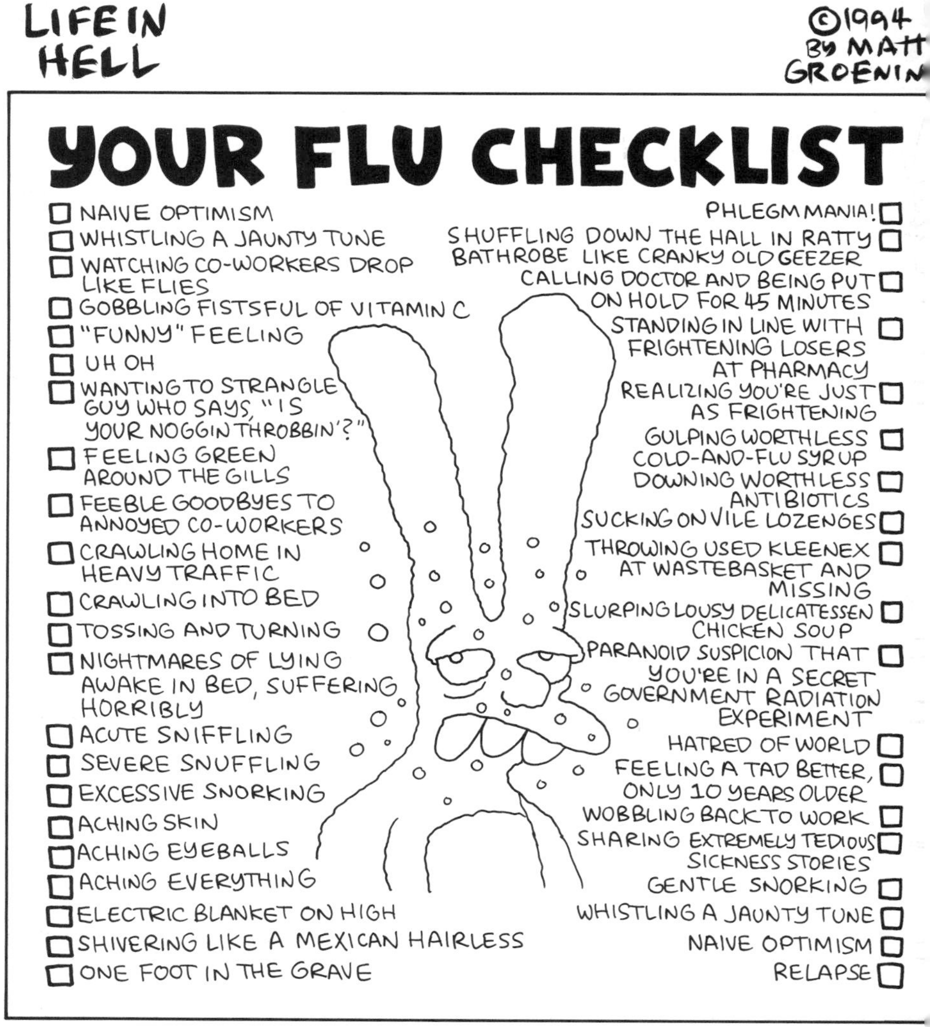
LIFE IN HELL
©1994 BY MATT GROENING
YOUR FLU CHECKLIST
NAIVE OPTIMISM
WHISTLING A JAUNTY TUNE
WATCHING CO-WORKERS DROP LIKE FLIES
GOBBLING FISTSFUL OF VITAMIN C
"FUNNY" FEELING
UH OH
WANTING TO STRANGLE GUY WHO SAYS, "IS YOUR NOGGIN THROBBIN'?"
FEELING GREEN AROUND THE GILLS
FEEBLE GOODBYES TO ANNOYED CO-WORKERS
CRAWLING HOME IN HEAVY TRAFFIC
CRAWLING INTO BED
TOSSING AND TURNING
NIGHTMARES OF LYING AWAKE IN BED, SUFFERING HORRIBLY
ACUTE SNIFFLING
SEVERE SNUFFLING
EXCESSIVE SNORKING
ACHING SKIN
ACHING EYEBALLS
ACHING EVERYTHING
ELECTRIC BLANKET ON HIGH
SHIVERING LIKE A MEXICAN HAIRLESS
ONE FOOT IN THE GRAVE
PHLEGMMANIA!
SHUFFLING DOWN THE HALL IN RATTY BATHROBE LIKE CRANKY OLD GEEZER
CALLING DOCTOR AND BEING PUT ON HOLD FOR 45 MINUTES
STANDING IN LINE WITH FRIGHTENING LOSERS AT PHARMACY
REALIZING YOU'RE JUST AS FRIGHTENING
GULPING WORTHLESS COLD-AND-FLU SYRUP
DOWNING WORTHLESS ANTIBIOTICS
SUCKING ON VILE LOZENGES
THROWING USED KLEENEX AT WASTEBASKET AND MISSING
SLURPING LOUSY DELICATESSEN CHICKEN SOUP
PARANOID SUSPICION THAT YOU'RE IN A SECRET GOVERNMENT RADIATION EXPERIMENT
HATRED OF WORLD
FEELING A TAD BETTER, ONLY 10 YEARS OLDER
WOBBLING BACK TO WORK
SHARING EXTREMELY TEDIOUS SICKNESS STORIES
GENTLE SNORKING
WHISTLING A JAUNTY TUNE
NAIVE OPTIMISM
RELAPSE

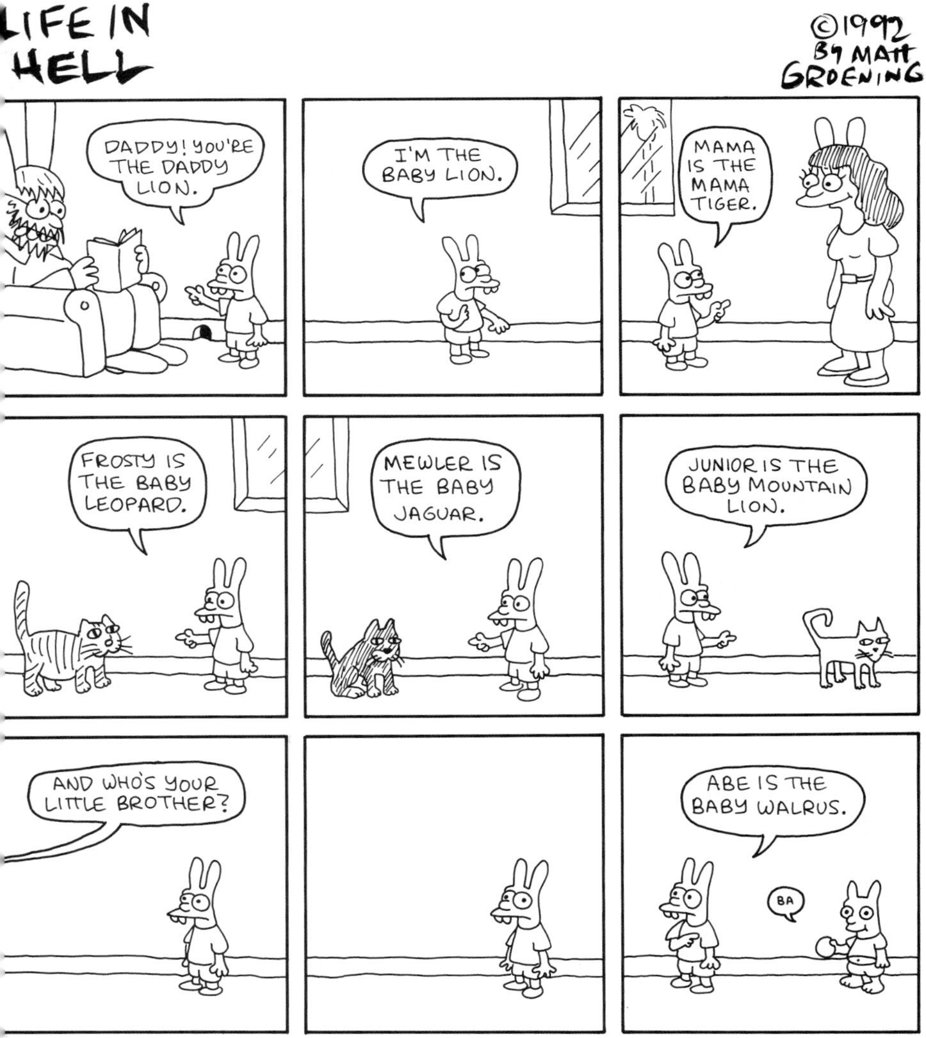
LIFE IN HELL
©1992 BY MATT GROENING
DADDY! YOU'RE THE DADDY LION.
I'M THE BABY LION.
MAMA IS THE MAMA TIGER.
FROSTY IS THE BABY LEOPARD.
MEWLER IS THE BABY JAGUAR.
JUNIOR IS THE BABY MOUNTAIN LION.
AND WHO'S YOUR LITTLE BROTHER?
ABE IS THE BABY WALRUS.
BA

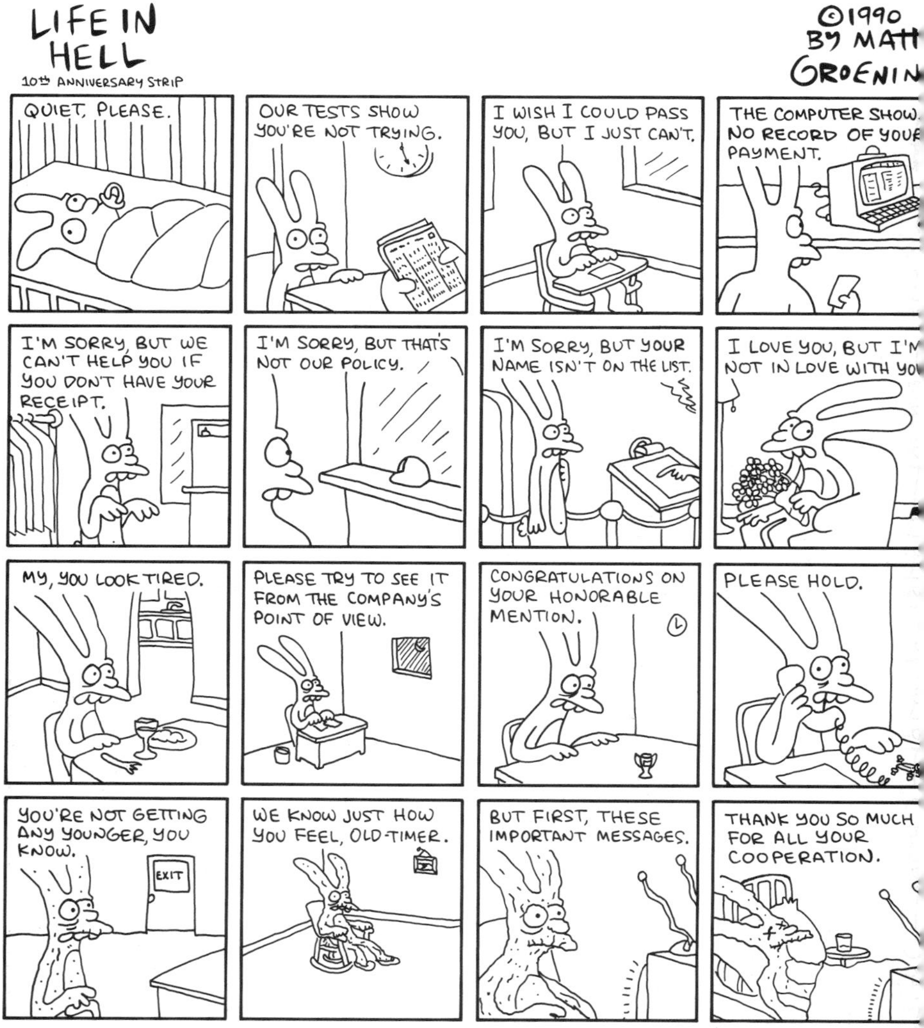

LIFE IN HELL
10th ANNIVERSARY STRIP
©1990 BY MATT GROENIN
QUIET, PLEASE.
OUR TESTS SHOW YOU'RE NOT TRYING.
I WISH I COULD PASS YOU, BUT I JUST CAN'T.
THE COMPUTER SHOWS NO RECORD OF YOUR PAYMENT.
I'M SORRY, BUT WE CAN'T HELP YOU IF YOU DON'T HAVE YOUR RECEIPT.
I'M SORRY, BUT THAT'S NOT OUR POLICY.
I'M SORRY, BUT YOUR NAME ISN'T ON THE LIST.
I LOVE YOU, BUT I'M NOT IN LOVE WITH YOU
MY, YOU LOOK TIRED.
PLEASE TRY TO SEE IT FROM THE COMPANY'S POINT OF VIEW.
CONGRATULATIONS ON YOUR HONORABLE MENTION.
PLEASE HOLD.
YOU'RE NOT GETTING ANY YOUNGER, YOU KNOW.
EXIT
WE KNOW JUST HOW YOU FEEL, OLD-TIMER.
BUT FIRST, THESE IMPORTANT MESSAGES.
THANK YOU SO MUCH FOR ALL YOUR COOPERATION.

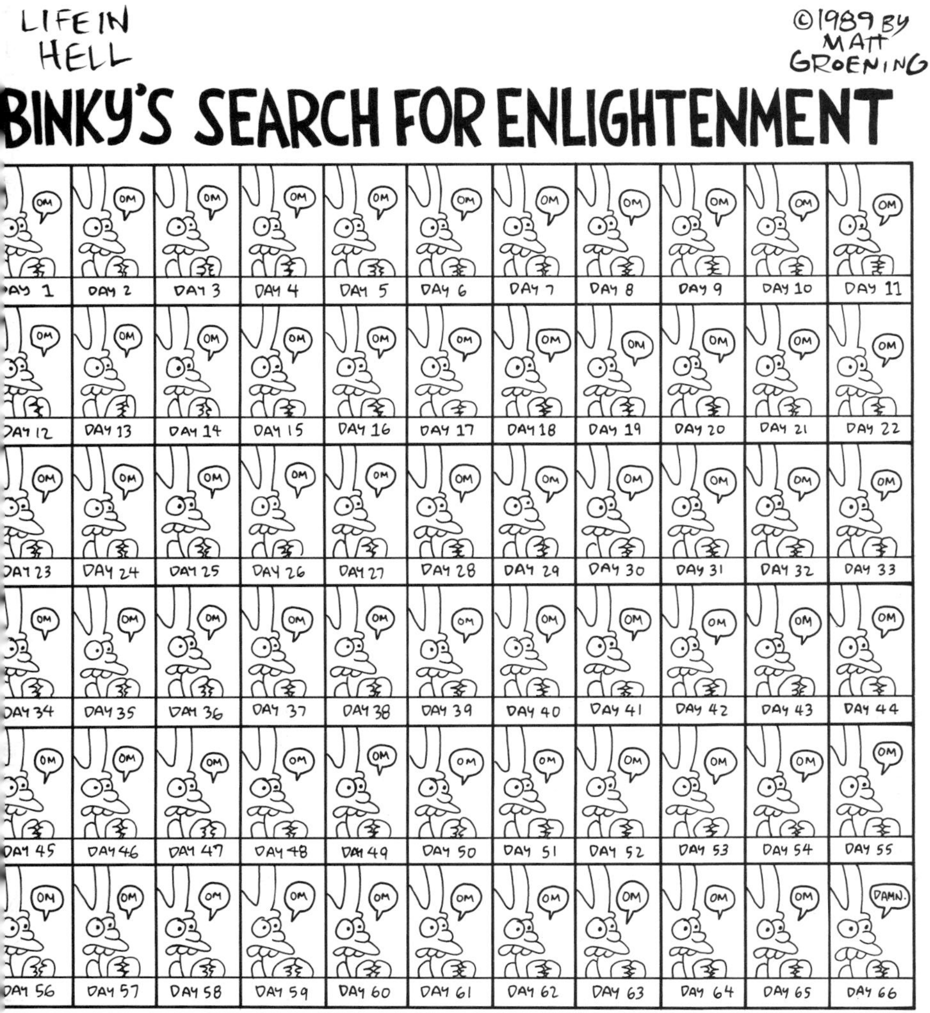
LIFE IN HELL
©1989 BY MATT GROENING
BINKY'S SEARCH FOR ENLIGHTENMENT
OM
DAY 1
OM
DAY 2
OM
DAY 3
OM
DAY 4
OM
DAY 5
OM
DAY 6
OM
DAY 7
OM
DAY 8
OM
DAY 9
OM
DAY 10
OM
DAY 11
OM
DAY 12
OM
DAY 13
OM
DAY 14
OM
DAY 15
OM
DAY 16
OM
DAY 17
OM
DAY 18
OM
DAY 19
OM
DAY 20
OM
DAY 21
OM
DAY 22
OM
DAY 23
OM
DAY 24
OM
DAY 25
OM
DAY 26
OM
DAY 27
OM
DAY 28
OM
DAY 29
OM
DAY 30
OM
DAY 31
OM
DAY 32
OM
DAY 33
OM
DAY 34
OM
DAY 35
OM
DAY 36
OM
DAY 37
OM
DAY 38
OM
DAY 39
OM
DAY 40
OM
DAY 41
OM
DAY 42
OM
DAY 43
OM
DAY 44
OM
DAY 45
OM
DAY 46
OM
DAY 47
OM
DAY 48
OM
DAY 49
OM
DAY 50
OM
DAY 51
OM
DAY 52
OM
DAY 53
OM
DAY 54
OM
DAY 55
OM
DAY 56
OM
DAY 57
OM
DAY 58
OM
DAY 59
OM
DAY 60
OM
DAY 61
OM
DAY 62
OM
DAY 63
OM
DAY 64
OM
DAY 65
DAMN.
DAY 66

LIFE IN HELL

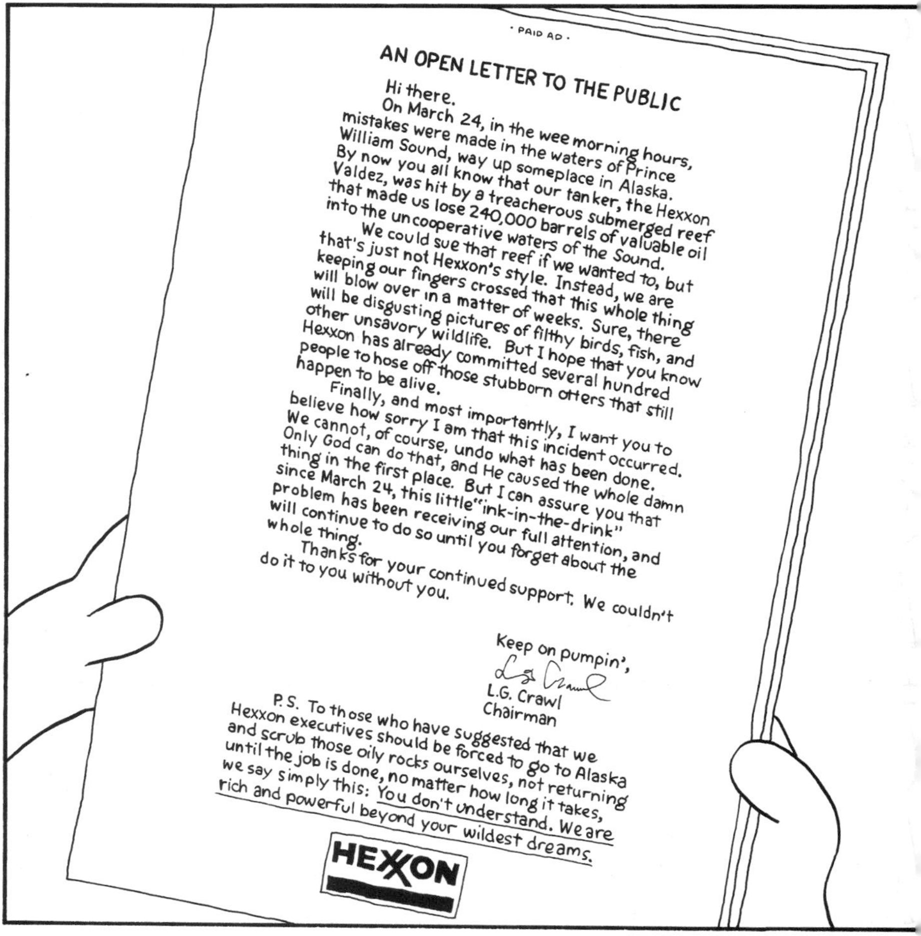
• PAID AD •
AN OPEN LETTER TO THE PUBLIC
Hi there.
On March 24, in the wee morning hours, mistakes were made in the waters of Prince William Sound, way up someplace in Alaska. By now you all know that our tanker, the Hexxon Valdez, was hit by a treacherous submerged reef that made us lose 240,000 barrels of valuable oil into the uncooperative waters of the Sound.
We could sue that reef if we wanted to, but that's just not Hexxon's style. Instead, we are keeping our fingers crossed that this whole thing will blow over in a matter of weeks. Sure, there will be disgusting pictures of filthy birds, fish, and other unsavory wildlife. But I hope that you know Hexxon has already committed several hundred people to hose off those stubborn otters that still happen to be alive.
Finally, and most importantly, I want you to believe how sorry I am that this incident occurred. We cannot, of course, undo what has been done. Only God can do that, and He caused the whole damn thing in the first place. But I can assure you that since March 24, this little "ink-in-the-drink" problem has been receiving our full attention, and will continue to do so until you forget about the whole thing.
Thanks for your continued support. We couldn't do it to you without you.
Keep on pumpin',
L.G. Crawl
Chairman
P.S. To those who have suggested that we Hexxon executives should be forced to go to Alaska and scrub those oily rocks ourselves, not returning until the job is done, no matter how long it takes, we say simply this: You don't understand. We are rich and powerful beyond your wildest dreams.
HEXXON

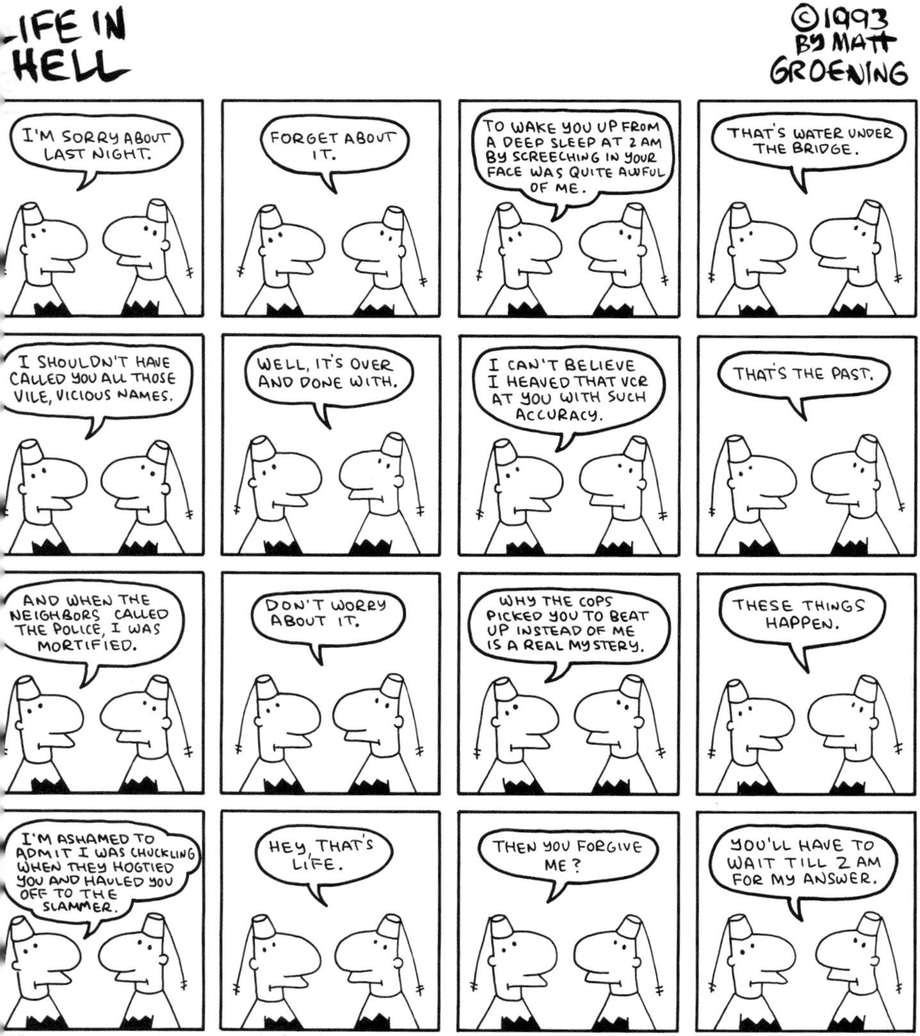
LIFE IN HELL
©1993 BY MATT GROENING
I'M SORRY ABOUT LAST NIGHT.
FORGET ABOUT IT.
TO WAKE YOU UP FROM A DEEP SLEEP AT 2 AM BY SCREECHING IN YOUR FACE WAS QUITE AWFUL OF ME.
THAT'S WATER UNDER THE BRIDGE.
I SHOULDN'T HAVE CALLED YOU ALL THOSE VILE, VICIOUS NAMES.
WELL, IT'S OVER AND DONE WITH.
I CAN'T BELIEVE I HEAVED THAT VCR AT YOU WITH SUCH ACCURACY.
THAT'S THE PAST.
AND WHEN THE NEIGHBORS CALLED THE POLICE, I WAS MORTIFIED.
DON'T WORRY ABOUT IT.
WHY THE COPS PICKED YOU TO BEAT UP INSTEAD OF ME IS A REAL MYSTERY.
THESE THINGS HAPPEN.
I'M ASHAMED TO ADMIT I WAS CHUCKLING WHEN THEY HOGTIED YOU AND HAULED YOU OFF TO THE SLAMMER.
HEY, THAT'S LIFE.
THEN YOU FORGIVE ME?
YOU'LL HAVE TO WAIT TILL 2 AM FOR MY ANSWER.

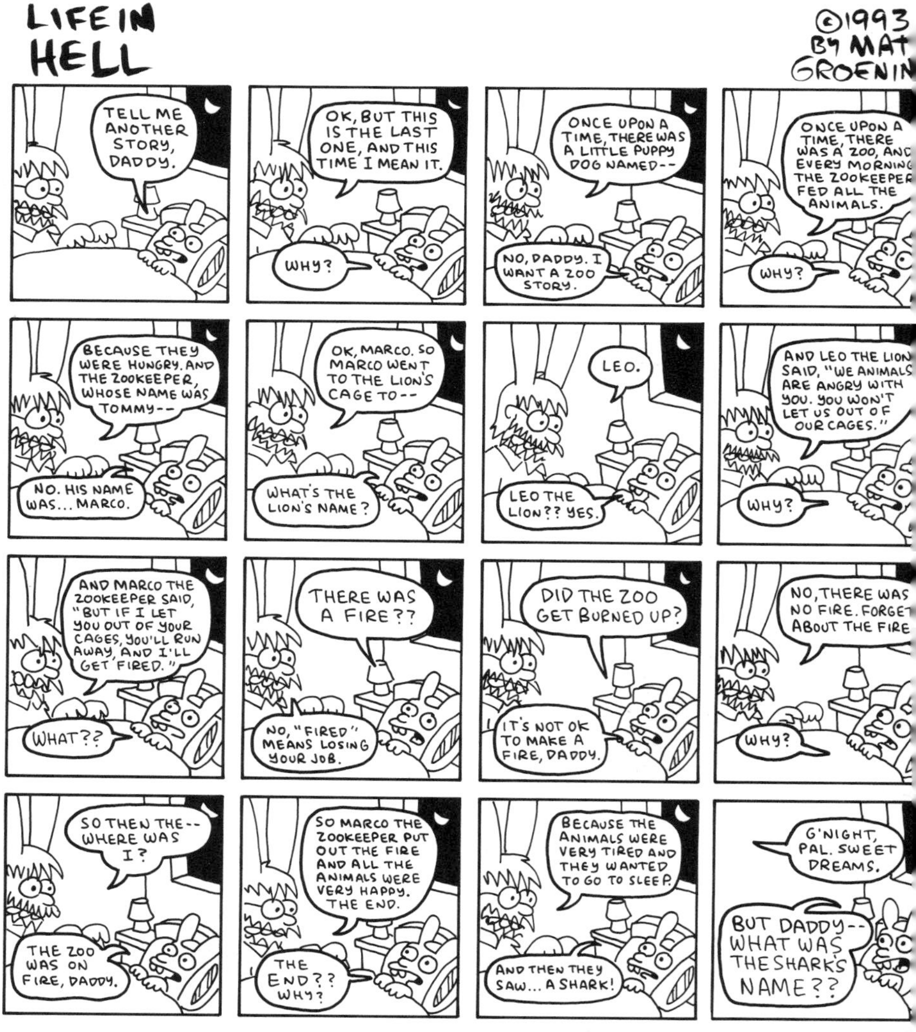
LIFE IN HELL
©1993 BY MAT GROENIN
TELL ME ANOTHER STORY, DADDY.
OK, BUT THIS IS THE LAST ONE, AND THIS TIME I MEAN IT.
WHY?
ONCE UPON A TIME, THERE WAS A LITTLE PUPPY DOG NAMED--
NO, DADDY. I WANT A ZOO STORY.
ONCE UPON A TIME, THERE WAS A ZOO, AND EVERY MORNING THE ZOOKEEPER FED ALL THE ANIMALS.
WHY?
BECAUSE THEY WERE HUNGRY. AND THE ZOOKEEPER, WHOSE NAME WAS TOMMY--
NO. HIS NAME WAS... MARCO.
OK, MARCO. SO MARCO WENT TO THE LION'S CAGE TO--
WHAT'S THE LION'S NAME?
LEO.
LEO THE LION?? YES.
AND LEO THE LION SAID, "WE ANIMALS ARE ANGRY WITH YOU. YOU WON'T LET US OUT OF OUR CAGES."
WHY?
AND MARCO THE ZOOKEEPER SAID, "BUT IF I LET YOU OUT OF YOUR CAGES, YOU'LL RUN AWAY, AND I'LL GET FIRED."
WHAT??
THERE WAS A FIRE??
NO, "FIRED" MEANS LOSING YOUR JOB.
DID THE ZOO GET BURNED UP?
IT'S NOT OK TO MAKE A FIRE, DADDY.
NO, THERE WAS NO FIRE. FORGET ABOUT THE FIRE
WHY?
SO THEN THE-- WHERE WAS I?
THE ZOO WAS ON FIRE, DADDY.
SO MARCO THE ZOOKEEPER PUT OUT THE FIRE AND ALL THE ANIMALS WERE VERY HAPPY. THE END.
THE END?? WHY?
BECAUSE THE ANIMALS WERE VERY TIRED AND THEY WANTED TO GO TO SLEEP.
AND THEN THEY SAW... A SHARK!
G'NIGHT, PAL. SWEET DREAMS.
BUT DADDY-- WHAT WAS THE SHARK'S NAME??

LIFE IN HELL

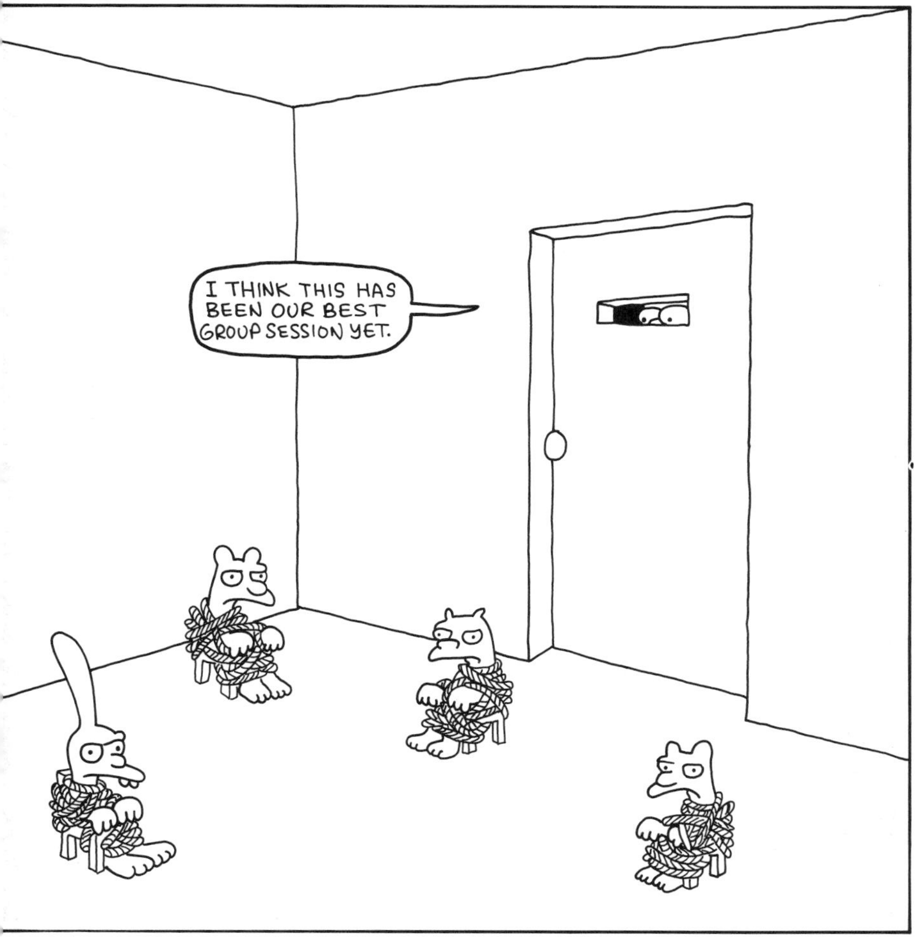
I THINK THIS HAS BEEN OUR BEST GROUP SESSION YET.

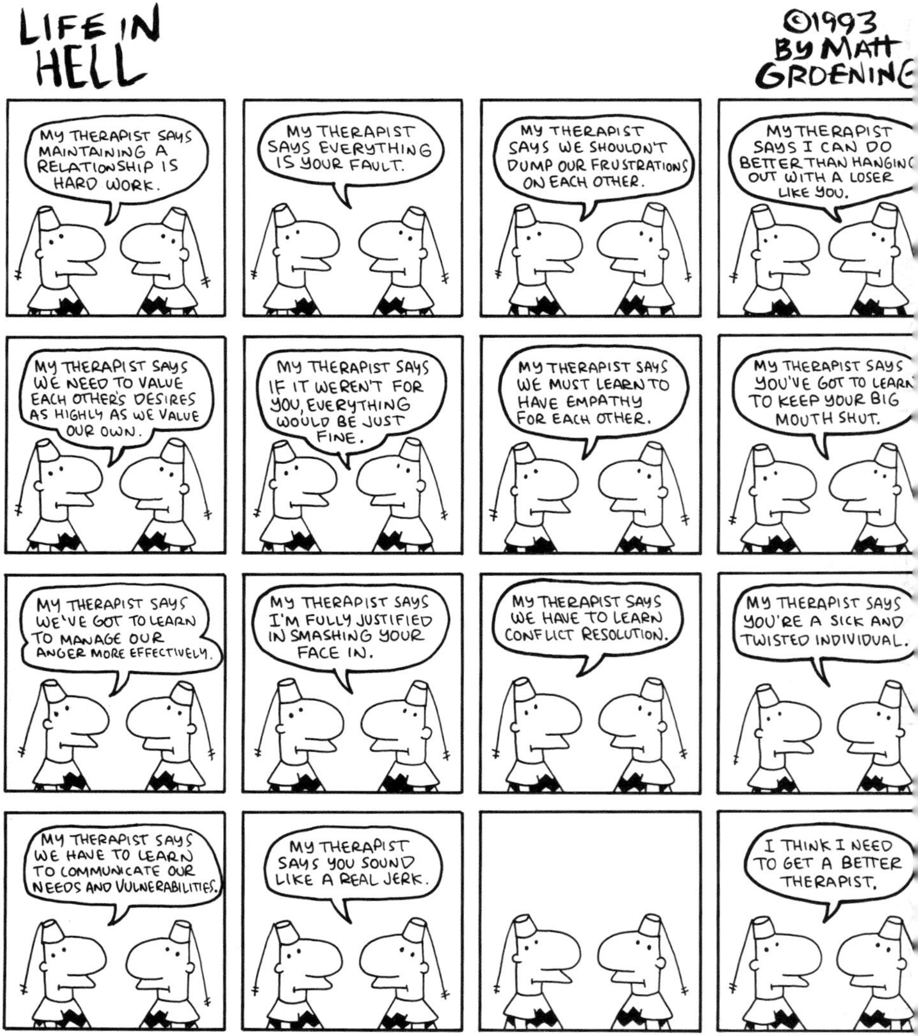
LIFE IN HELL
©1993 BY MATT GROENING
MY THERAPIST SAYS MAINTAINING A RELATIONSHIP IS HARD WORK.
MY THERAPIST SAYS EVERYTHING IS YOUR FAULT.
MY THERAPIST SAYS WE SHOULDN'T DUMP OUR FRUSTRATIONS ON EACH OTHER.
MY THERAPIST SAYS I CAN DO BETTER THAN HANGING OUT WITH A LOSER LIKE YOU.
MY THERAPIST SAYS WE NEED TO VALUE EACH OTHER'S DESIRES AS HIGHLY AS WE VALUE OUR OWN.
MY THERAPIST SAYS IF IT WEREN'T FOR YOU, EVERYTHING WOULD BE JUST FINE.
MY THERAPIST SAYS WE MUST LEARN TO HAVE EMPATHY FOR EACH OTHER.
MY THERAPIST SAYS YOU'VE GOT TO LEARN TO KEEP YOUR BIG MOUTH SHUT.
MY THERAPIST SAYS WE'VE GOT TO LEARN TO MANAGE OUR ANGER MORE EFFECTIVELY.
MY THERAPIST SAYS I'M FULLY JUSTIFIED IN SMASHING YOUR FACE IN.
MY THERAPIST SAYS WE HAVE TO LEARN CONFLICT RESOLUTION.
MY THERAPIST SAYS YOU'RE A SICK AND TWISTED INDIVIDUAL.
MY THERAPIST SAYS WE HAVE TO LEARN TO COMMUNICATE OUR NEEDS AND VULNERABILITIES.
MY THERAPIST SAYS YOU SOUND LIKE A REAL JERK.
I THINK I NEED TO GET A BETTER THERAPIST.

LIFE IN HELL

©1993 BY MATT GROENING

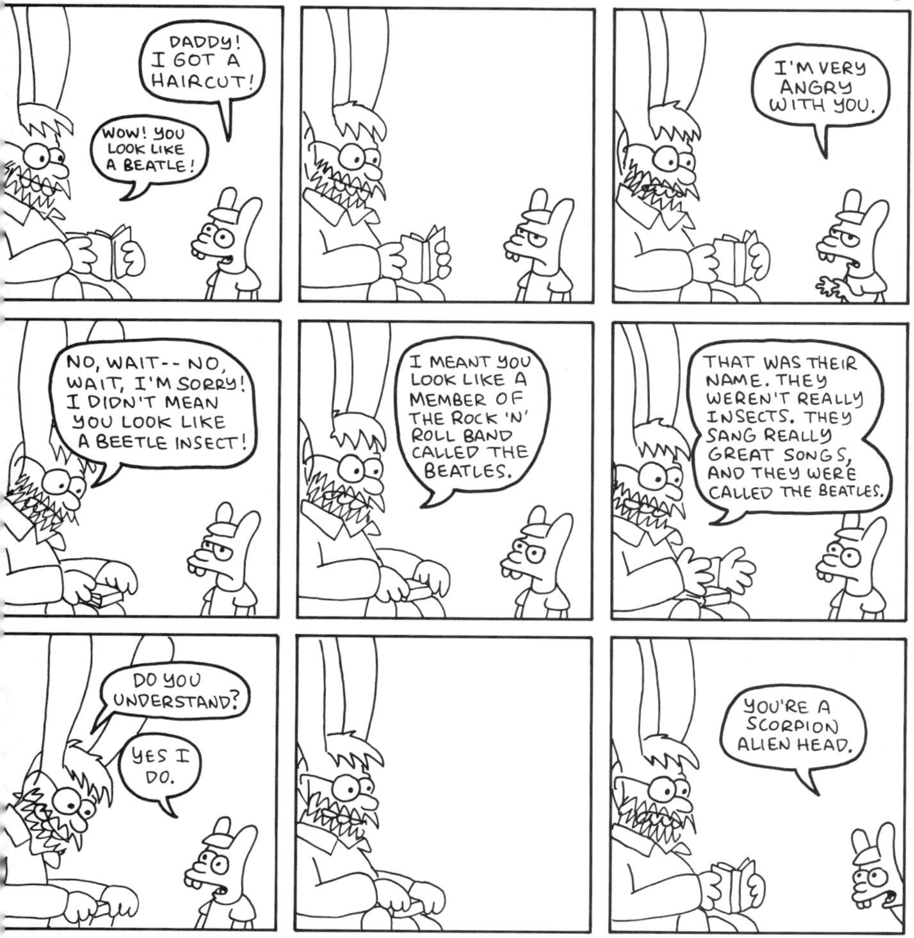
DADDY! I GOT A HAIRCUT!
WOW! YOU LOOK LIKE A BEATLE!
I'M VERY ANGRY WITH YOU.
NO, WAIT-- NO, WAIT, I'M SORRY! I DIDN'T MEAN YOU LOOK LIKE A BEETLE INSECT!
I MEANT YOU LOOK LIKE A MEMBER OF THE ROCK 'N' ROLL BAND CALLED THE BEATLES.
THAT WAS THEIR NAME. THEY WEREN'T REALLY INSECTS. THEY SANG REALLY GREAT SONGS, AND THEY WERE CALLED THE BEATLES.
DO YOU UNDERSTAND?
YES I DO.
YOU'RE A SCORPION ALIEN HEAD.

LIFE IN HELL

©1993 BY MATT GROENING

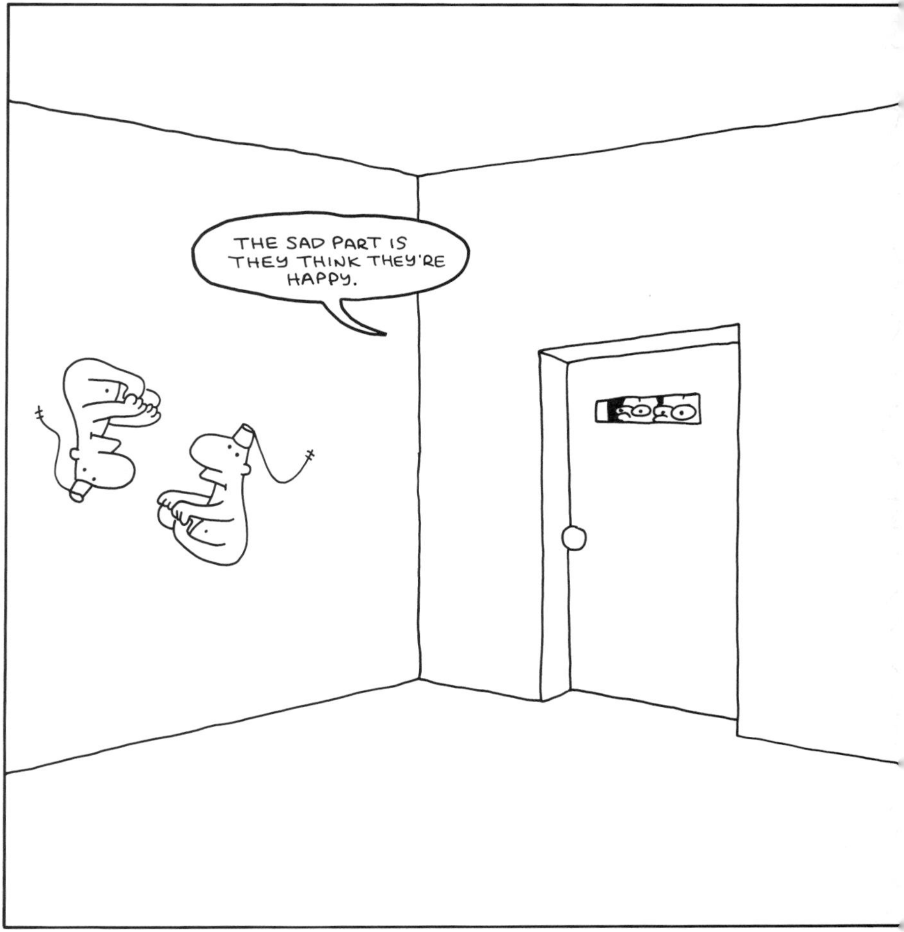
THE SAD PART IS THEY THINK THEY'RE HAPPY.

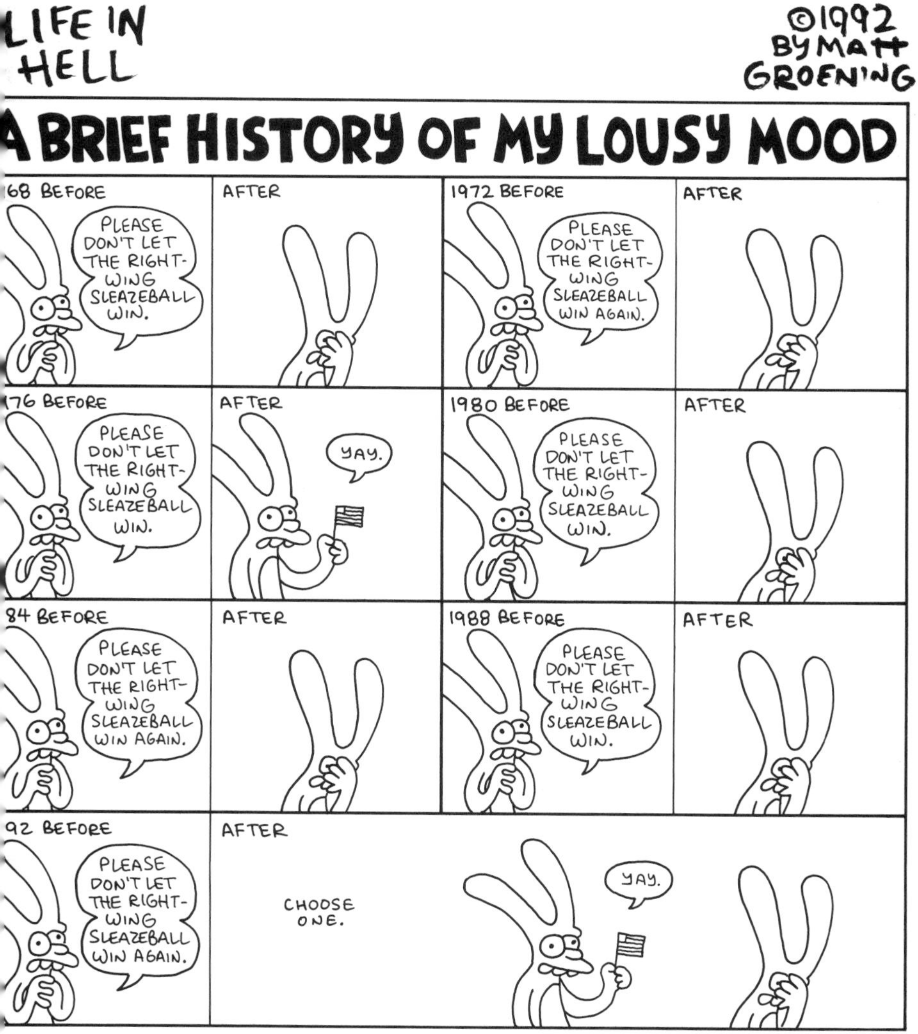
LIFE IN HELL
©1992 BY MATT GROENING
A BRIEF HISTORY OF MY LOUSY MOOD
68 BEFORE
PLEASE DON'T LET THE RIGHT-WING SLEAZEBALL WIN.
AFTER
1972 BEFORE
PLEASE DON'T LET THE RIGHT-WING SLEAZEBALL WIN AGAIN.
AFTER
76 BEFORE
PLEASE DON'T LET THE RIGHT-WING SLEAZEBALL WIN.
AFTER
YAY.
1980 BEFORE
PLEASE DON'T LET THE RIGHT-WING SLEAZEBALL WIN.
AFTER
84 BEFORE
PLEASE DON'T LET THE RIGHT-WING SLEAZEBALL WIN AGAIN.
AFTER
1988 BEFORE
PLEASE DON'T LET THE RIGHT-WING SLEAZEBALL WIN.
AFTER
92 BEFORE
PLEASE DON'T LET THE RIGHT-WING SLEAZEBALL WIN AGAIN.
AFTER
CHOOSE ONE.
YAY.

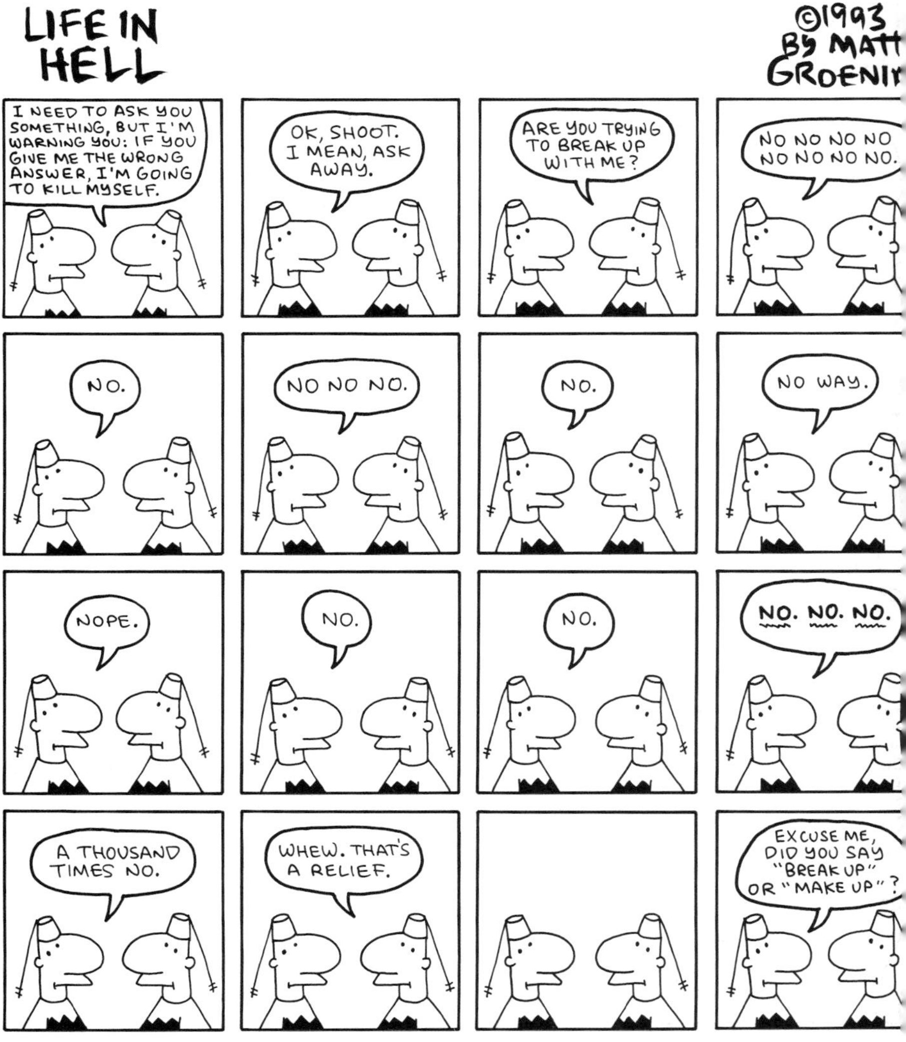
LIFE IN HELL
©1993 BY MATT GROENI
I NEED TO ASK YOU SOMETHING, BUT I'M WARNING YOU: IF YOU GIVE ME THE WRONG ANSWER, I'M GOING TO KILL MYSELF.
OK, SHOOT. I MEAN, ASK AWAY.
ARE YOU TRYING TO BREAK UP WITH ME?
NO NO NO NO NO NO NO NO.
NO.
NO NO NO.
NO.
NO WAY.
NOPE.
NO.
NO.
NO. NO. NO.
A THOUSAND TIMES NO.
WHEW. THAT'S A RELIEF.
EXCUSE ME, DID YOU SAY "BREAK UP" OR "MAKE UP"?

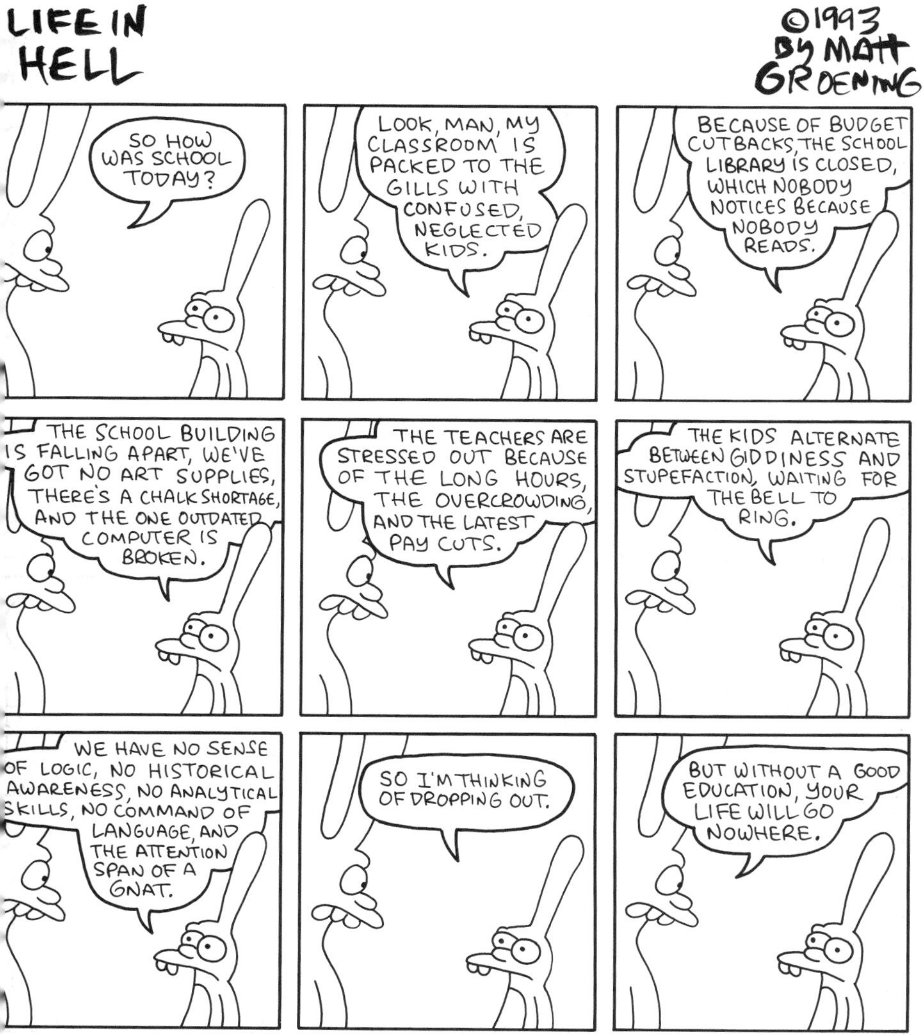
LIFE IN HELL
©1993 BY MATT GROENING
SO HOW WAS SCHOOL TODAY?
LOOK, MAN, MY CLASSROOM IS PACKED TO THE GILLS WITH CONFUSED, NEGLECTED KIDS.
BECAUSE OF BUDGET CUTBACKS, THE SCHOOL LIBRARY IS CLOSED, WHICH NOBODY NOTICES BECAUSE NOBODY READS.
THE SCHOOL BUILDING IS FALLING APART, WE'VE GOT NO ART SUPPLIES, THERE'S A CHALK SHORTAGE, AND THE ONE OUTDATED COMPUTER IS BROKEN.
THE TEACHERS ARE STRESSED OUT BECAUSE OF THE LONG HOURS, THE OVERCROWDING, AND THE LATEST PAY CUTS.
THE KIDS ALTERNATE BETWEEN GIDDINESS AND STUPEFACTION, WAITING FOR THE BELL TO RING.
WE HAVE NO SENSE OF LOGIC, NO HISTORICAL AWARENESS, NO ANALYTICAL SKILLS, NO COMMAND OF LANGUAGE, AND THE ATTENTION SPAN OF A GNAT.
SO I'M THINKING OF DROPPING OUT.
BUT WITHOUT A GOOD EDUCATION, YOUR LIFE WILL GO NOWHERE.

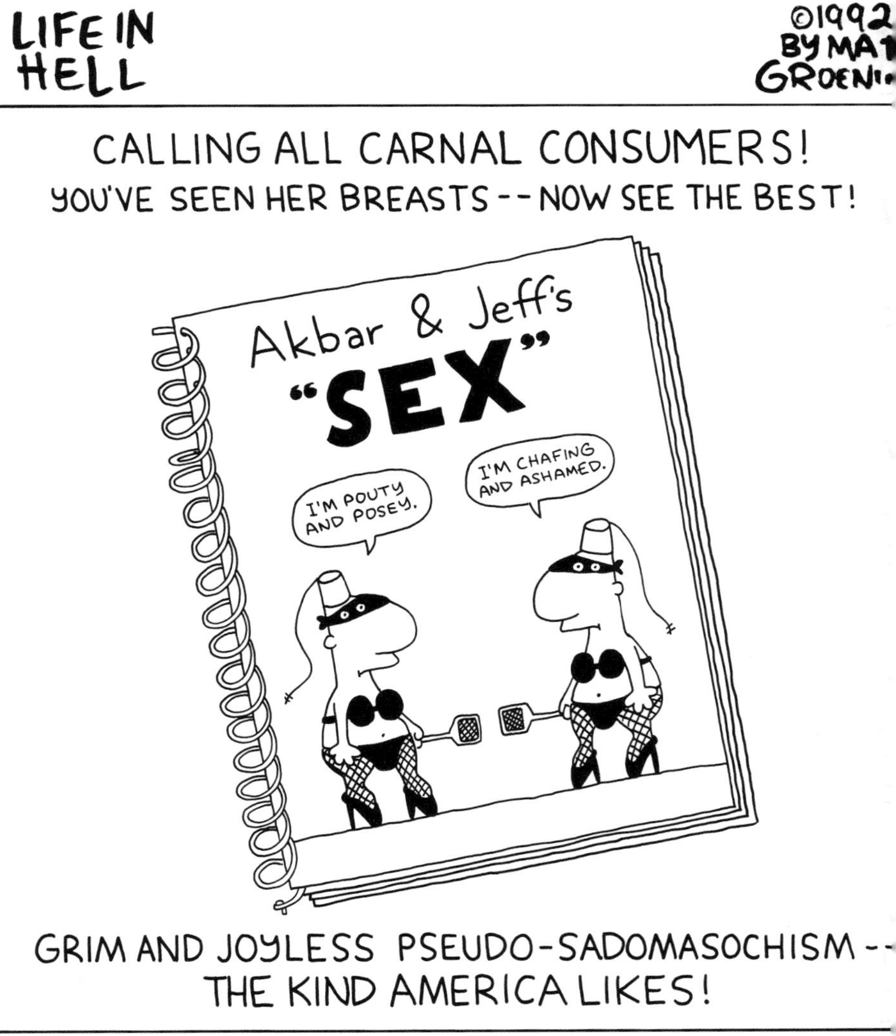
LIFE IN HELL
©1992
BY MA
GROEN
CALLING ALL CARNAL CONSUMERS!
YOU'VE SEEN HER BREASTS -- NOW SEE THE BEST!
Akbar & Jeff's
"SEX"
I'M POUTY AND POSEY.
I'M CHAFING AND ASHAMED.
GRIM AND JOYLESS PSEUDO-SADOMASOCHISM --
THE KIND AMERICA LIKES!

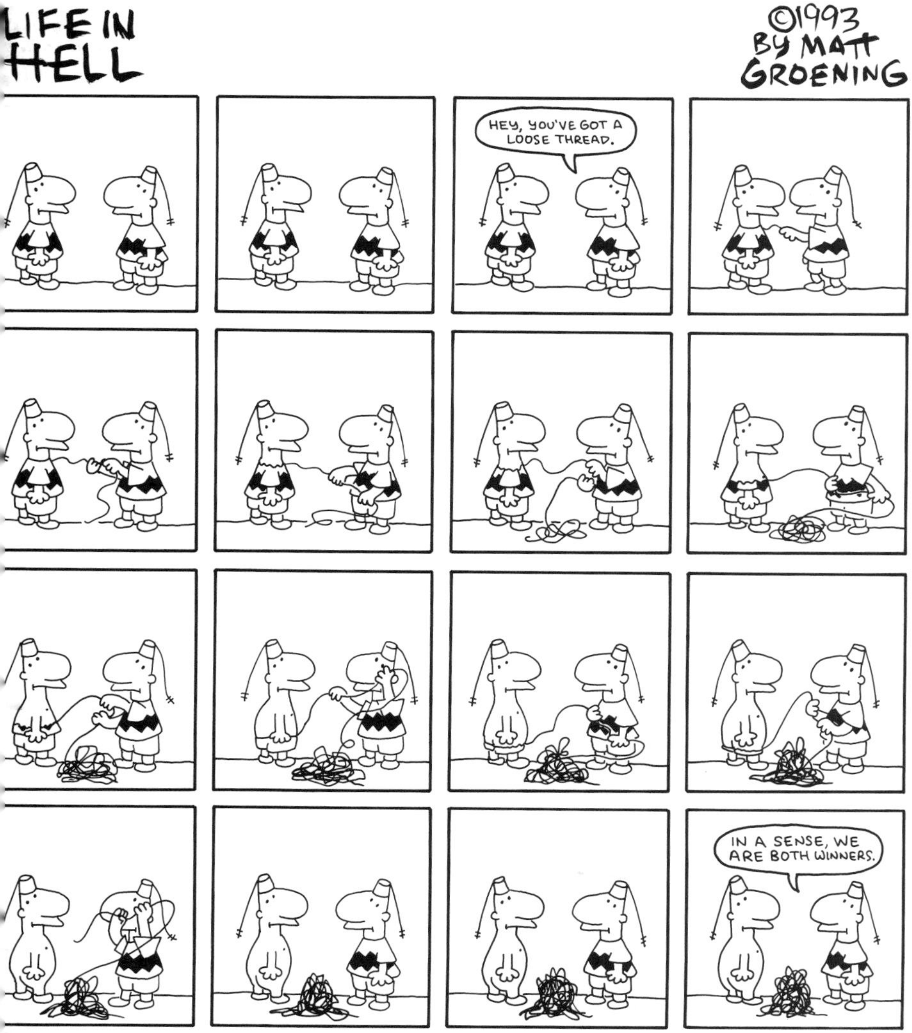
LIFE IN HELL
©1993 BY MATT GROENING
HEY, YOU'VE GOT A LOOSE THREAD.
IN A SENSE, WE ARE BOTH WINNERS.

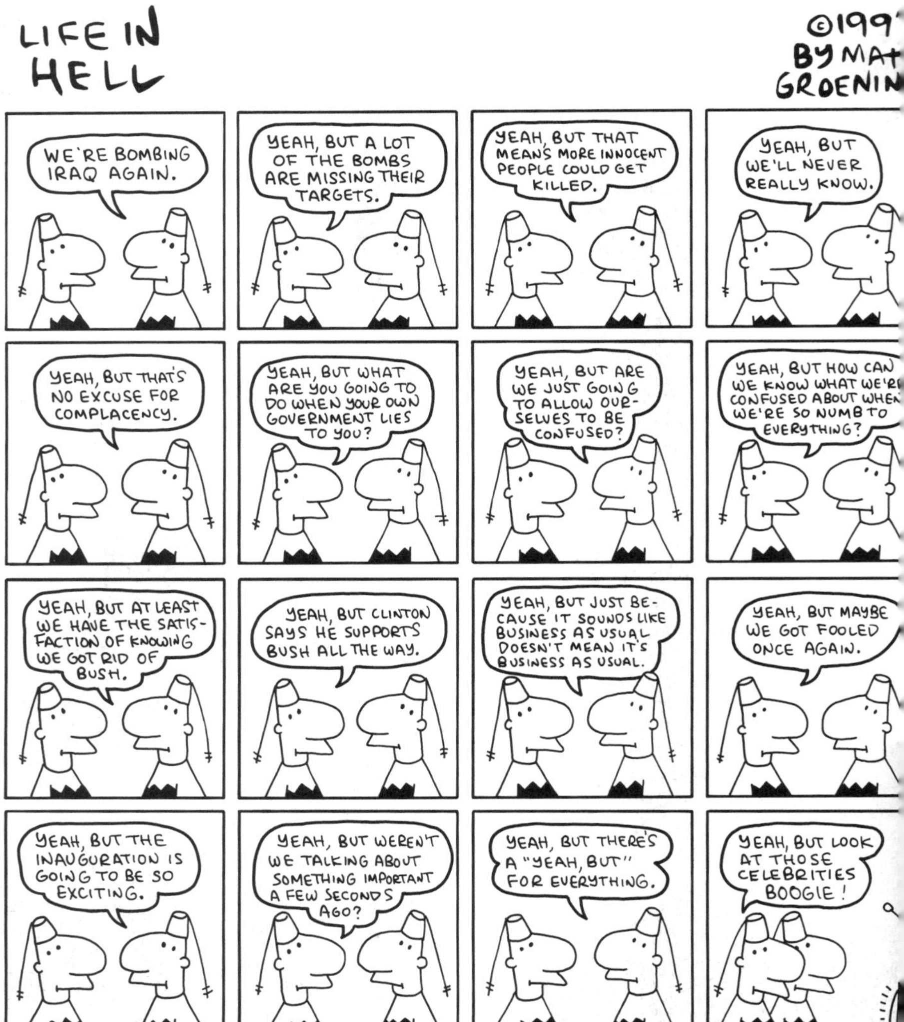
LIFE IN HELL
©199
BY MAT
GROENIN
WE'RE BOMBING IRAQ AGAIN.
YEAH, BUT A LOT OF THE BOMBS ARE MISSING THEIR TARGETS.
YEAH, BUT THAT MEANS MORE INNOCENT PEOPLE COULD GET KILLED.
YEAH, BUT WE'LL NEVER REALLY KNOW.
YEAH, BUT THAT'S NO EXCUSE FOR COMPLACENCY.
YEAH, BUT WHAT ARE YOU GOING TO DO WHEN YOUR OWN GOVERNMENT LIES TO YOU?
YEAH, BUT ARE WE JUST GOING TO ALLOW OURSELVES TO BE CONFUSED?
YEAH, BUT HOW CAN WE KNOW WHAT WE'R CONFUSED ABOUT WHEN WE'RE SO NUMB TO EVERYTHING?
YEAH, BUT AT LEAST WE HAVE THE SATISFACTION OF KNOWING WE GOT RID OF BUSH.
YEAH, BUT CLINTON SAYS HE SUPPORTS BUSH ALL THE WAY.
YEAH, BUT JUST BECAUSE IT SOUNDS LIKE BUSINESS AS USUAL DOESN'T MEAN IT'S BUSINESS AS USUAL.
YEAH, BUT MAYBE WE GOT FOOLED ONCE AGAIN.
YEAH, BUT THE INAUGURATION IS GOING TO BE SO EXCITING.
YEAH, BUT WEREN'T WE TALKING ABOUT SOMETHING IMPORTANT A FEW SECONDS AGO?
YEAH, BUT THERE'S A "YEAH, BUT" FOR EVERYTHING.
YEAH, BUT LOOK AT THOSE CELEBRITIES BOOGIE!

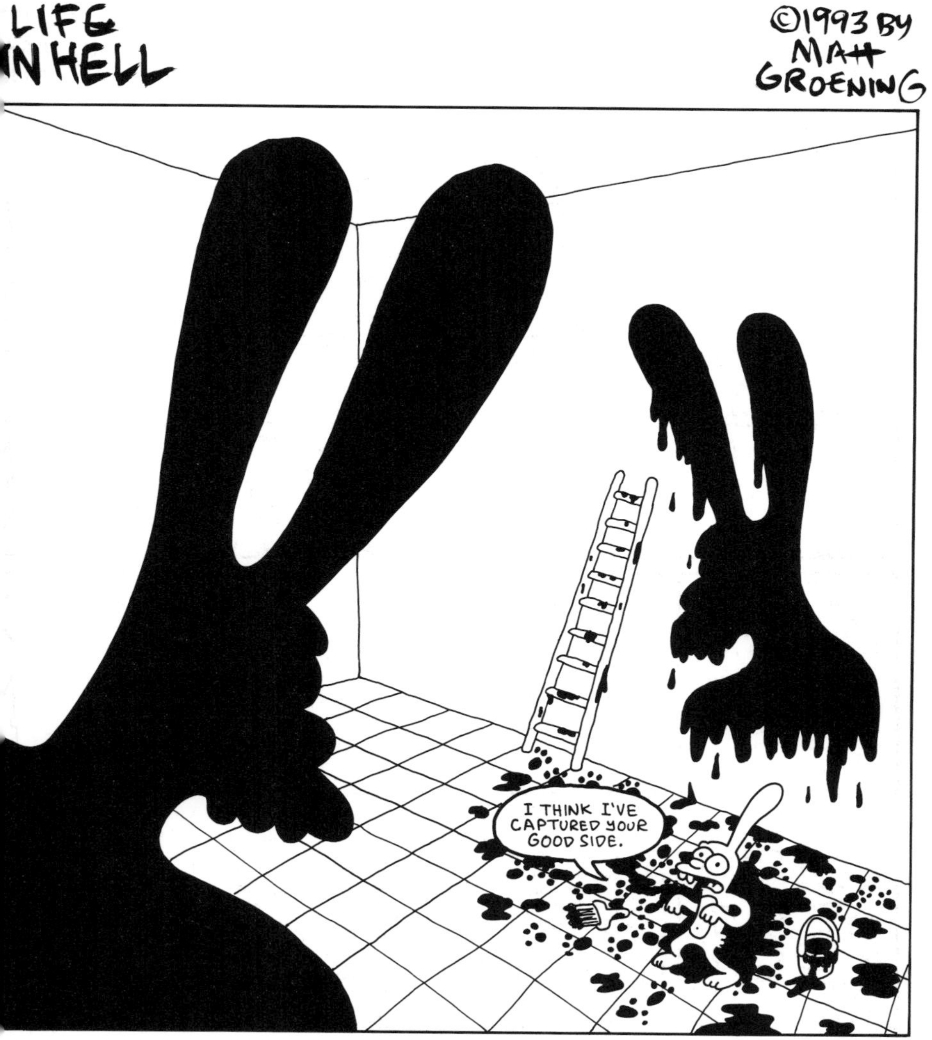
LIFE IN HELL
©1993 BY MATT GROENING
I THINK I'VE CAPTURED YOUR GOOD SIDE.

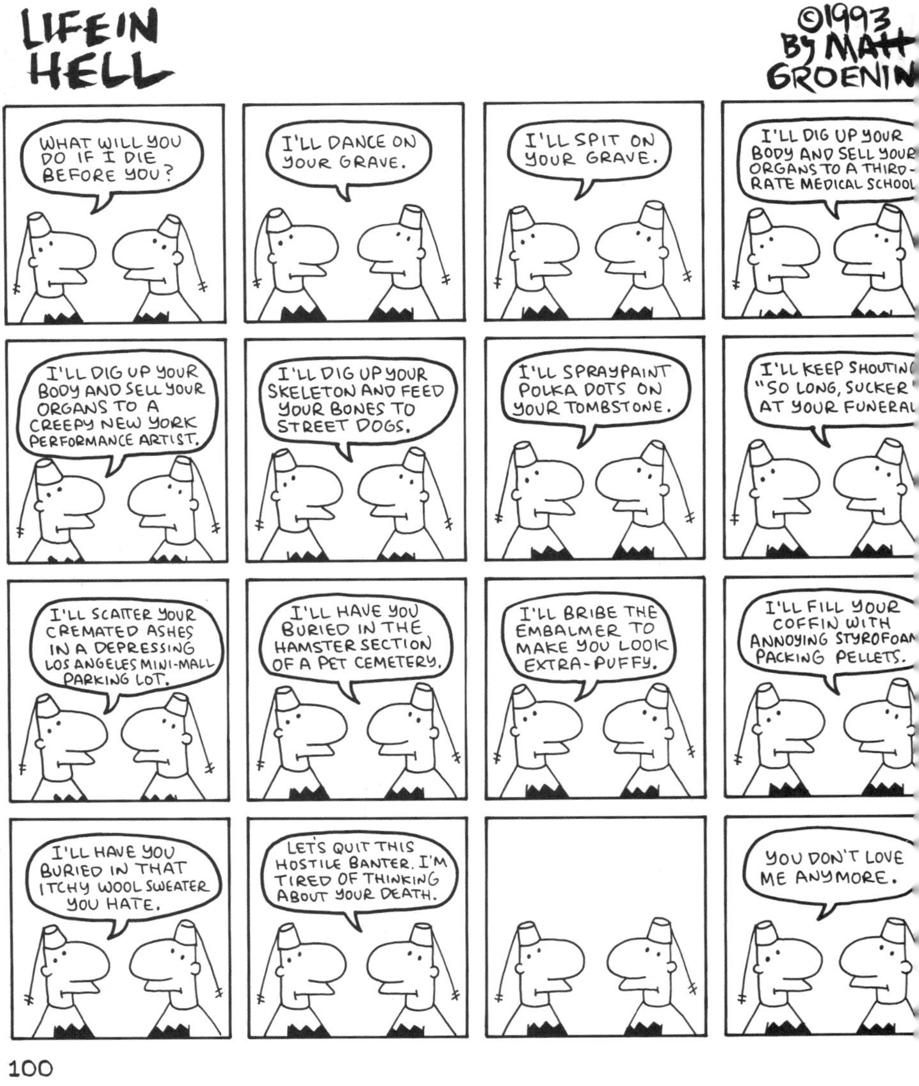
LIFE IN HELL
©1993 BY MATT GROENIN
WHAT WILL YOU DO IF I DIE BEFORE YOU?
I'LL DANCE ON YOUR GRAVE.
I'LL SPIT ON YOUR GRAVE.
I'LL DIG UP YOUR BODY AND SELL YOUR ORGANS TO A THIRD-RATE MEDICAL SCHOOL
I'LL DIG UP YOUR BODY AND SELL YOUR ORGANS TO A CREEPY NEW YORK PERFORMANCE ARTIST.
I'LL DIG UP YOUR SKELETON AND FEED YOUR BONES TO STREET DOGS.
I'LL SPRAYPAINT POLKA DOTS ON YOUR TOMBSTONE.
I'LL KEEP SHOUTIN "SO LONG, SUCKER" AT YOUR FUNERAL
I'LL SCATTER YOUR CREMATED ASHES IN A DEPRESSING LOS ANGELES MINI-MALL PARKING LOT.
I'LL HAVE YOU BURIED IN THE HAMSTER SECTION OF A PET CEMETERY.
I'LL BRIBE THE EMBALMER TO MAKE YOU LOOK EXTRA-PUFFY.
I'LL FILL YOUR COFFIN WITH ANNOYING STYROFOA PACKING PELLETS.
I'LL HAVE YOU BURIED IN THAT ITCHY WOOL SWEATER YOU HATE.
LET'S QUIT THIS HOSTILE BANTER. I'M TIRED OF THINKING ABOUT YOUR DEATH.
YOU DON'T LOVE ME ANYMORE.

LIFE IN HELL

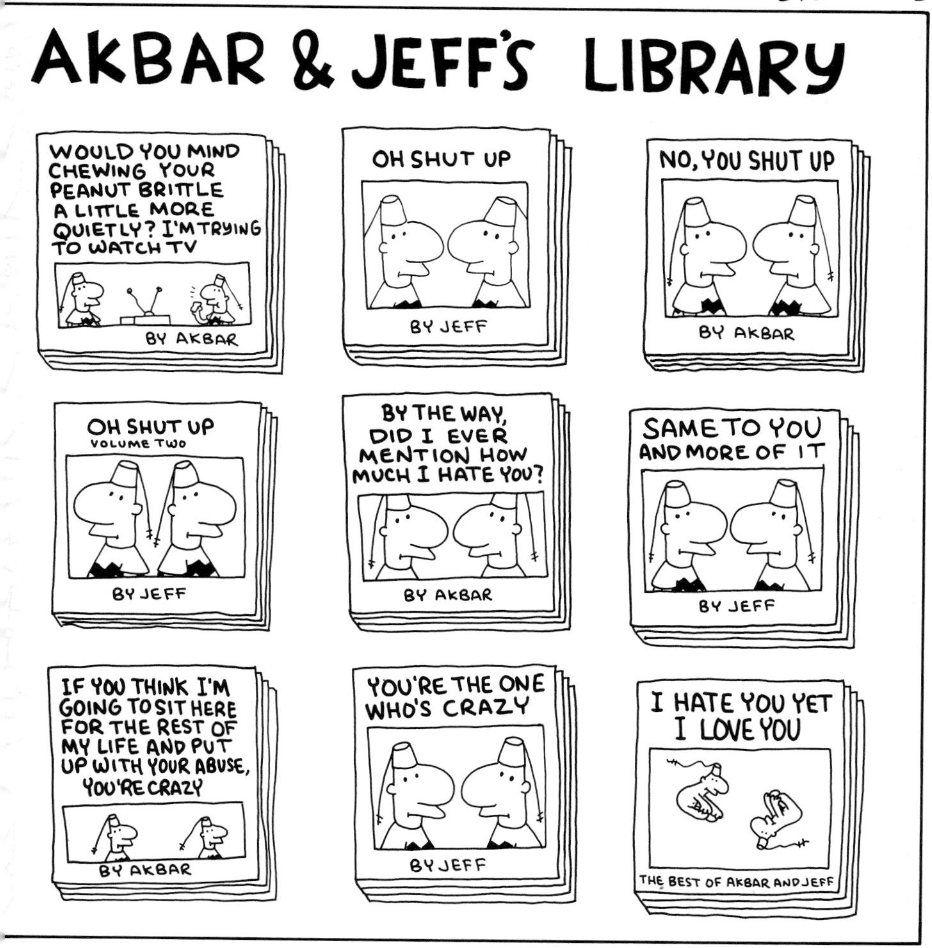
AKBAR & JEFF'S LIBRARY
WOULD YOU MIND CHEWING YOUR PEANUT BRITTLE A LITTLE MORE QUIETLY? I'M TRYING TO WATCH TV
BY AKBAR
OH SHUT UP
BY JEFF
NO, YOU SHUT UP
BY AKBAR
OH SHUT UP
VOLUME TWO
BY JEFF
BY THE WAY, DID I EVER MENTION HOW MUCH I HATE YOU?
BY AKBAR
SAME TO YOU AND MORE OF IT
BY JEFF
IF YOU THINK I'M GOING TO SIT HERE FOR THE REST OF MY LIFE AND PUT UP WITH YOUR ABUSE, YOU'RE CRAZY
BY AKBAR
YOU'RE THE ONE WHO'S CRAZY
BY JEFF
I HATE YOU YET I LOVE YOU
THE BEST OF AKBAR AND JEFF

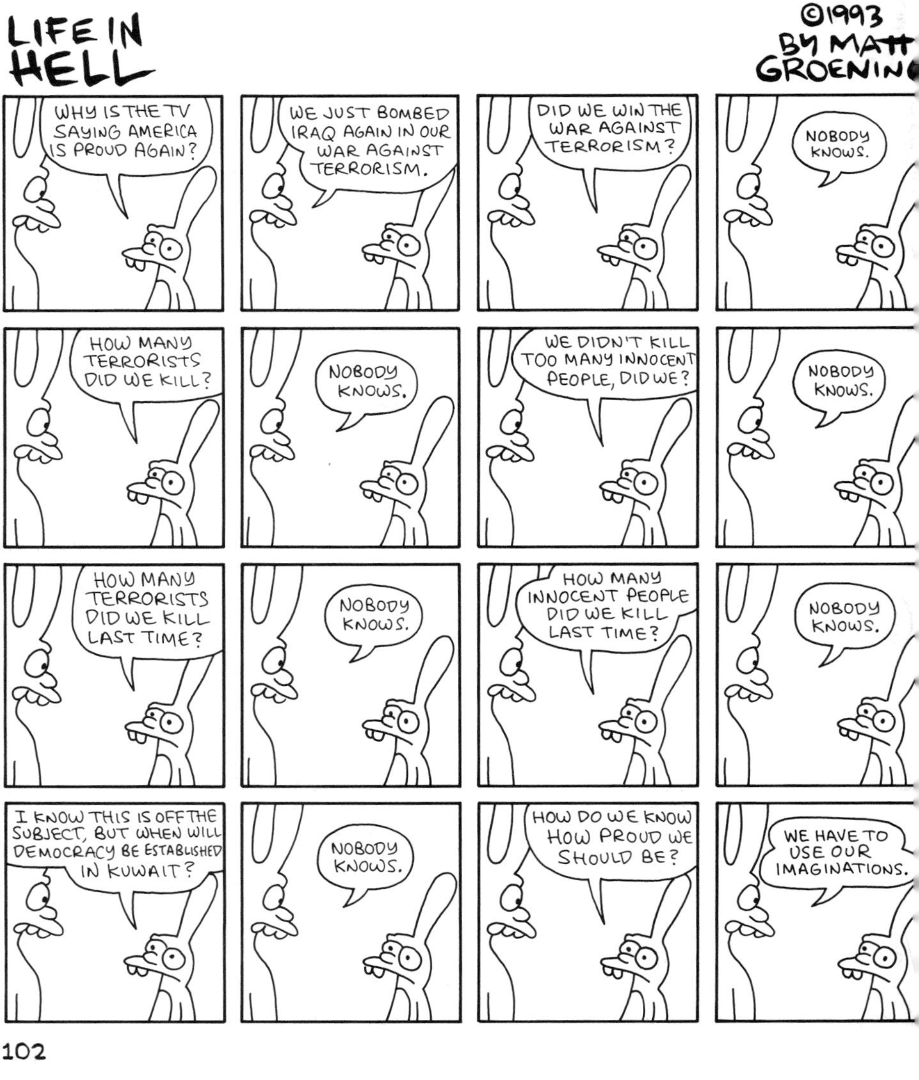
LIFE IN HELL
©1993 BY MATT GROENING
WHY IS THE TV SAYING AMERICA IS PROUD AGAIN?
WE JUST BOMBED IRAQ AGAIN IN OUR WAR AGAINST TERRORISM.
DID WE WIN THE WAR AGAINST TERRORISM?
NOBODY KNOWS.
HOW MANY TERRORISTS DID WE KILL?
NOBODY KNOWS.
WE DIDN'T KILL TOO MANY INNOCENT PEOPLE, DID WE?
NOBODY KNOWS.
HOW MANY TERRORISTS DID WE KILL LAST TIME?
NOBODY KNOWS.
HOW MANY INNOCENT PEOPLE DID WE KILL LAST TIME?
NOBODY KNOWS.
I KNOW THIS IS OFF THE SUBJECT, BUT WHEN WILL DEMOCRACY BE ESTABLISHED IN KUWAIT?
NOBODY KNOWS.
HOW DO WE KNOW HOW PROUD WE SHOULD BE?
WE HAVE TO USE OUR IMAGINATIONS.

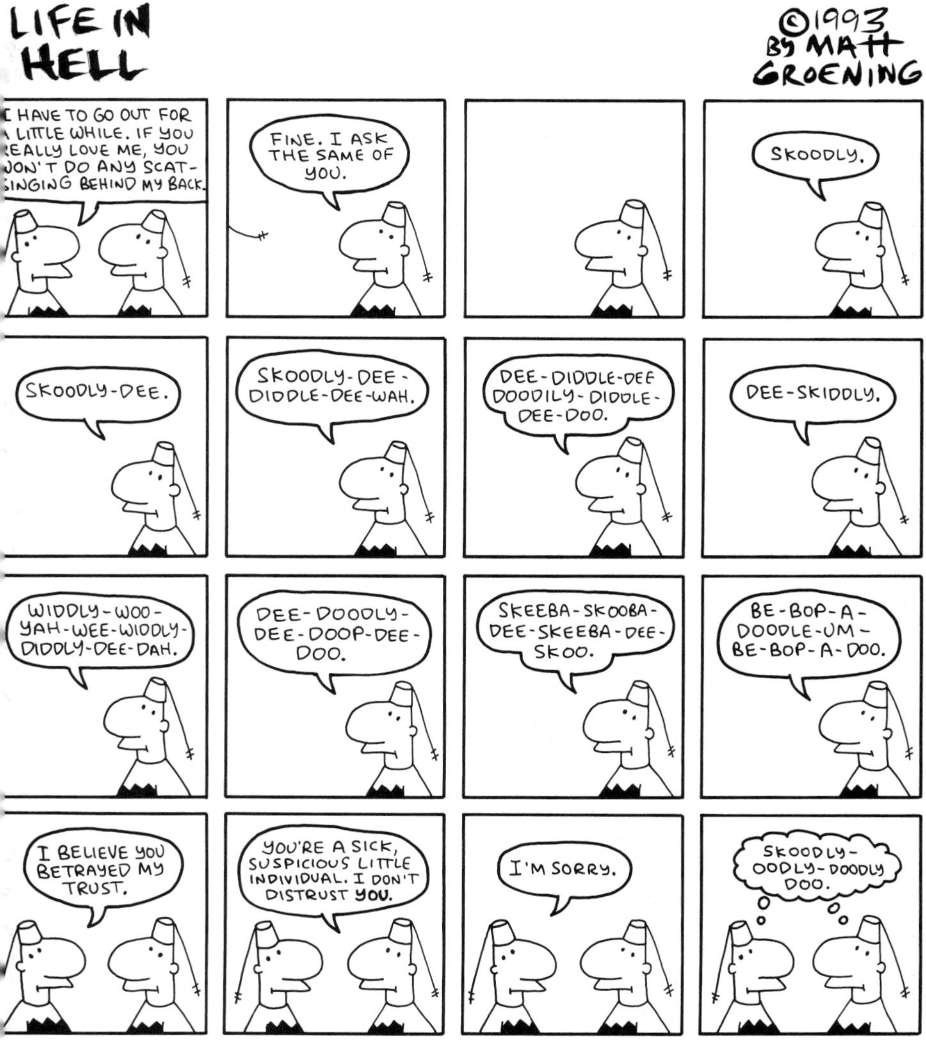
LIFE IN HELL
©1993 BY MATT GROENING
I HAVE TO GO OUT FOR A LITTLE WHILE. IF YOU REALLY LOVE ME, YOU WON'T DO ANY SCAT-SINGING BEHIND MY BACK.
FINE. I ASK THE SAME OF YOU.
SKOODLY.
SKOODLY-DEE.
SKOODLY-DEE-DIDDLE-DEE-WAH.
DEE-DIDDLE-DEE DOODILY-DIDDLE-DEE-DOO.
DEE-SKIDDLY.
WIDDLY-WOO-YAH-WEE-WIDDLY-DIDDLY-DEE-DAH.
DEE-DOODLY-DEE-DOOP-DEE-DOO.
SKEEBA-SKOOBA-DEE-SKEEBA-DEE-SKOO.
BE-BOP-A-DOODLE-UM-BE-BOP-A-DOO.
I BELIEVE YOU BETRAYED MY TRUST.
YOU'RE A SICK, SUSPICIOUS LITTLE INDIVIDUAL. I DON'T DISTRUST YOU.
I'M SORRY.
SKOODLY-OODLY-DOODLY DOO.

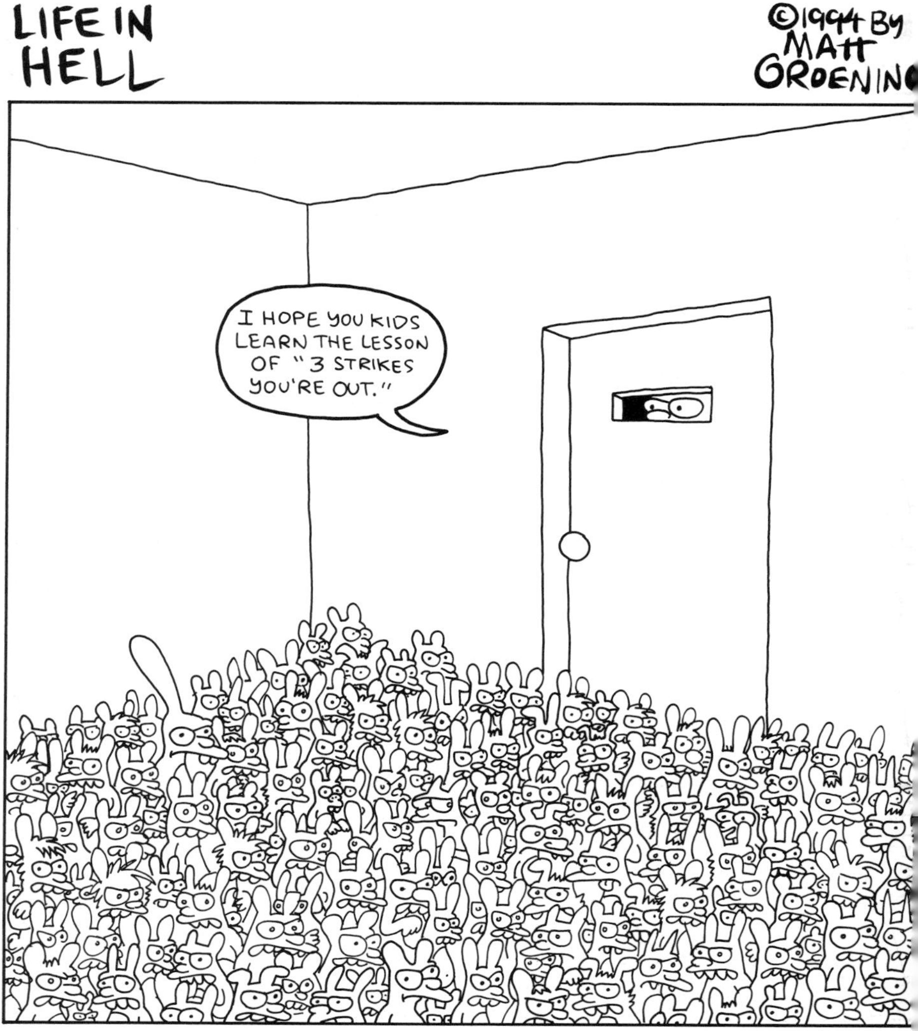
LIFE IN HELL
©1994 BY MATT GROENING
I HOPE YOU KIDS LEARN THE LESSON OF "3 STRIKES YOU'RE OUT."

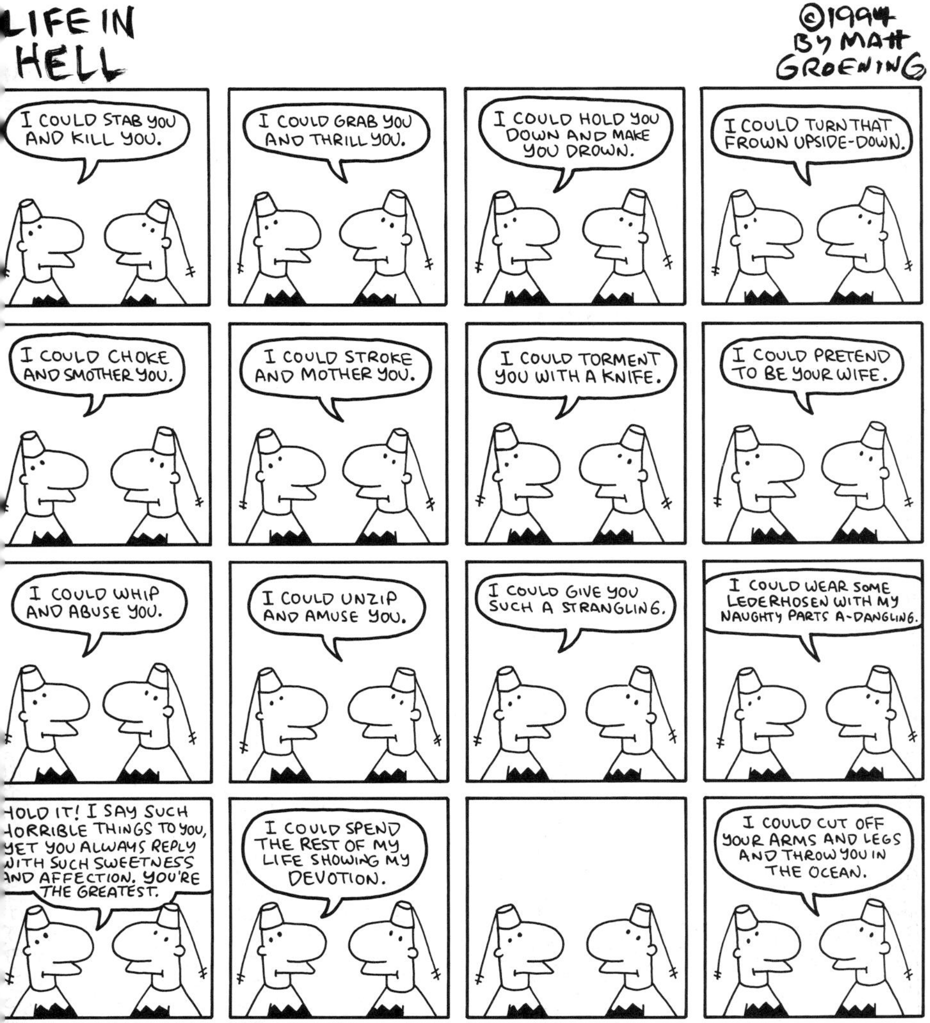
LIFE IN HELL
©1994 BY MATT GROENING
I COULD STAB YOU AND KILL YOU.
I COULD GRAB YOU AND THRILL YOU.
I COULD HOLD YOU DOWN AND MAKE YOU DROWN.
I COULD TURN THAT FROWN UPSIDE-DOWN.
I COULD CHOKE AND SMOTHER YOU.
I COULD STROKE AND MOTHER YOU.
I COULD TORMENT YOU WITH A KNIFE.
I COULD PRETEND TO BE YOUR WIFE.
I COULD WHIP AND ABUSE YOU.
I COULD UNZIP AND AMUSE YOU.
I COULD GIVE YOU SUCH A STRANGLING.
I COULD WEAR SOME LEDERHOSEN WITH MY NAUGHTY PARTS A-DANGLING.
HOLD IT! I SAY SUCH HORRIBLE THINGS TO YOU, YET YOU ALWAYS REPLY WITH SUCH SWEETNESS AND AFFECTION. YOU'RE THE GREATEST.
I COULD SPEND THE REST OF MY LIFE SHOWING MY DEVOTION.
I COULD CUT OFF YOUR ARMS AND LEGS AND THROW YOU IN THE OCEAN.

LIFE IN HELL

©1993 By MATT GROENING

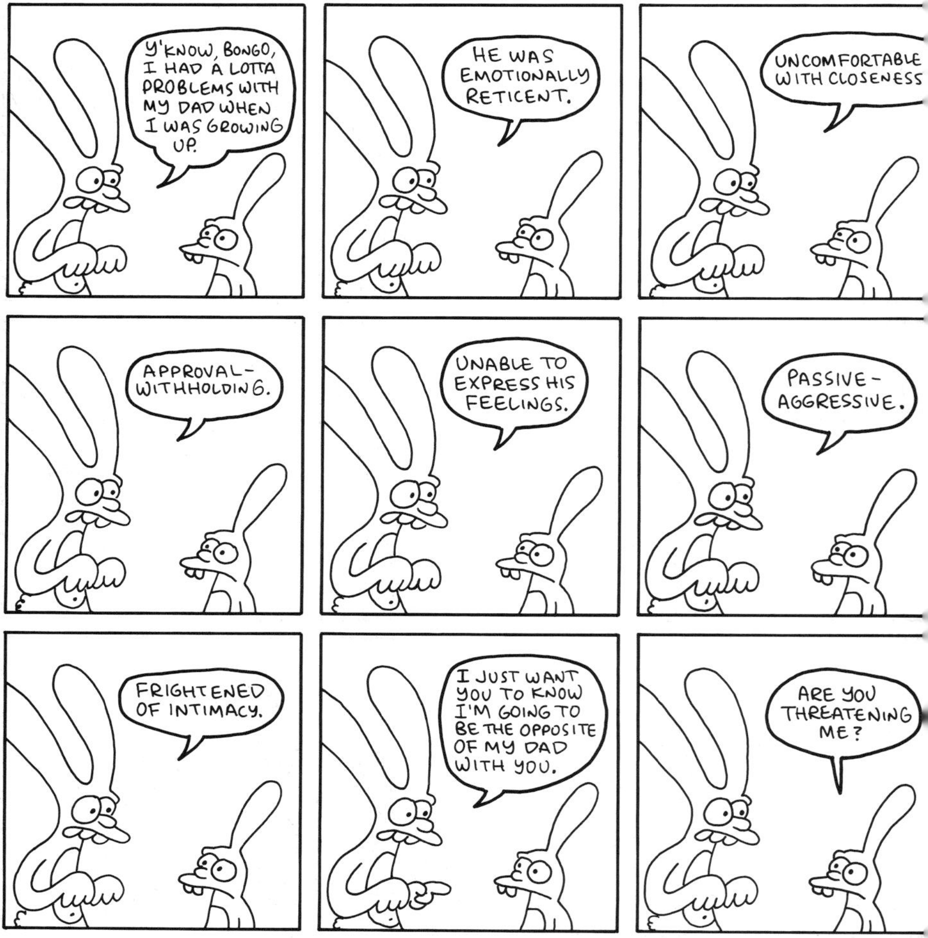

Y'KNOW, BONGO, I HAD A LOTTA PROBLEMS WITH MY DAD WHEN I WAS GROWING UP.
HE WAS EMOTIONALLY RETICENT.
UNCOMFORTABLE WITH CLOSENESS
APPROVAL-WITHHOLDING.
UNABLE TO EXPRESS HIS FEELINGS.
PASSIVE-AGGRESSIVE.
FRIGHTENED OF INTIMACY.
I JUST WANT YOU TO KNOW I'M GOING TO BE THE OPPOSITE OF MY DAD WITH YOU.
ARE YOU THREATENING ME?

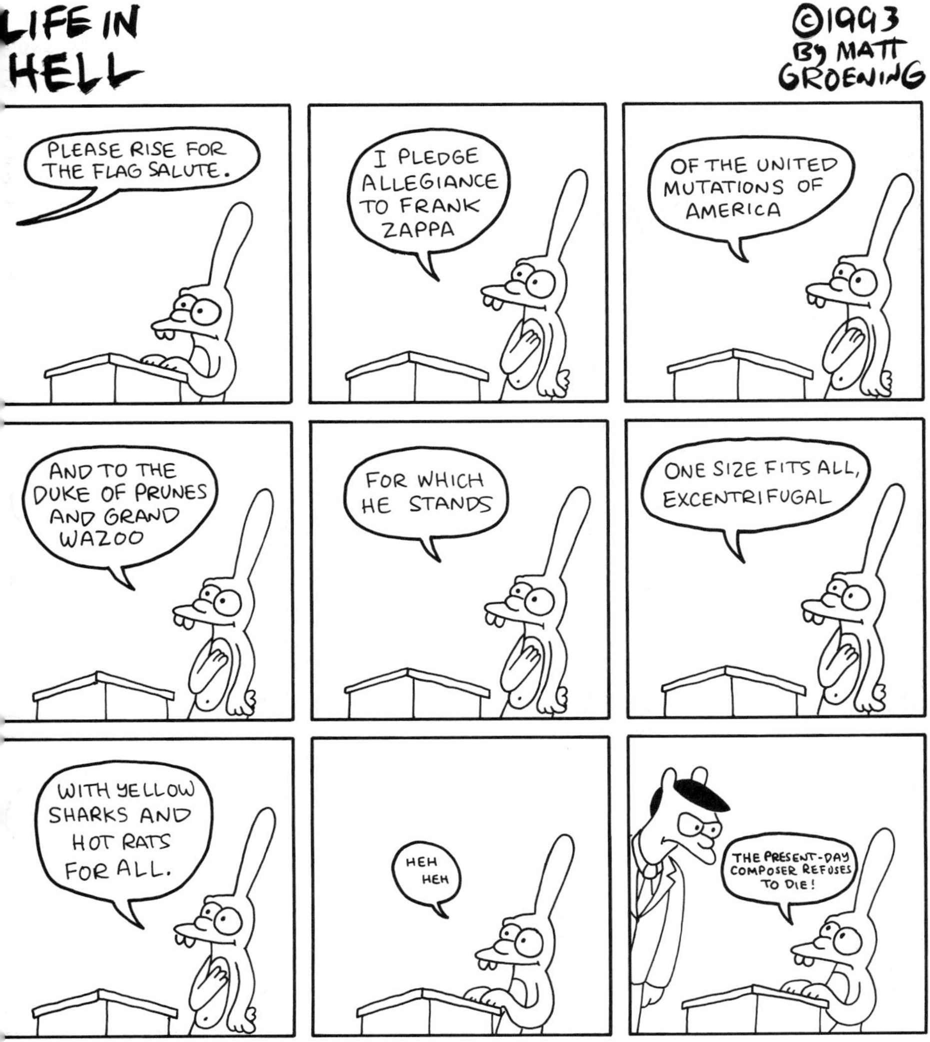
LIFE IN HELL
©1993 BY MATT GROENING
PLEASE RISE FOR THE FLAG SALUTE.
I PLEDGE ALLEGIANCE TO FRANK ZAPPA
OF THE UNITED MUTATIONS OF AMERICA
AND TO THE DUKE OF PRUNES AND GRAND WAZOO
FOR WHICH HE STANDS
ONE SIZE FITS ALL, EXCENTRIFUGAL
WITH YELLOW SHARKS AND HOT RATS FOR ALL.
HEH HEH
THE PRESENT-DAY COMPOSER REFUSES TO DIE!

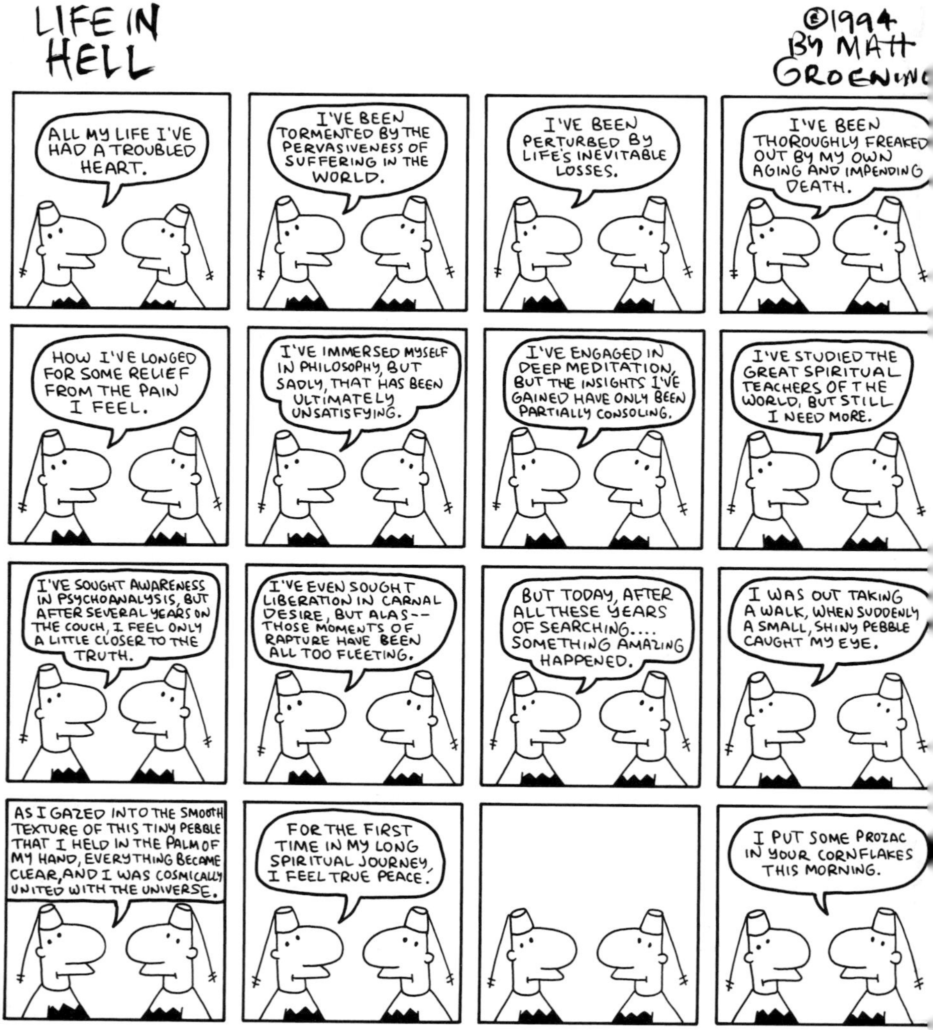
LIFE IN HELL
©1994 BY MATT GROENING
ALL MY LIFE I'VE HAD A TROUBLED HEART.
I'VE BEEN TORMENTED BY THE PERVASIVENESS OF SUFFERING IN THE WORLD.
I'VE BEEN PERTURBED BY LIFE'S INEVITABLE LOSSES.
I'VE BEEN THOROUGHLY FREAKED OUT BY MY OWN AGING AND IMPENDING DEATH.
HOW I'VE LONGED FOR SOME RELIEF FROM THE PAIN I FEEL.
I'VE IMMERSED MYSELF IN PHILOSOPHY, BUT SADLY, THAT HAS BEEN ULTIMATELY UNSATISFYING.
I'VE ENGAGED IN DEEP MEDITATION, BUT THE INSIGHTS I'VE GAINED HAVE ONLY BEEN PARTIALLY CONSOLING.
I'VE STUDIED THE GREAT SPIRITUAL TEACHERS OF THE WORLD, BUT STILL I NEED MORE.
I'VE SOUGHT AWARENESS IN PSYCHOANALYSIS, BUT AFTER SEVERAL YEARS ON THE COUCH, I FEEL ONLY A LITTLE CLOSER TO THE TRUTH.
I'VE EVEN SOUGHT LIBERATION IN CARNAL DESIRE, BUT ALAS-- THOSE MOMENTS OF RAPTURE HAVE BEEN ALL TOO FLEETING.
BUT TODAY, AFTER ALL THESE YEARS OF SEARCHING.... SOMETHING AMAZING HAPPENED.
I WAS OUT TAKING A WALK, WHEN SUDDENLY A SMALL, SHINY PEBBLE CAUGHT MY EYE.
AS I GAZED INTO THE SMOOTH TEXTURE OF THIS TINY PEBBLE THAT I HELD IN THE PALM OF MY HAND, EVERYTHING BECAME CLEAR, AND I WAS COSMICALLY UNITED WITH THE UNIVERSE.
FOR THE FIRST TIME IN MY LONG SPIRITUAL JOURNEY, I FEEL TRUE PEACE.
I PUT SOME PROZAC IN YOUR CORNFLAKES THIS MORNING.

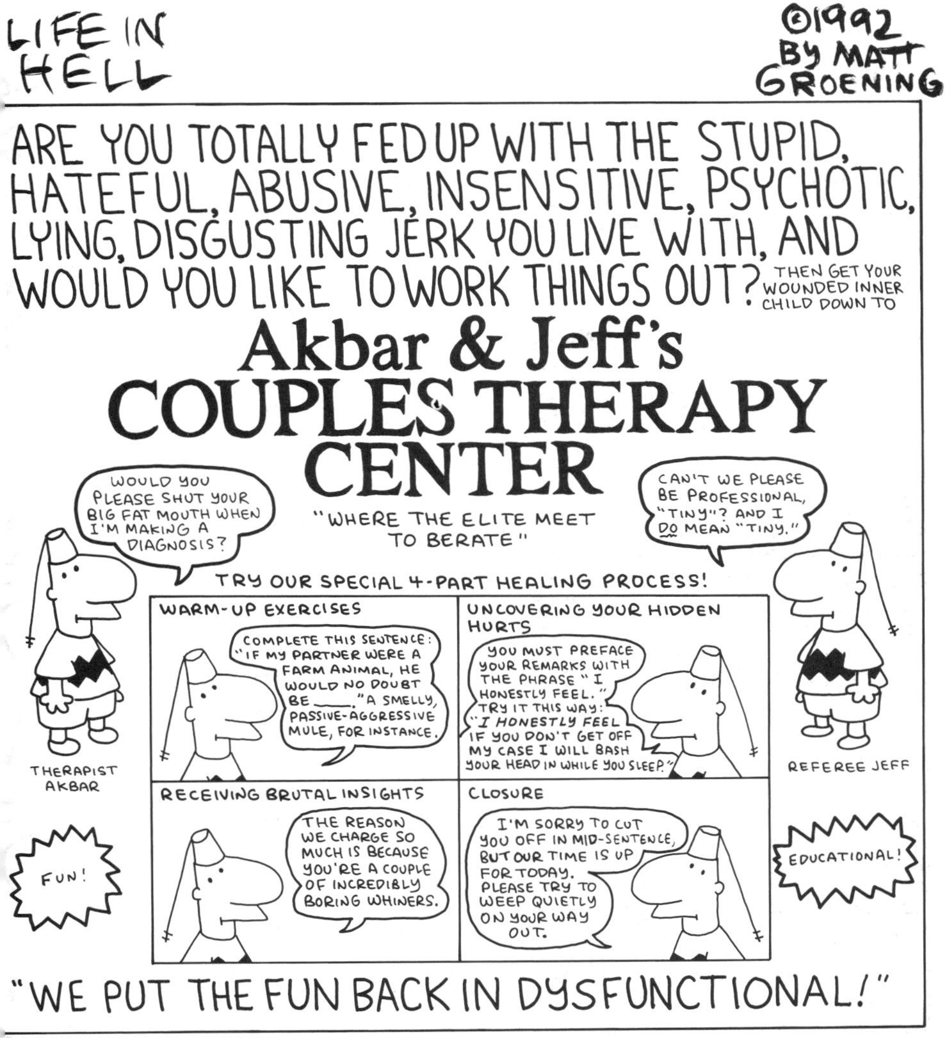

LIFE IN HELL
©1992 BY MATT GROENING
ARE YOU TOTALLY FED UP WITH THE STUPID, HATEFUL, ABUSIVE, INSENSITIVE, PSYCHOTIC, LYING, DISGUSTING JERK YOU LIVE WITH, AND WOULD YOU LIKE TO WORK THINGS OUT?
THEN GET YOUR WOUNDED INNER CHILD DOWN TO
Akbar & Jeff's COUPLES THERAPY CENTER
"WHERE THE ELITE MEET TO BERATE"
WOULD YOU PLEASE SHUT YOUR BIG FAT MOUTH WHEN I'M MAKING A DIAGNOSIS?
CAN'T WE PLEASE BE PROFESSIONAL, "TINY"? AND I DO MEAN "TINY."
THERAPIST AKBAR
REFEREE JEFF
TRY OUR SPECIAL 4-PART HEALING PROCESS!
WARM-UP EXERCISES
COMPLETE THIS SENTENCE: "IF MY PARTNER WERE A FARM ANIMAL, HE WOULD NO DOUBT BE ____." A SMELLY, PASSIVE-AGGRESSIVE MULE, FOR INSTANCE.
UNCOVERING YOUR HIDDEN HURTS
YOU MUST PREFACE YOUR REMARKS WITH THE PHRASE "I HONESTLY FEEL." TRY IT THIS WAY: "I HONESTLY FEEL IF YOU DON'T GET OFF MY CASE I WILL BASH YOUR HEAD IN WHILE YOU SLEEP."
RECEIVING BRUTAL INSIGHTS
THE REASON WE CHARGE SO MUCH IS BECAUSE YOU'RE A COUPLE OF INCREDIBLY BORING WHINERS.
CLOSURE
I'M SORRY TO CUT YOU OFF IN MID-SENTENCE, BUT OUR TIME IS UP FOR TODAY. PLEASE TRY TO WEEP QUIETLY ON YOUR WAY OUT.
FUN!
EDUCATIONAL!
"WE PUT THE FUN BACK IN DYSFUNCTIONAL!"

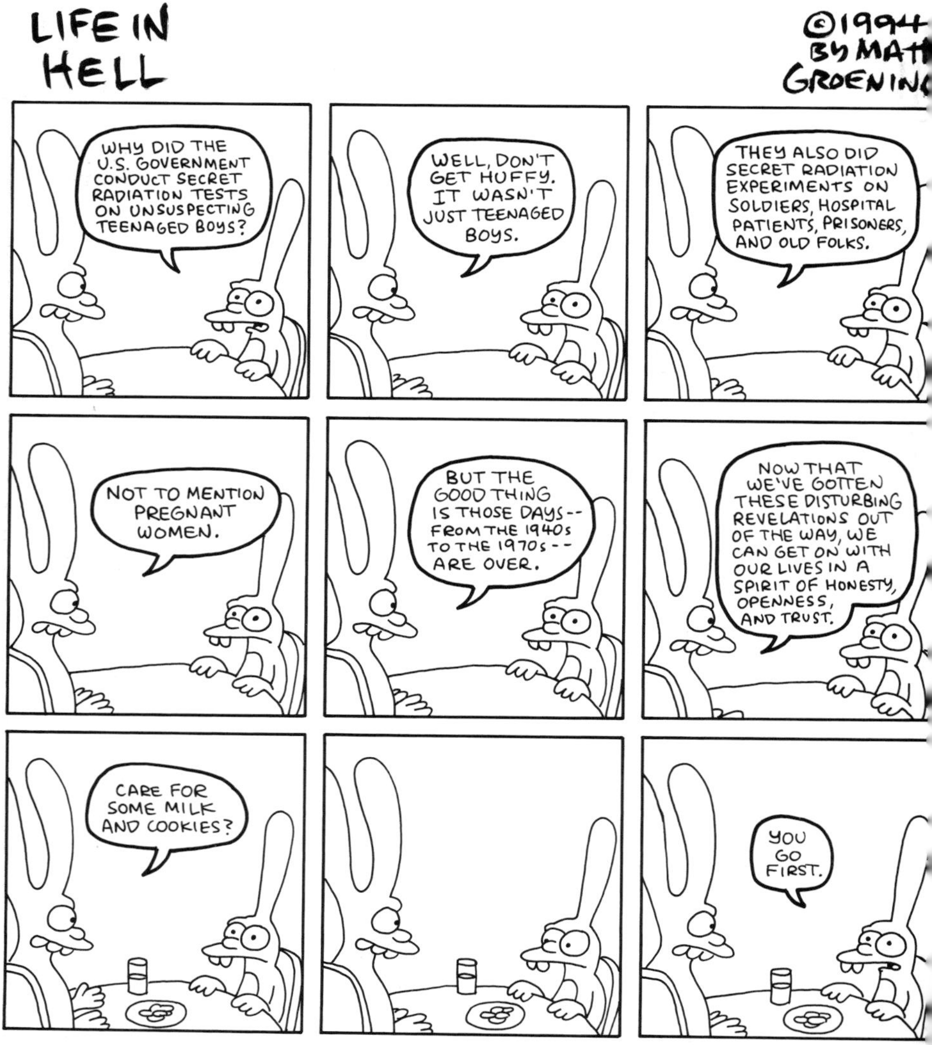
LIFE IN HELL
©1994 BY MATT GROENING
WHY DID THE U.S. GOVERNMENT CONDUCT SECRET RADIATION TESTS ON UNSUSPECTING TEENAGED BOYS?
WELL, DON'T GET HUFFY. IT WASN'T JUST TEENAGED BOYS.
THEY ALSO DID SECRET RADIATION EXPERIMENTS ON SOLDIERS, HOSPITAL PATIENTS, PRISONERS, AND OLD FOLKS.
NOT TO MENTION PREGNANT WOMEN.
BUT THE GOOD THING IS THOSE DAYS-- FROM THE 1940s TO THE 1970s-- ARE OVER.
NOW THAT WE'VE GOTTEN THESE DISTURBING REVELATIONS OUT OF THE WAY, WE CAN GET ON WITH OUR LIVES IN A SPIRIT OF HONESTY, OPENNESS, AND TRUST.
CARE FOR SOME MILK AND COOKIES?
YOU GO FIRST.

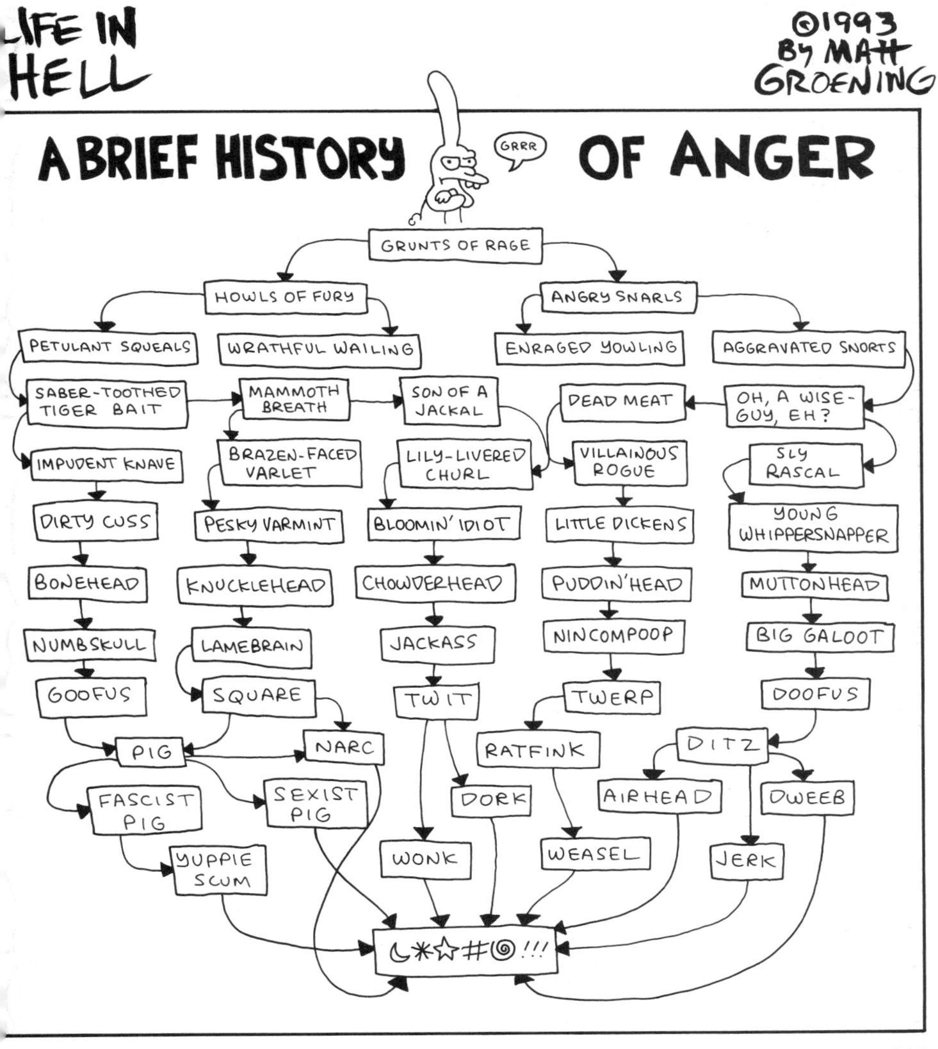

LIFE IN HELL
©1993 BY MATT GROENING
A BRIEF HISTORY OF ANGER
GRRR
GRUNTS OF RAGE
HOWLS OF FURY
ANGRY SNARLS
PETULANT SQUEALS
WRATHFUL WAILING
ENRAGED YOWLING
AGGRAVATED SNORTS
SABER-TOOTHED TIGER BAIT
MAMMOTH BREATH
SON OF A JACKAL
DEAD MEAT
OH, A WISE-GUY, EH?
IMPUDENT KNAVE
BRAZEN-FACED VARLET
LILY-LIVERED CHURL
VILLAINOUS ROGUE
SLY RASCAL
DIRTY CUSS
PESKY VARMINT
BLOOMIN' IDIOT
LITTLE DICKENS
YOUNG WHIPPERSNAPPER
BONEHEAD
KNUCKLEHEAD
CHOWDERHEAD
PUDDIN'HEAD
MUTTONHEAD
NUMBSKULL
LAMEBRAIN
JACKASS
NINCOMPOOP
BIG GALOOT
GOOFUS
SQUARE
TWIT
TWERP
DOOFUS
PIG
NARC
RATFINK
DITZ
FASCIST PIG
SEXIST PIG
DORK
AIRHEAD
DWEEB
YUPPIE SCUM
WONK
WEASEL
JERK
☾*☆#◎!!!

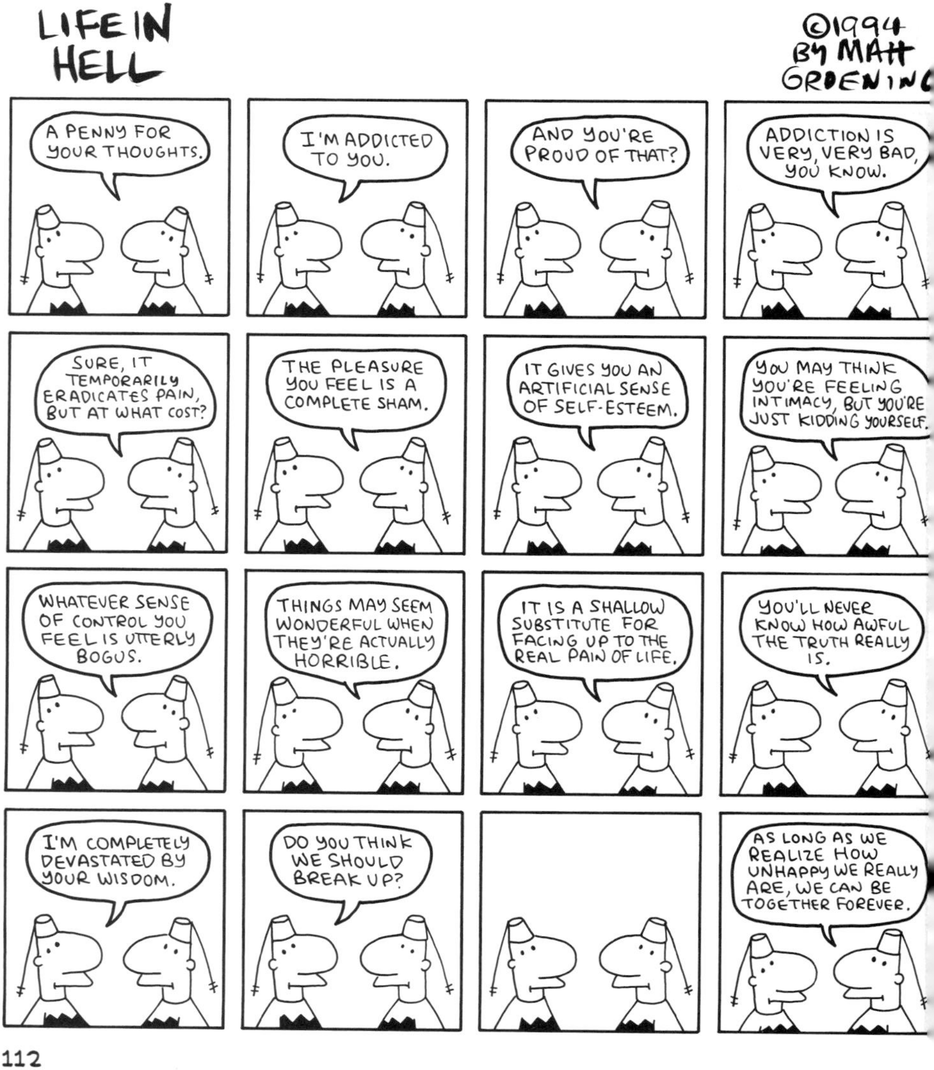
LIFE IN HELL
©1994 BY MATT GROENING
A PENNY FOR YOUR THOUGHTS.
I'M ADDICTED TO YOU.
AND YOU'RE PROUD OF THAT?
ADDICTION IS VERY, VERY BAD, YOU KNOW.
SURE, IT TEMPORARILY ERADICATES PAIN, BUT AT WHAT COST?
THE PLEASURE YOU FEEL IS A COMPLETE SHAM.
IT GIVES YOU AN ARTIFICIAL SENSE OF SELF-ESTEEM.
YOU MAY THINK YOU'RE FEELING INTIMACY, BUT YOU'RE JUST KIDDING YOURSELF.
WHATEVER SENSE OF CONTROL YOU FEEL IS UTTERLY BOGUS.
THINGS MAY SEEM WONDERFUL WHEN THEY'RE ACTUALLY HORRIBLE.
IT IS A SHALLOW SUBSTITUTE FOR FACING UP TO THE REAL PAIN OF LIFE.
YOU'LL NEVER KNOW HOW AWFUL THE TRUTH REALLY IS.
I'M COMPLETELY DEVASTATED BY YOUR WISDOM.
DO YOU THINK WE SHOULD BREAK UP?
AS LONG AS WE REALIZE HOW UNHAPPY WE REALLY ARE, WE CAN BE TOGETHER FOREVER.

LIFE IN HELL

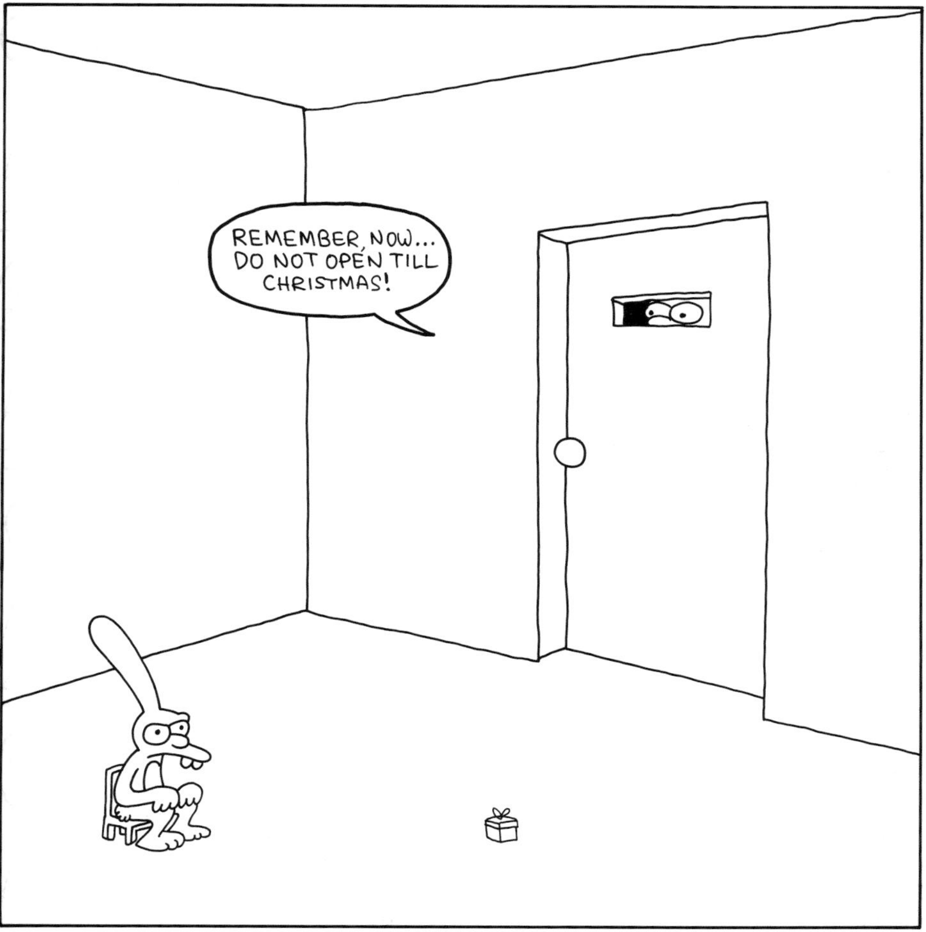
REMEMBER, NOW... DO NOT OPEN TILL CHRISTMAS!

TRUE-LIFE IN HELL

©1994 BY MATT GROENING

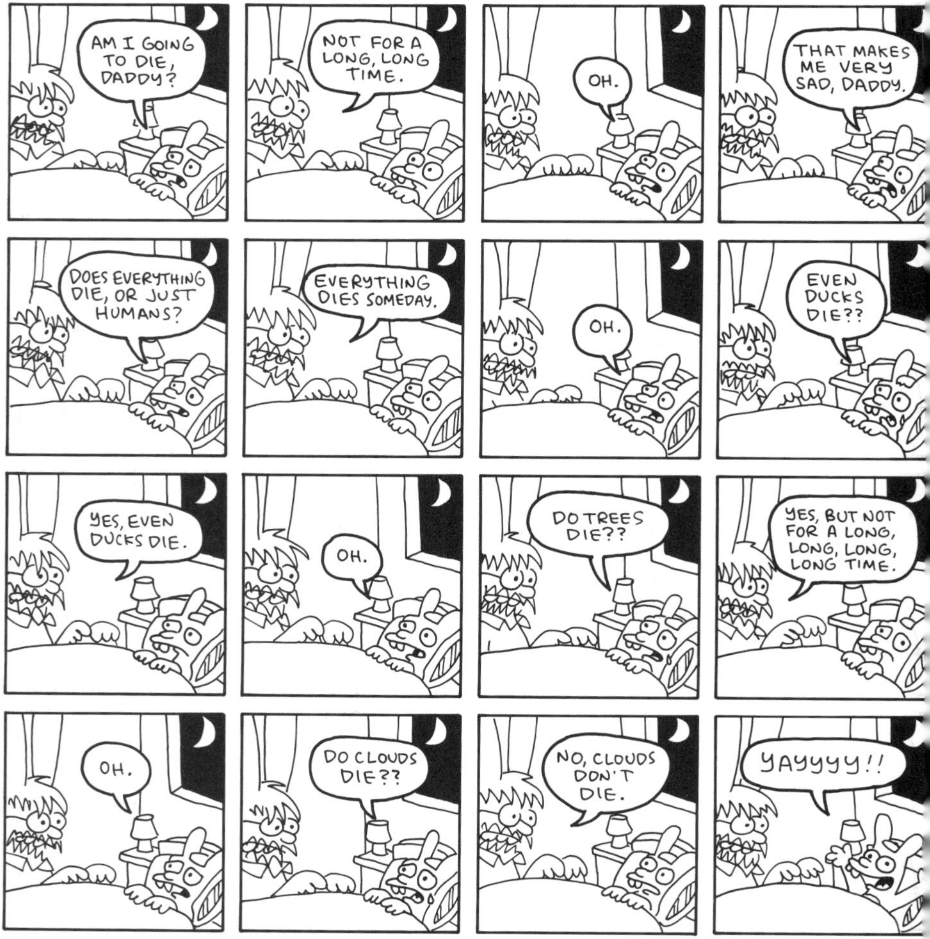
AM I GOING TO DIE, DADDY?
NOT FOR A LONG, LONG TIME.
OH.
THAT MAKES ME VERY SAD, DADDY.
DOES EVERYTHING DIE, OR JUST HUMANS?
EVERYTHING DIES SOMEDAY.
OH.
EVEN DUCKS DIE??
YES, EVEN DUCKS DIE.
OH.
DO TREES DIE??
YES, BUT NOT FOR A LONG, LONG, LONG, LONG TIME.
OH.
DO CLOUDS DIE??
NO, CLOUDS DON'T DIE.
YAYYYY!!

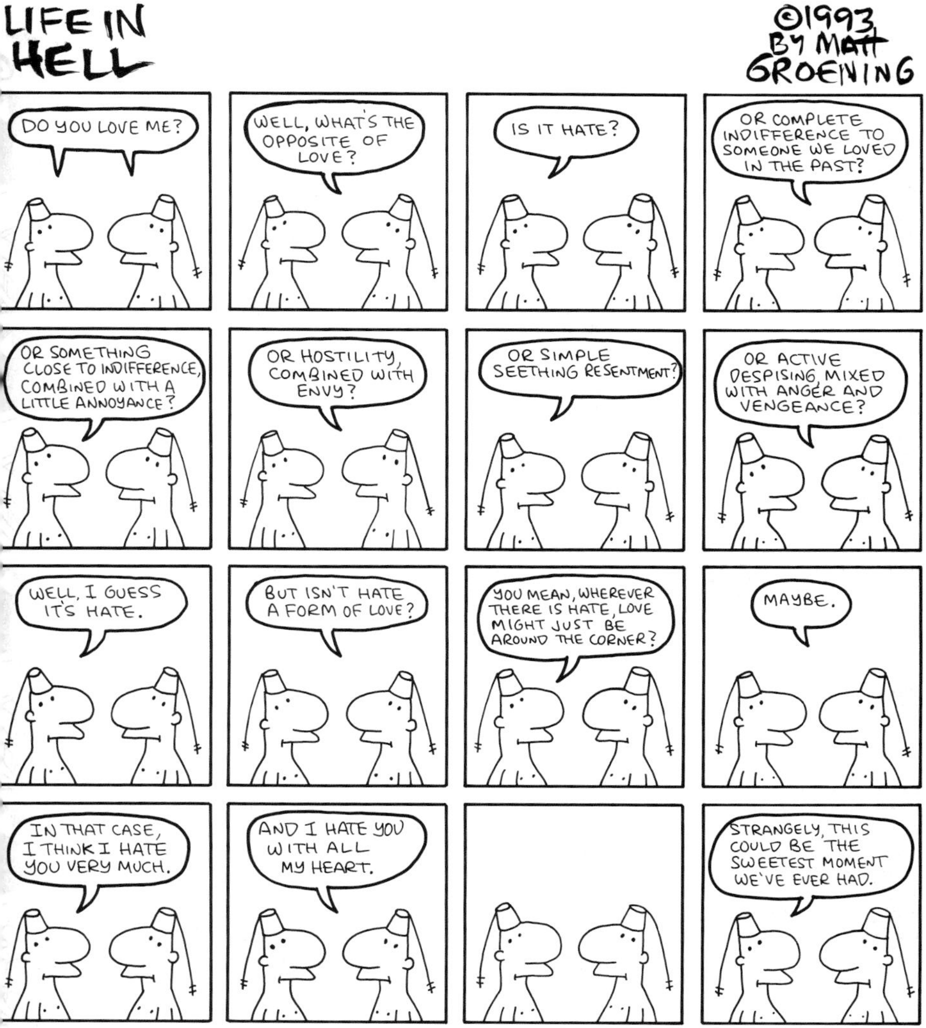
LIFE IN HELL
©1993 BY MATT GROENING
DO YOU LOVE ME?
WELL, WHAT'S THE OPPOSITE OF LOVE?
IS IT HATE?
OR COMPLETE INDIFFERENCE TO SOMEONE WE LOVED IN THE PAST?
OR SOMETHING CLOSE TO INDIFFERENCE, COMBINED WITH A LITTLE ANNOYANCE?
OR HOSTILITY, COMBINED WITH ENVY?
OR SIMPLE SEETHING RESENTMENT?
OR ACTIVE DESPISING, MIXED WITH ANGER AND VENGEANCE?
WELL, I GUESS IT'S HATE.
BUT ISN'T HATE A FORM OF LOVE?
YOU MEAN, WHEREVER THERE IS HATE, LOVE MIGHT JUST BE AROUND THE CORNER?
MAYBE.
IN THAT CASE, I THINK I HATE YOU VERY MUCH.
AND I HATE YOU WITH ALL MY HEART.
STRANGELY, THIS COULD BE THE SWEETEST MOMENT WE'VE EVER HAD.

LIFE IN HELL

©1993 BY MATT GROENING

I'LL GIVE YOU 30 SECONDS TO SAY I LOVE YOU OR I'M LEAVING YOU FOREVER.

STARTING RIGHT NOW.

YOU CAN'T THREATEN ME.

25 SECONDS.

I CAN'T SAY WHAT I DON'T FEEL.

20 SECONDS.

I STRONGLY RESENT THESE PRESSURE TACTICS.

15 SECONDS.

YOU'VE GOT DEEP MENTAL PROBLEMS.

10 SECONDS.

I DON'T EVEN KNOW WHAT LOVE IS.

5 SECONDS.

I HATE YOU.

1 SECOND.

I LOVE YOU.

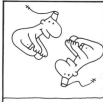

116

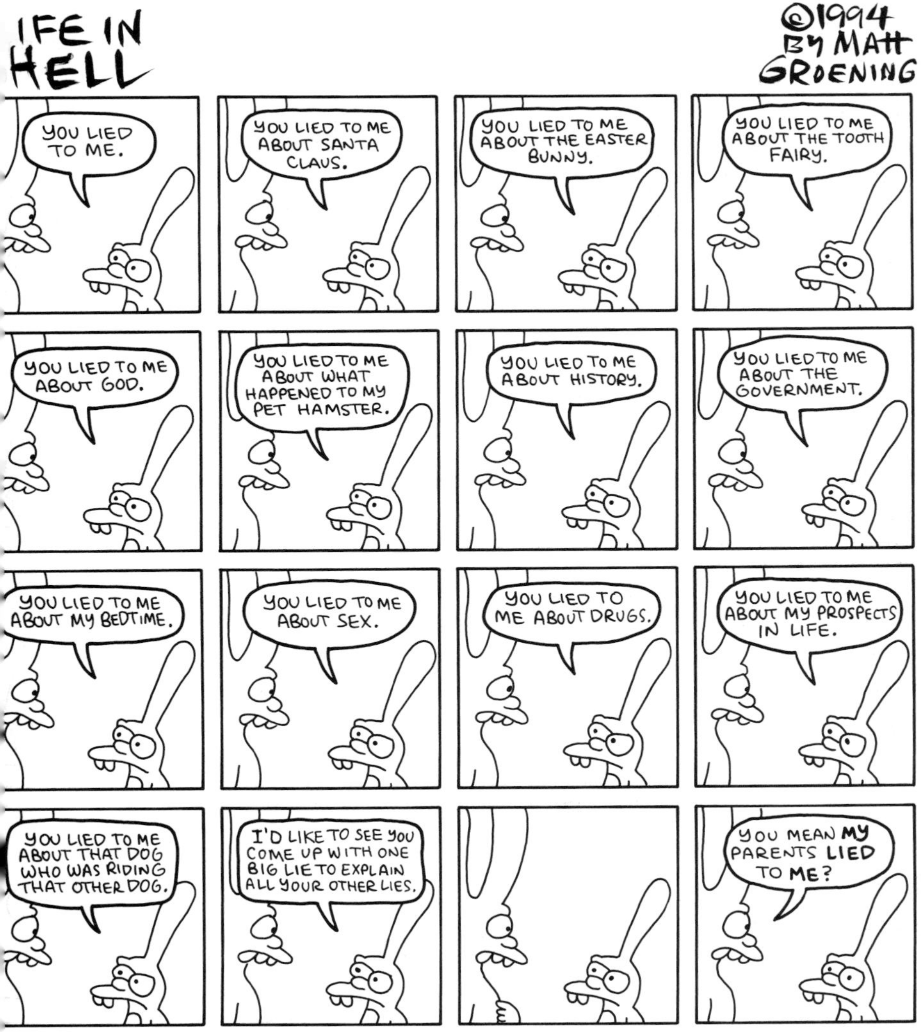
LIFE IN HELL
©1994 BY MATT GROENING
YOU LIED TO ME.
YOU LIED TO ME ABOUT SANTA CLAUS.
YOU LIED TO ME ABOUT THE EASTER BUNNY.
YOU LIED TO ME ABOUT THE TOOTH FAIRY.
YOU LIED TO ME ABOUT GOD.
YOU LIED TO ME ABOUT WHAT HAPPENED TO MY PET HAMSTER.
YOU LIED TO ME ABOUT HISTORY.
YOU LIED TO ME ABOUT THE GOVERNMENT.
YOU LIED TO ME ABOUT MY BEDTIME.
YOU LIED TO ME ABOUT SEX.
YOU LIED TO ME ABOUT DRUGS.
YOU LIED TO ME ABOUT MY PROSPECTS IN LIFE.
YOU LIED TO ME ABOUT THAT DOG WHO WAS RIDING THAT OTHER DOG.
I'D LIKE TO SEE YOU COME UP WITH ONE BIG LIE TO EXPLAIN ALL YOUR OTHER LIES.
YOU MEAN **MY** PARENTS **LIED** TO **ME**?

LIFE IN HELL

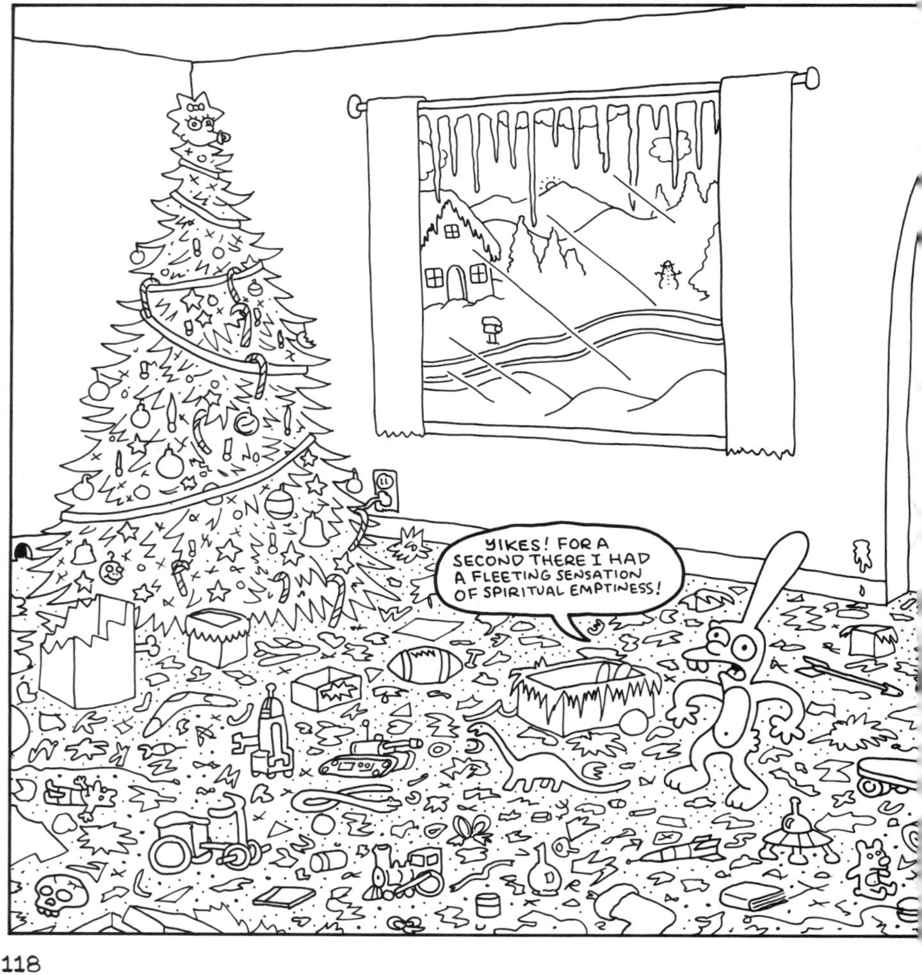
YIKES! FOR A SECOND THERE I HAD A FLEETING SENSATION OF SPIRITUAL EMPTINESS!

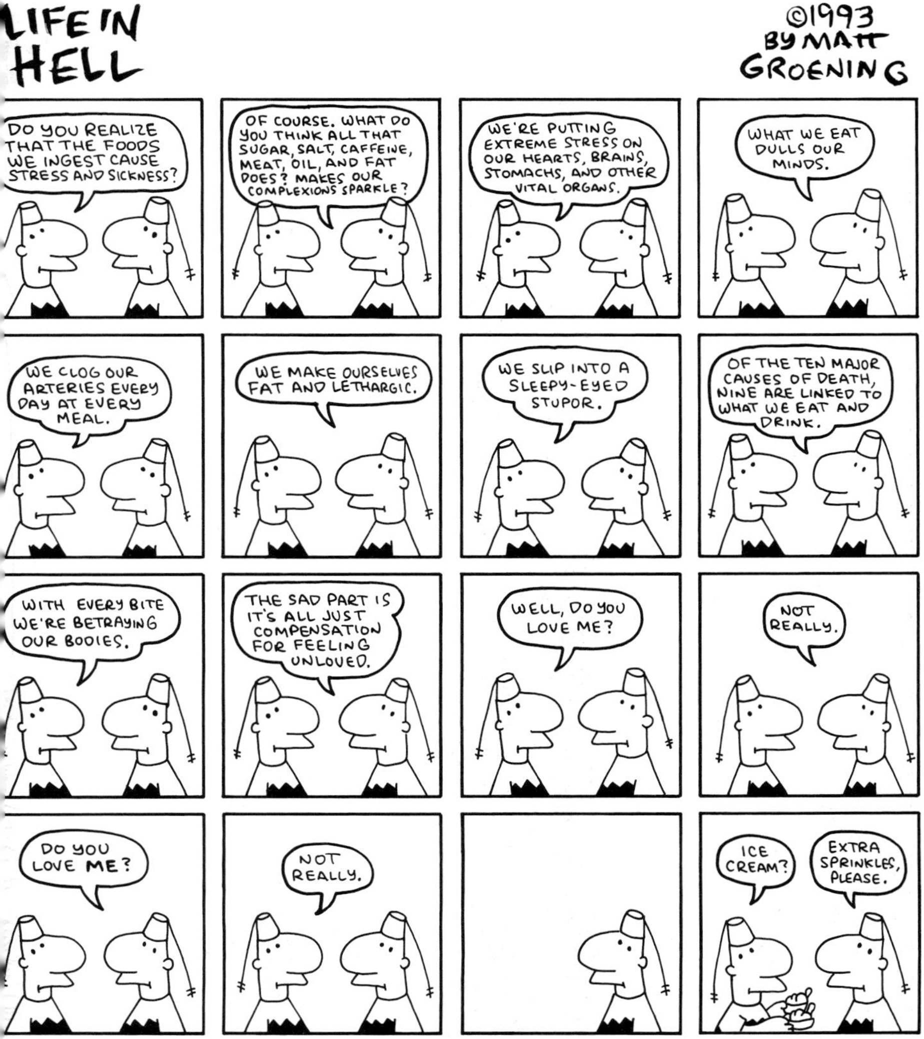
LIFE IN HELL
©1993 BY MATT GROENING
DO YOU REALIZE THAT THE FOODS WE INGEST CAUSE STRESS AND SICKNESS?
OF COURSE. WHAT DO YOU THINK ALL THAT SUGAR, SALT, CAFFEINE, MEAT, OIL, AND FAT DOES? MAKES OUR COMPLEXIONS SPARKLE?
WE'RE PUTTING EXTREME STRESS ON OUR HEARTS, BRAINS, STOMACHS, AND OTHER VITAL ORGANS.
WHAT WE EAT DULLS OUR MINDS.
WE CLOG OUR ARTERIES EVERY DAY AT EVERY MEAL.
WE MAKE OURSELVES FAT AND LETHARGIC.
WE SLIP INTO A SLEEPY-EYED STUPOR.
OF THE TEN MAJOR CAUSES OF DEATH, NINE ARE LINKED TO WHAT WE EAT AND DRINK.
WITH EVERY BITE WE'RE BETRAYING OUR BODIES.
THE SAD PART IS IT'S ALL JUST COMPENSATION FOR FEELING UNLOVED.
WELL, DO YOU LOVE ME?
NOT REALLY.
DO YOU LOVE **ME**?
NOT REALLY.
ICE CREAM?
EXTRA SPRINKLES, PLEASE.

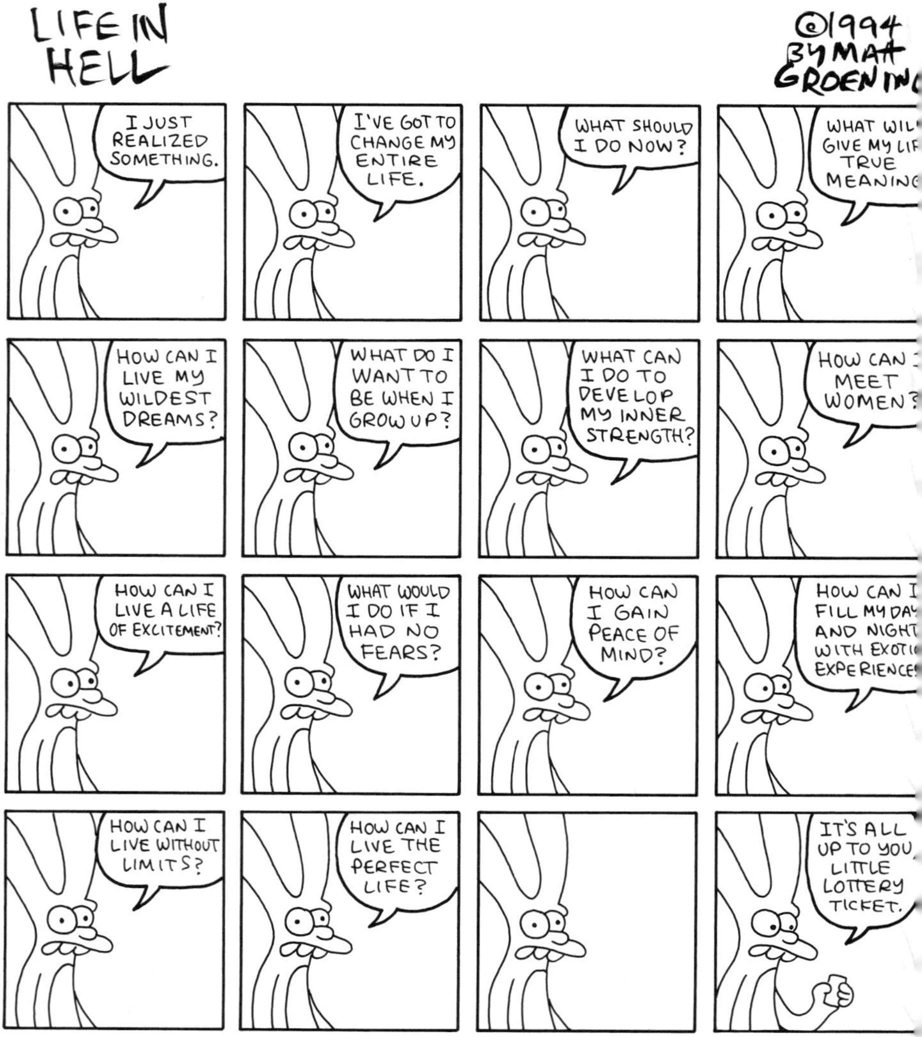
LIFE IN HELL
©1994 BY MATT GROENIN
I JUST REALIZED SOMETHING.
I'VE GOT TO CHANGE MY ENTIRE LIFE.
WHAT SHOULD I DO NOW?
WHAT WIL
GIVE MY LIF
TRUE
MEANING
HOW CAN I LIVE MY WILDEST DREAMS?
WHAT DO I WANT TO BE WHEN I GROW UP?
WHAT CAN I DO TO DEVELOP MY INNER STRENGTH?
HOW CAN
MEET WOMEN
HOW CAN I LIVE A LIFE OF EXCITEMENT?
WHAT WOULD I DO IF I HAD NO FEARS?
HOW CAN I GAIN PEACE OF MIND?
HOW CAN I
FILL MY DAY
AND NIGHT
WITH EXOTI
EXPERIENCE
HOW CAN I LIVE WITHOUT LIMITS?
HOW CAN I LIVE THE PERFECT LIFE?
IT'S ALL UP TO YOU, LITTLE LOTTERY TICKET.

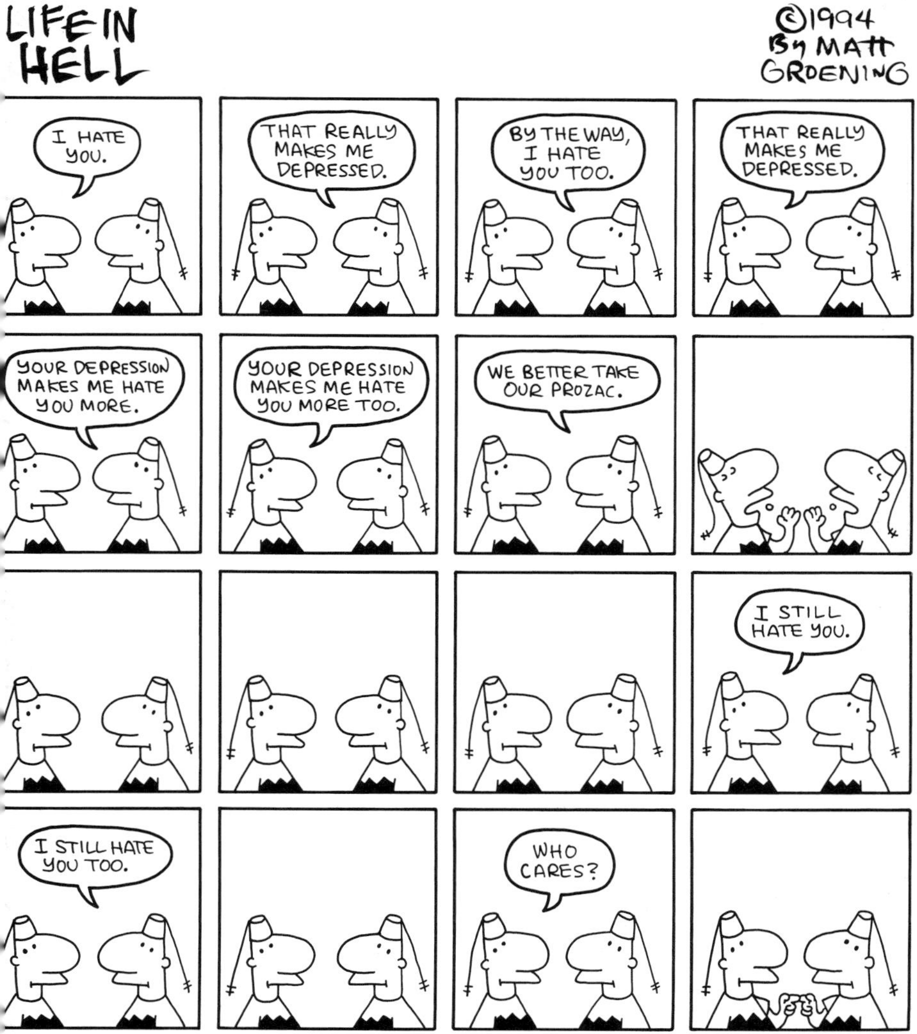
LIFE IN HELL
©1994 BY MATT GROENING
I HATE YOU.
THAT REALLY MAKES ME DEPRESSED.
BY THE WAY, I HATE YOU TOO.
THAT REALLY MAKES ME DEPRESSED.
YOUR DEPRESSION MAKES ME HATE YOU MORE.
YOUR DEPRESSION MAKES ME HATE YOU MORE TOO.
WE BETTER TAKE OUR PROZAC.
I STILL HATE YOU.
I STILL HATE YOU TOO.
WHO CARES?

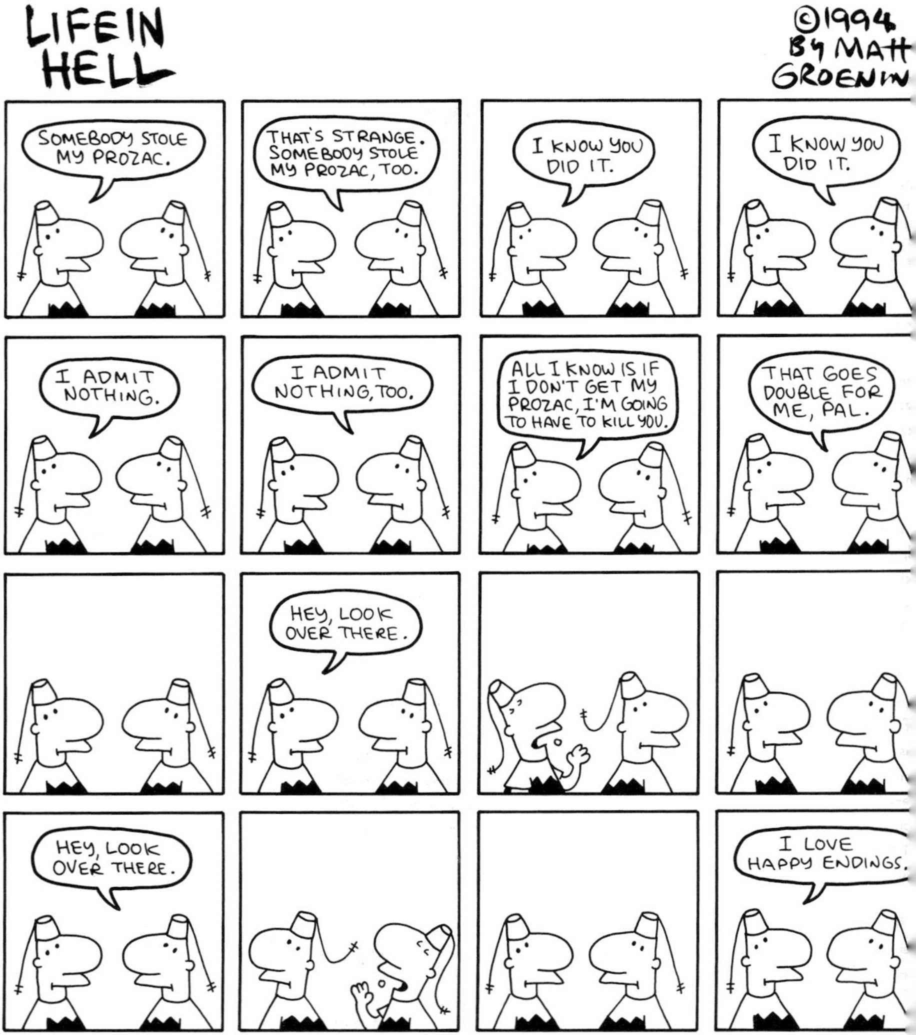
LIFE IN HELL
©1994 BY MATT GROENIN
SOMEBODY STOLE MY PROZAC.
THAT'S STRANGE. SOMEBODY STOLE MY PROZAC, TOO.
I KNOW YOU DID IT.
I KNOW YOU DID IT.
I ADMIT NOTHING.
I ADMIT NOTHING, TOO.
ALL I KNOW IS IF I DON'T GET MY PROZAC, I'M GOING TO HAVE TO KILL YOU.
THAT GOES DOUBLE FOR ME, PAL.
HEY, LOOK OVER THERE.
HEY, LOOK OVER THERE.
I LOVE HAPPY ENDINGS.